HARVARD EAST ASIAN MONOGRAPHS
69

THE RUSSIAN ECCLESIASTICAL MISSION IN PEKING
DURING THE EIGHTEENTH CENTURY

THE RUSSIAN ECCLESIASTICAL MISSION IN PEKING DURING THE EIGHTEENTH CENTURY

by
Eric Widmer

Published by
East Asian Research Center
Harvard University

Distributed by
Harvard University Press
Cambridge, Massachusetts
and
London, England
1976

The East Asian Research Center at Harvard University administers research projects designed to further scholarly understanding of China, Japan, Korea, Vietnam, Inner Asia, and adjacent areas. These studies have been assisted by grants from the Ford Foundation.

Library of Congress Cataloging in Publication Data

Widmer, Eric, 1940-
    The Russian ecclesiastical mission in Peking during the eighteenth century.

    (Harvard East Asian monographs; 69)
    Bibliography: p.
    Includes index.
    1. Missions—China. 2. Missions, Russian. 3. Russia—Relations (general) with China. 4. China—Relations (general) with Russia. I. Title. II. Series.
BV3417,W46   266'.1'951   76-12575
ISBN   0-674-78129-5

To my mother
Carolyn Ladd Widmer

CONTENTS

FOREWORD

Chinese-Russian relations began in the seventeenth century, contemporary with the settling of the Thirteen Colonies in America. But the first Americans reached Canton only in 1784, almost a century after the rulers of Russia and China had made their first treaty in 1689. The Sino-Soviet relationship of today has a long history behind it, some knowledge of which might mitigate the disaster rate as we develop our side of the superpower triangle.

Yet the American historians who read Chinese and Russian can still be counted on your fingers. The American build-up of recent decades in Soviet studies, Chinese studies, and studies of contemporary international relations has foreshortened our view: two centuries of political and economic contact between Russia and China have been generally lost to sight.

As Eric Widmer's account makes clear, Sino-Russian intercourse was a managed happening based partly on treaties and guided by *raisons d'état* on both sides. The reasons differed but the contact was maintained. The Russian ecclesiastical mission in Peking fitted into the interstices between the respective state policies. By not trying too hard, it survived as a unique outpost of Europe at the center of the Ch'ing empire. Indeed the mission has long been a historical celebrity known to everyone by name but to almost no one in factual detail. This book now pulls its biography together and shows its central role in Sino-Russian relations.

Dr. Widmer began his Russian studies at Williams College where he graduated in 1961, and his Chinese studies at Harvard, where he took his Ph.D. in 1969. He has since been teaching Chinese and Inner Asian history at Brown University.

John K. Fairbank

ACKNOWLEDGEMENTS

For a work of such modest size my list of debts is considerable. In enumerating them I shall try to be brief, lest the reader's hopes for what follows in the text of this study are raised unnecessarily.

I am indebted, in the first order of magnitude, to the teaching and scholarship of three people: John Fairbank, Joseph Fletcher, and Francis Cleaves. To the extent within my powers to do so, I have revealed what I owe to them in writing this book.

From two redoubtable figures—Mark Mancall and Ellis Joffe —I got the inspiration to undertake a history of the Russian mission in Peking. To others, who read the manuscript copy, or who helped earlier along the way, or who otherwise contributed their time and attention, I am also grateful: David Arkush, Chen Yu-shih, Fred Drake, Alison Dray-Novey, Jerry Grieder, Beate Hill-Paulus, Owen Lattimore, Madeline Levine, Li Hsueh-chih, Peter Seybolt, Denis Sinor, Ranbir Vohra, Ellen Widmer, and Lea Williams.

Summer money from Brown University, and from the East Asian Research Center at Harvard, helped my work on this book progress from one academic year to the next. Here I should also say that I greatly appreciate the fellowship of those people at Brown and Harvard among whom I have been situated.

Michael Dalby gave the book, when it appeared to me to be finished, the thorough going-over that it obviously still needed. His extraordinary efforts deserve a special citation. Sharon Coppa typed the whole of the manuscript, and Olive Holmes subjected it to the editorial scrutiny for which she is now deservedly famous.

E. W.

Providence, Rhode Island
March 1976

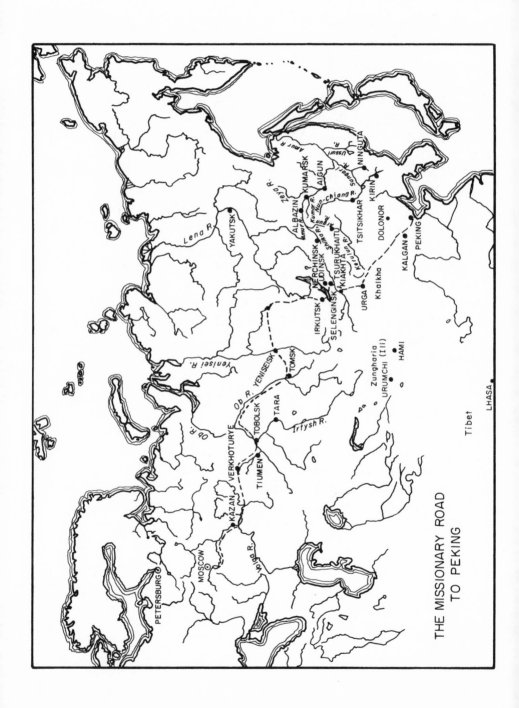

THE MISSIONARY ROAD
TO PEKING

INTRODUCTION

In the midsummer of 1683, a Russian freebooter named Grigorii Mylnikov was groping his way through the forest along the Amur River, not far beyond the outermost Siberian garrison of Albazin. He had with him seventy men and a parish priest from Albazin, Maksim Leont'ev.

Mylnikov's mission, like that of other Cossack parties that summer, was to push Russian power further into the Amur River Valley, where Siberian fur merchants needed protection if they were to make a success of their efforts to collect tribute (or *iasak*) from local Mongol and Tungus peoples. For this Albazin served as a convenient base of operations, situated on the bank of the Amur near the confluence of the Argun, and facing downriver to the Pacific over a thousand miles away. From here, forty years earlier, Vasilii Poiarkov had made a lightning advance down the Amur, reaching the ocean in 1643. A decade later he had been followed by another redoubtable pioneer, Erofei Khabarov, who fortified his position at Albazin in the spring of 1651 and spent the rest of the year fighting his way into the Amur River Valley. But in March, 1652, Khabarov's approach had been contested by a new and superior force of "bogdoiskii people"—a term which he and those who read about his adventures were, without knowing it, applying to the Manchu conquerors of China.[1]

Khabarov's skirmishes with the Manchus ended inconclusively, although the significance that Russian historians have been ready to accord them has grown tremendously in recent years. At the time, the only clear result of these events was the knowledge that what Poiarkov and Khabarov had begun to accomplish should now be undertaken more slowly and more carefully. The Amur region could truly be won only by more painstaking efforts at penetrating the forests and extracting professions of fealty from the native peoples, whom frontiersmen like Grigorii Mylnikov were no doubt well qualified to intimidate. This in turn presupposed a well-coordinated deployment of men, military governors, blockhouses, and winter shelters. Thirty years after Khabarov, enough had been done to allow the feeling that cis-Amuriia was secure and, if no unkind fate intervened, that the river valley itself would succumb before long.

But what of those "bogdoiskii people" who had not been so compliant? The residents of the town of Nerchinsk, where the local governor, or voevoda, lived, had already caught a glimpse of them in 1669 when several inquisitive Manchus turned up pretending to be merchants, and making vague offers of trade coupled with demands for repatriating fugitives.[2] Neither proposal was readily intelligible to the Russians in this stronghold: tribute, not trade, formed the basis of their relations with Siberian natives, and the idea that fugitives could be sought by a people still largely beyond their view was not at first taken very seriously. Nevertheless, by 1683 there was growing evidence that Russia was indeed close to a more substantial meeting with a force disinclined to collapse at first musket shot—a force, in fact, which possessed an alarming supply of muskets of its own. Had this not been the troubling significance of Spafarii's embassy to Peking in 1676?[3] In the simple act of taking a route that led through Manchuria had Spafarii not demonstrated once and for all the ominous identity of the "bogdoiskii people" with the "kitaiskii" rulers of China? The summer weather in Albazin brought with it the presentiment of a cloudburst: the question that hung over the garrison was soon to be resolved one way or the other.

Quite suddenly Mylnikov's party came face to face in the middle of the woods with a contingent of Manchus. No questions needed asking, for Mylnikov knew at once that he was in the presence of a "bogdoiskii" detachment, and worse, that he was outnumbered. And if one can impute to him a sense of fascination with his helplessness, perhaps he also knew that his life, and the history that it carried, were about to undergo a dramatic change. With a number of his companions and Father Maksim, Mylnikov was invited into a clearing to break bread with his opposites. They entered the Manchu camp and had lunch. But when the Russians rose to leave they discovered predictably that Manchu hospitality could not easily be overstayed. Instead they were escorted deeper into the forest and, several weeks later, surfaced in Peking as guests of the K'ang-hsi emperor himself. Two of them were given new clothes and hats and sent straight back to the frontier to announce the fate that had befallen their expedition.[4]

One of the letters they carried was from a companion, now marooned in Peking. It was addressed to his liege in Albazin:

> I, Grishka Stefanov, prostrate myself before my sovereign, friend, my absent benefactor, Ignatii Ivanovich. How merciful is God to you? You were so good to inquire after me, but for my sins the Bogdoi have seized me at the River Amur. And now I am living in the Chinese empire under surveillance. I was shod and clothed by the Bogdoi tsar, but as for the future, I put my trust in the grace of God. I do not know the duration of this existence of mine ... but I heard from the interpreters that we will never be freed; and now I am quite ruined. The little money I had, about a hundred rubles, and what I had on hand, everything is lost ... As for my arms, take them and sell them ... Only may God have mercy on you, my sovereign Ignatii Ivanovich, do not abandon my children, but be as a father to them. Give Stenka and Orinka each my blessing and prostrate yourself before all my friends. I greet you in the name of Christ ... It was said to us that we were to remain in this kingdom forever. May it please you, my good friends, do not abandon my children Stenka and Orinka.[5]

Those like Grishka Stefanov, who remained in Peking, were to be provided with food and drink, K'ang-hsi said, "in order to show Our intention of taking good care of them."[6] It was an imperial way of saying that the Albazinian wars had begun.

K'ang-hsi explained that his benevolence to the prisoners was conceived as an effort to "comply with the will of Heaven,"[7] perhaps not oblivious of the fact that a man of God was among them. And whatever Father Maksim may have thought about his descent into the middle of Peking, he was now the man to ready the deracinated bunch of Russians for the difficult times ahead. For this purpose he was soon given an old Buddhist prayer house, which he promptly converted into an Orthodox chapel. By late September of 1683, while Manchus and Russians were mobilizing along the Amur, K'ang-hsi and Maksim Leont'ev together had brought to life an institution that would one day become the Russian ecclesiastical mission in Peking.

Not many years later, Albazin itself fell and more Russians turned up in Peking, where they were settled around the makeshift church. In 1713, after the death of Leont'ev, the Manchus invited Russia to send more priests to the now languishing émigré quarter; however, it was not until the treaty of Kiakhta, exchanged in 1728, that the Russian ecclesiastical mission was given its legal underpinnings. The fifth article of the treaty provided for four priests and six students to live in Peking until they felt like returning to Russia, at which time they would be replaced by a new contingent. The mission was to be supported, in various ways, by both countries. In return, it answered a mutual need for continuous contact between the capitals of St. Petersburg and Peking. And the question of tenure in China was therefore not as freely decided as the language of the treaty suggests, for most members of the mission in the demoralized eighteenth century would surely have elected to return to Russia on the morrow of their arrival in Peking. It was not a higher calling but instead the Russian government that had cajoled them into the adventure, and that thereafter refused to retrieve them for approximately ten years.

Because the missionary traditions of the Orthodox church, so actively followed in Siberia, had not yet been transmitted to China, the ecclesiastical mission, once established, was left with little to do except to keep its Albazinian communicants from plunging into that oceanic "gloom of heathendom" by which they were surrounded. But despite its modest function in Peking, or rather because of it, the mission became the most durable "sinoforeign" institution in modern Chinese history and one that was, after 1728, located in the very center of the Chinese capital. Self-concerned in a religious sense, it did not engage in active proselytization among

the Chinese and Manchu population of the city, and therefore
avoided the heroic persecutions that Roman Catholics underwent
in the eighteenth century and Protestants as well in the nineteenth.

It is not hard to imagine the jealousy that the mission's
exclusive position excited among other Western powers before
1858, when they at last won an equivalent privilege. To get to
Peking, to remain there for a decade, and then to return! Who else
in the world could boast such a franchise but the clerics and
students of the Russian mission? Roman Catholics in the eighteenth
century had gained their entree into China at the expense of giving
up any expectation of leaving again.[8] By the nineteenth century
this was too high a price for most Europeans to pay, since it meant
that to spend any time in the interior one would have to become
Chinese, a metamorphosis which was not at all in keeping either
with up-to-date diplomatic practice or with the cooling European
enthusiasm for China. That Russia had somehow managed to find
a loophole was a source of irritation; even worse was the shameful
fact that Russia, with a mission in Peking, had turned it to practically no use at all. Here is the remark of one Englishman in the
nineteenth century: "It will be seen, that by the treaty of 1728,
the Russian government have had, for more than a century, a
regularly established religious and scientific mission at Peking; and
to their disgrace it must be told that, with the exception of a
geographical description of China, in 1820, by Father Hyacinth
[Bichurin], not a single advantage has either science or literature
derived, after enjoying an opportunity that no other Christian
nation has possessed, notwithstanding the example set them by
the Jesuits. It is needless to say, how different the result would
have been, had the natives of England and France been allowed to
remain ten years in the capital . . . As Russia possesses a college
and mission, at Peking, the English, French, and other nations are
equally entitled to hold a similar position."[9]

After 1858 such spiteful feelings subsided. The unique place
that the Russian mission once occupied became a curiosity,
remembered in Western literature in the cautious practice of foot-
noting the apparently more important events of history. Because

the mission never obtruded impatiently onto the Chinese scene and contributed none of those celebrated nineteenth-century "missionary cases," and because it left little behind when it disappeared from that scene in 1949, it has rarely achieved more than a sentimental significance in the historiography of modern China. Latourette, in his monumental history of Christian missions in China,[10] gives the Russian mission seven pages and three other scattered references.

To be sure, even sentiments will vary enormously. In Russia there was once a quite understandable national pride in the fact that the mission did survive continuously from the time of K'anghsi under the most oppressively heathen conditions. Nikolai Adoratskii, whose history of the Russian mission in Peking was published in 1887,[11] excuses its failures in the "spiritual wasteland of China" by maintaining that it served the fatherland by "bringing together the two neighboring monarchies."[12] In this century it was more often argued that the mission had played a great role in the cultural exchange "between the two peoples,"[13] and that its communicants in Peking "promoted the strengthening of the cultural ties of the Chinese and Russian peoples."[14] But now, even such gamely offered opinions as these are no longer heard. Instead, the silence has suddenly been broken in China; and instead of being praised, the Russian mission is blamed for being "in every sense a tool of aggression" against the Chinese state. Not only were Russian missionaries a "flock of rapacious underlings fed and used by the Tsarist government to invade China," among them were also those who "came to be known as the leading ... Confucian worshippers in the eighteenth century."[15] These are all titles that a member of the Russian mission would wear proudly, if only he felt deserving of them. But until the case is better made, they must remain purely honorary.

The most recent bourgeois thinking on this subject is confined more to the simple destitution of the mission. R. K. I. Quested writes of its "sordid nature,"[16] and Clifford Foust remarks facetiously, in his superb study of Sino-Russian trade relations in the eighteenth century, that "not all of the Russians in Peking were dissolute, licentious, lazy, rude, perverted, dishonest, or deceitful, only most of them."[17] The origins of the Russian mission were too circumstantial, its sense of mission too uncompetitive, its behavior far too debauched, for it to be taken seriously in our China missiology. It began as an unsolicited gesture from a Manchu emperor and, unlike most foreign missions in modern Chinese history, was connected with a war that China had managed to win. In more peaceful times, when Russia sent its venerable archimandrites to Peking, life in China did indeed have a way of bringing out their incontinence instead of their piety.

This essay will attempt to say more. For one thing, by obstinately continuing its long march into the nineteenth and twentieth centuries, by outlasting everything else the Kiakhta Treaty had provided for, and by requiring bureaucratic attention to the replacement of personnel at scheduled intervals, the Russian mission contributed greatly to the regularity of contact between Russia and China. Whatever else went wrong in Sino-Russian relations, there would always be Russian missionaries to negotiate over. Furthermore, in the obscure and innocuous life of this institution (indeed Peter the Great had once instructed his China missionaries to be unostentatious) lay interesting possibilities, for it could then invite the pretense of being an equivalent of Russian diplomatic outposts in places like Constantinople or Paris, but too far from St. Petersburg for anyone to notice the functional and formal discrepancies. The mission made Russia's relations with China appear closer to normal than they ever, in fact, were before 1860. The Manchu rulers of China could appreciate the subtlety of this point because they were looking upon the Russian mission in quite the same way. There was, however, one important difference. It was a sinocentric normality with which they were concerned, not the establishment of diplomatic outposts abroad. And it was in particular their self-image as sovereigns of Inner Asia that required constant embellishment. For the Manchus the Russian mission accordingly became a lamasery of bearded mendicants which, situated next to the Mongol camping grounds in the city, gave visible substance to the sense that Peking was the booming metrop-

olis of an Inner Asian empire. The more pretense, the less willingness to ask too pointedly in either Russia or China what the mission
was really doing in Peking, for what it was doing there was answering the opposite needs of two contending empires, and two international systems.

That Romanov Russia and Ch'ing China had radically different
traditions of foreign relations will not come as news to anyone.
Russia under Peter belonged to the age of European expansion, and
was making mercantilist demands upon northern China that
resembled what other Europeans sought on the China coast. The
China upon which these demands were being made was itself as
culturally certain in refusing most of what Russia wanted as it was
in dealing with any other nation that came knocking at its doors.
These are themes that we now take for granted. What lends a special
interest to the study of early Sino-Russian relations is not the idea
of cultural encounter *per se,* but the time and the place in which this
encounter occurred. Briefly and plainly stated, Russia met China at
a time when China, under its new Manchu rulers, was also an
expansionistic power; and in a place where the control of territory
and people was greatly at issue. In the volatile setting of Inner Asia
in the seventeenth and eighteenth centuries, values and appearances
were as necessary to the stability of Sino-Russian relations as were
treaties. Continuous contact was as necessary as intermittent embassies. These were the needs that the Russian ecclesiastical mission in
Peking was silently asked to fill. And in answering the call perhaps
the mission did achieve a kind of sublimation that was always well
out of the reach of its uncertain spiritual powers. Nothing, after all,
could be more sublime than to be recognized by the latest edition
of the *Guinness Book of World Records,* where it is noted that the
old Russian ecclesiastical mission in Peking, now appropriated by
the Soviet Union, has become the site of the largest embassy in the
world. [18]

Chapter I

THE BEGINNINGS OF THE
ECCLESIASTICAL MISSION IN CHINA

There can be no doubt that the Russian ecclesiastical mission in Peking owed its origins to the Russian constituency in that city during the early Ch'ing period, to the historical process by which Russians were made citizens of the Manchu state, and to the reasons why the Manchus themselves felt obliged to take seriously the religious predicament of a people who were now at the mercy of the K'ang-hsi emperor. It was a coincidence of history that Russia and China had become Inner Asian empires in the course of the seventeenth century, for both countries had reached a point in their historical development where territorial expansion became possible because of political and economic developments within their own borders. But expansion into Inner Asia also had the more elemental significance of reversing a tide of history; here vast stretches of land now lay beckoning at least partly for the reason that they no longer inspired the fear of nomadic supremacy over the sedentary civilizations that rimmed the interior of the continent. The military power of the nomads had greatly subsided in the sixteenth century, and by the seventeenth Russia and China were equally carrying forward the process of subjecting the steppe to the sown. It is therefore in the seventeenth century that we may begin to speak properly of a Russian or Chinese imperialism, for it was then that the institutions of empire—those that dealt specifically with the problem of relating new possessions or new frontiers to an imperial superstructure—made their modern historical appearance. In a loose sense the Russian ecclesiastical mission in Peking was eventually destined to be such an imperialistic institution for both Russia and China. But more important for their immediate purposes was the respective establishment, almost simultaneously in the seventeenth century, of the Sibirskii Prikaz (the Siberian Department) and the Li-fan yuan (the Mongolian

9

Superintendancy). The Sibirskii Prikaz dates from 1637, the Li-fan yuan from 1638; it was in these offices that the details of empire-building were managed, whether through the administration of subject territories and peoples (in China) or by promoting colonization as well (in Russia).[1]

The Meeting of the Manchu and Russian Empires

Since neither the Li-fan yuan nor the Sibirskii Prikaz was prepared to take any interest in the world beyond its bureaucratically confined horizons, there was little room to conceive that events in Siberia, or on the expanding Inner Asian frontier of China, might give rise to a delicate international affair in which two established monarchies would end in contesting a remote and desolate tract of land on the Amur frontier. The conduct of foreign relations in a general sense belonged to other chanceries. For the Li-fan yuan and the Sibirskii Prikaz, steppe and forest lands receded from the center of the empire; their job was to define them in terms of the center. Neither was intellectually armed to suspect that these lands, getting further away from one metropolis, might be getting nearer to another. Indeed, these limitations were so natural that it took years for both Russia and China to appreciate the enormity of the fact that they had, in the middle of the seventeenth century, come into contact with one another in the Amur River valley.

For Manchu China the problem of recognition—that is, of ascertaining that the Siberians (or *lo-ch'a*[2]) on the Amur were Russians—was made easier by the fact that the newcomers looked so outlandish. Thereafter the Manchus tried to comprehend the relationship between outlying stockades like Albazin or Nerchinsk on the one hand and Moscow on the other—the capital from which a number of Russian envoys had, by 1670, already arrived in China (notably Petlin in 1618, Baikov in 1656, Ablin in 1654, 1662, and 1668). Since, in Manchu geography, Russia belonged somewhere near Holland,[3] it was properly concluded that Russian power must be very loosely strung out along the immense overland distance to the Siberian frontier. The question was really whether the frontier was taking orders from Moscow at all. Getting an answer was important, for the means of dealing with the problem that Albazin posed would obviously depend on a certain knowledge of where authority was located. By 1670 K'ang-hsi had his evidence that Nerchinsk, at least, was well within the tsarist line of command.[4] Thereafter the Manchu task was to get the tsar to behave like the autocrat he announced himself to be, and keep his far-flung subjects under control. This was best accomplished by writing him embarrassing letters which implied that K'ang-hsi knew more about what was going on in Eastern Siberia than did Aleksei Mikhailovich.

The Manchu strategy, however, was too subtle. In 1670 (the date of K'ang-hsi's first letter to Aleksei[5]) Russia was still far from fathoming the importance of the events on its Siberian frontier, for the task of sorting out the geography and ethnography of Inner Asia had scarcely begun.[6] No one in Moscow could yet be sure whether China was more than remotely concerned with the Amur territories. Until the proper questions were asked, or until the situation was even taken to be the puzzle that it was, the correct answers could not be arrived at. As much as any other, the difficulty was a bureaucratic one: the Russian envoys who went to Peking to develop commercial and diplomatic relations between the two countries were sent off not by the Sibirskii Prikaz but by the Posol'skii Prikaz (the Ambassadorial Department), an office which had no wish to inquire into the unglamorous goings-on in Siberia. In the mid-seventeenth century the information on China that was ultimately retrieved by the Posol'skii Prikaz was still in the grip of the Mongol terminology that had given so much trouble to an earlier generation of Europeans who had sought Marco Polo's "Cathay" somewhere beyond the Ming horizon. Envoys from Moscow who were on their way to "Kitai" were escorted by Mongol guides, crossed the steppe lands of Western Mongolia after turning south from Tobolsk, and expected to end their journey in a city they still called "Khanbalik." The emperor they were prepared to encounter was "of Mongol stock" and supposedly spoke the same language as the Mongols.[7]

Meanwhile the route into Eastern Siberia, having divided so soon and so sharply from that which led across Mongolia to "Khanbalik" (or Peking), brought its different travelers into an entirely different world, where a disagreeable Manchu (or "bogdoiskii") people apparently still waited to be pacified by men like Khabarov. No one yet supposed that the rulers of China also took themselves to be rulers of the Amur, or that the distance between the Amur frontier and Peking would narrow considerably in the remote eastern horizon. Baikov, in 1656, could not know that the recent fighting on the Amur in fact had involved agents of the very emperor to whom he was accredited. The Amur, after all, was the business of the Sibirskii Prikaz. Baikov and the Posol'skii Prikaz had Russian foreign relations to attend to, not the intractability of some Amurian natives as seemingly far from China as they were from metropolitan Russia. Russia, in other words, had a two-China policy without realizing it.[8]

The Milovanov mission of 1671 stumbled upon the truth,[9] but even then its full significance was not easily digested in Moscow. Instead of recognizing the worst—that Russian expansion had met its match on the Amur—Russian officials preferred to believe that the Manchus could not possibly prevail in China and on the frontier at the same time. The Spafarii embassy of 1675–1678, the first official mission to cross into China at the Manchurian border, might have shown more interest than it did in the fact that Peking was easily reached by the northeastern waterways. But Spafarii did not pursue the logic of his observations. He did not acknowledge that his new and rapid route to China could just as well be traversed in the opposite direction by Manchu armies headed for the northern frontier. Quite the contrary; the important news for Spafarii was that the Manchus were a quite finite group of conquerors now engaged in a desperate struggle with an infinite number of Chinese (his reference being to the San-fan rebellion).[10] Surely the San-fan affair was a menace to Manchu hegemony, probably the greatest danger the Manchus faced before the Taiping rebellion. But the Three Feudatories had been put down by the time Spafarii brought word of the revolt back to Moscow. Matters were now moving too fast for either the Posol'skii Prikaz or the Sibirskii Prikaz (even if we assume they were by now pooling their information)[11] to keep up with them. The price of their lack of coordination was the rapid and violent loss of Albazin, and what is now viewed in the Soviet Union as the dictated, humiliating, and "unequal" treaty of Nerchinsk in 1689—circumstances which, in the first instance, contributed many new members to the Russian community in Peking and, in the second, worked to leave them there forever.[12] But here we are anticipating the events that were so crucial to the origin of the ecclesiastical mission.

The "Pacification" of Albazin

Before the capture of Grigorii Mylnikov and the final arrival of destitute Albazinians in Peking after the fall of the outpost in 1685, a number of Russians had already put themselves within the Ch'ing empire, whether by accidentally straying across a frontier that was only dimly perceived in the confusion of converging expansionism in the seventeenth century, or by quite wittingly taking the opportunity to flee a harrowing existence in Siberia. The first Russian reported to be living in China was a deserter named Wu-lang-ko-li, who had "submitted voluntarily" in 1651. One may well suppose that Wu-lang-ko-li was Ananii Uruslanov, a Christianized Moslem who had served the voevoda of Yakutsk, Dmitrii Andreevich Frantsbekov. The latter, a man who did not shrink from whatever tasks he may have felt it his duty to undertake, sent off a delegation to the Manchus on July 27, 1651, to invite them to pledge their allegiance to the Russian tsar. Uruslanov was part of the troupe (perhaps an interpreter); he had gone on ahead and, for unexplained reasons, had never returned.[13] He reappeared in the summer of 1670, when Ignatii Milovanov, on identical diplomatic business in Peking, reported that he was visited by "the traitor Anashka Uruslanov ... who had fled from Dauria, from the Amur River, into China some years ago."[14]

But by then there were other Russian expatriates in China, for Milovanov also encountered a man named Pakhom, once the bondsman of a boyar-son in Yakutsk. Pakhom was no less a "traitor," even though he had been fleeing the renegade Cossack settler of Albazin, Nikifor Romanovich Chernigovskii. According to Milovanov, "the traitors Anashko and Pakhomka have married, are professing a Chinese faith, are getting their food from the Bogdokhan [emperor], and live in their own homes." And quite apart from these two, mention is made in the *Annals of the Eight Banners* (the *Pa-ch'i t'ung-chih*) of the defection of a Russian named I-fan (Ivan) and his companions in 1668.[15] Spafarii, in 1676, derived the following count from his sources of information in Peking: "There are now thirteen Russians in China, of whom only two were actually taken captive on the Amur, while all the rest are fugitives from the stockades on the frontier, especially from Albazin. Three years ago three men deserted by managing an escape down the Amur to the mouth of the Shingala [Sungari] River. Here the Chinese take the deserters, and send them straightway to Peking, where the bugdykhan pays them a salary, marries them off, and enlists them in his services."[16]

After the Manchus had organized their campaign against the Russian encroachments on the Amur (Russia having shrugged off the responsibility of keeping its garrisons under control), many more prisoners were taken beyond the two that Spafarii had heard of. By 1683 K'ang-hsi was offering them inducements to settle in China. The distinction between "traitor" and "prisoner" therefore became blurred, which was indeed the practical intent of the policy of "favor and awe" (*en wei*) that K'ang-hsi now wished to apply to the pacification of Albazin.[17] K'ang-hsi himself was taking a punctilious interest in the contest for the Amur, the more so because the recently concluded Manchu operations in Taiwan, notwithstanding their brutality, had taken much too long. The problem of the northern frontier, waiting thirty years for a resolution, consequently was approached with more sophistication, more probably than it deserved. Even as the fate of Albazin was busily being planned in Peking, "favor and awe" meant in practical terms that captives like Grigorii Mylnikov and Maksim Leont'ev, instead of being put to the sword, would receive rewards, rank, homes, and women. Needless to say, Manchu magnanimity had nothing to do with battlefield heroics, for no battles had yet been fought; but it was a part of their pacification theory, and undoubtedly it affected the morale of the defenders of Albazin, where women (for example) were in chronically short supply.

For many of these Cossacks, the choice had once been between living inside or outside the law in Siberia; now, when even their well-known endurance was reaching an end, a new alternative was suddenly available to them: a choice between Russia itself and China. There can be no doubt that they knew of the possibility of another life beyond the frontier, for in 1684 twenty-one Russians deserted to China.[18] Early in the following year two more were incarcerated by a Tungus chieftain from whom they were attempting to collect *iasak*. Taken before the Manchu commander, they were asked if they would not rather serve the emperor of China and were promised tempting rewards, which included two wives apiece, and two servants each (with wives). In this case, surely an exception, the offer was refused. With "favor and awe" the Russians were sent back to Albazin carrying Manchu propaganda with them and undoubtedly a few tall stories of their own.[19] The final, and by far the largest group of Russians to cross into China after the fall of Albazin in 1685 was responding only to Manchu blandishments. Nevertheless, metropolitan officials and religious authorities in Russia now began to regard them all as prisoners of China, a convenient means of dealing with a troublesome historical reality.[20]

By mid-1685 there were upwards of one hundred Russian "prisoners" in China, enough to constitute a full company in the Manchu banner organization. Whether or not one accepts this figure (for it is far from unchallengeable),[21] or whether it is taken to be a relatively large or relatively small number, there can be no dispute that many of these expatriates functioned in the Manchu service in more important ways than as passive victims of good psychological warfare. To be sure, no Albazinians were ever put into the field to fight against their former countrymen, but the use of them in Manchu intelligence operations may be taken as a case in point. After he was in Peking (a second time) to announce the coming of Spafarii's embassy, Ignatii Milovanov reported that the

Ch'ing officials had "forcibly removed from him the instructions given him in Nerchinsk . . . and [had] had them translated by Russian traitors who had lived there a long time and had translated for the Khan himself."[22] And of the thirteen Russians he had counted in Peking, Spafarii said that "they are now instructing the Chinese to shoot their harquebuses on horseback as well as foot, as one of their number, a man of Tobolsk, wrote to his brother; he has now been hired as a translator in the Ambassadorial Department [the Li-fan yuan] because he is literate in Russian, has learned Chinese, and can translate any Russian letter."[23]

By the 1680s some of these Russians were being used as interpreters, and even as *agents provocateurs,* for the Manchu command on the Amur. One account[24] of the capture of Grigorii Mylnikov states accusingly that it was "the Chinese translators, traitors formerly of Albazin, [who] invited the whole party to come over to China." Two of Mylnikov's Cossacks (their names were Mishka Ivanov and Ivashko Zakharov) were taken to the Manchu camp where they were interrogated by "the traitors of the tsar, Ivashko Artem'ev, Agafonko Zyrian, and Stenka Verkhotur." Then, after several weeks in captivity, they were told by still another Russian, Pakhom Stepanovich Kornoukh (whom we have met earlier, but now know by his full name), that the Manchus were planning a major campaign against Albazin. Kornoukh gave them a letter, ostensibly from Mylnikov, to take back to Albazin, making clear the alternatives of withdrawal or full hostilities, and not forgetting to mention the "obedient *lo-ch'a*" who had become subjects of the Ch'ing emperor. In the course of this adventure, Mishka Ivanov and Ivashko Zakharov had confronted several of their countrymen who were now in the service of China, and had performed a useful service for the Manchus by delivering an ominous note to the beleaguered Russian stockade. The impact was considerable, not only because it was the first formal Manchu ultimatum against Russia's eastward expansion, but also because it had arrived in translation! Ivanov and Zakharov at length presented themselves at the more important garrison town of Yeniseisk, where they spelled out a definitive version of their story.

At the same time two other Russians in Mylnikov's detachment were sent to the headquarters of Sabsu, the Manchu commander, "so they may be used to bring others to submit."[25] On the Russian side there was simply no counterpart to people like them. The handful of Manchu prisoners that were taken near Albazin in 1686 (when hostilities threatened to resume) spoke a language that was still unintelligible to the Russians,[26] who lacked that capacity for the gathering of intelligence and dispensing of propaganda that had characterized Manchu military planning. The success of the Manchu campaign against Albazin was indeed advanced considerably by the Russians whom it so adroitly employed.

As helpful as they were in making war on Russia, Albazinians could be instruments of peace, too. In May, 1685, three liberated prisoners left Peking with a package of six messages (in Russian, Latin, and Mongol) "and a letter from Stenka Kozmin to his father and mother."[27] Inside the carefully translated notes, addressed to the tsars Peter and Ivan, was the offer of a peace conference. They were delivered half a year later[28] (after the destruction of Albazin) and caused the assembling of Fedor Golovin's embassy to the frontier. As it turned out, the prisoners of war who carried the Manchu mail were the last to return to Russia from Peking. The Albazinians had accomplished everything the Manchus could have expected of them, and it only remained to be seen whether Russia was interested in getting them back.

It is conceivable that they would, in fact, have been repatriated had it not been for the celebrated case of Ghantimur, an important Daghur Mongol chieftain. Until 1667 Ghantimur had received an annual stipend from K'ang-hsi. In that year he became dissatisfied with the terms of his investiture by the Manchus and fled into Siberia with about forty of his relatives and tribesmen, stopping on the way to assist Chernigovskii in the building of Albazin. Russia protected him jealously from the persistent Ch'ing diplomatic efforts to get him back; symbolically he was important to both sides, since both Russian and Manchu territorial claims at that time depended as much on local tribal allegiances as on a military presence. And since, by contrast, the Albazinians could symbolize no such thing, it is quite obvious that K'ang-hsi would have parted with them gladly for the return of Ghantimur. The messages taken to the Siberian garrisons by released prisoners like Ivashko Zakharov and Mishka Ivanov never failed to mention Ghantimur. He was an *idée fixe* of Ch'ing diplomacy. Variety appeared only when the Manchus forgot how to spell his name, as they had by the summer of 1685 when another "I-fan" and his four companions were sent back to Siberia with the demand for the return of "Chi-erh-meng-a."[29]

Meanwhile, Ghantimur and his son Katanaem were converted to Russian Orthodoxy in 1684. At that time they were given the baptismal names of Petr and Pavel, respectively, with the last name of Gantimurov (not any easier for Russians to spell, however, as Spafarii and Golovin both demonstrate when they passed through his territory).[30] Russia obviously had no intention of surrendering them. As far as Ghantimur himself was concerned, this resolve was made easier when he died, shortly afterwards, on his way to Moscow to present himself to the tsars. The leadership of the clan thus fell to Pavel Petrovich Gantimurov, who until his death in 1700 remained a well-known, if not entirely welcome, citizen of Nerchinsk. In 1688 the voevoda of Nerchinsk, Ivan Vlasov, instructing his assistants on how to manage things in his absence, ordered them to "treat the Muscovite *dvorianin* [nobleman] Prince Pavel Gantimurov with kindness and respect so that no insult or indignity will be done him."[31]

The stubborn refusal of Russia to give up Ghantimur had the effect of making the Manchus more stubborn with their Albazinians. None of Golovin's advance party, who had come to Peking to announce his embassy, were allowed to see them, although a servant of Ferdinand Verbiest did reveal to the Russians that two Albazinians were helping the Jesuit with the casting of cannon and shells, whose destination for the northern frontier was perfectly plain should peace not be concluded soon.[32] Meanwhile, Golovin's final instructions had given him the power to negotiate the exchange of Manchu fugitives in Russia for the Russian "prisoners" in China (preferably without compensation, or, at the most, paying thirty rubles for each Russian retrieved); but the Gantimurovs were excepted. Here Russia stood firm, and here the fate of the Albazinians was sealed.

The fourth article of the Treaty of Nerchinsk, which was signed on August 28, 1689, disposed of the whole issue in one lifeless sentence. "Those subjects of the Russian empire who are now in China, and those of the Chinese empire now in Russia, shall remain in that condition." The Manchu text is hardly preferable, but it is more straightforward: "The Russians now living in China and the Chinese subjects who are in Russia shall be left there for the rest of their lives."[33] Such language meant, of course, that Pavel Gantimurov, citizen of Russia, was no longer negotiable under any circumstances. With a peace treaty in hand, the Manchus promptly ceased (but surely did not forget) their long effort to get him back. For its part, however, Russia had a more difficult time reconciling itself to the loss of the Albazinians (as well as to the loss of Albazin itself, provided for in the third article of the treaty). Shortly after the signing of the treaty a boyar-son named Grigorii Lonshchakov visited Peking asking for their release; and soon another envoy, Plotnikov, went to Peking for the same purpose. The old offer of thirty rubles apiece still stood, but neither man had any success. Perhaps Russia considered that now, when commercial relations with China were resuming, a traffic in Albazinians was theoretically possible without reference to the treaty of Nerchinsk. Yet for better or for worse, the Albazinians of Peking were there to stay, and the Manchus could now freely, and quite spitefully, refer to them as "our Russians."[34]

The Russian Company

The practical question of integrating the Manchu-Russians into Peking society had been asked much earlier and was another matter altogether. Here K'ang-hsi, expounding on the subject in 1683, decided that segregation was the better idea. On November 15 of that year the Board of Revenue suggested that "the *lo-ch'a* who had surrendered, Chi-li-kuo-li [Grigorii Mylnikov] and his companions, should be assigned to the Plain White Banner and enrolled in the companies that are undermanned." But to this the emperor replied that "the surrendered *lo-ch'a* are quite numerous; they should constitute a company of their own and, by depending on each other, help us all out."[35] It was from this edict that the seventeenth company (*tso-ling*) of the fourth regiment (*ts'an-ling*) of the Manchu Bordered Yellow Banner was formed. At first at only half-strength, its *lo-ch'a* enlistment was complete by 1685.

The decision to form a banner company of Russians was one of great importance, the more so since historical evidence clearly reveals that K'ang-hsi made the decision himself. In making it, he was obviously mindful of the fact that he was taking his Russians into a principal Manchu institution, which had already been used to enroll Chinese and Mongol adherents of the Ch'ing much earlier in the seventeenth century. One effect of this arrangement was to suggest that the Manchu government was supple enough to find an honorable place in its military organization for the non-Manchus who supported it; and by extension, to suggest to those Russians who remained "unpacified" that submission was preferable to resistance. The Russian company was, accordingly, supposed to retain its identity, not lose it. Russians were not to become Manchus, they were to remain foreigners, serving happily in the Manchu service. But by taking in the Albazinians in this fashion, K'ang-hsi was implicitly giving something as well. From 1683 on, he would be bound to provide for them exactly as he provided for his Chinese and Mongol bannermen. Among other things this meant making available to them a place in which to practice their religion. Ultimately it also bound him, in a sense, to receive Russian priests from outside China.

In Peking the "Russian company" was settled in the extreme northeast corner of the Tartar City, at the very bottom of the city wall. This was the section reserved for the Bordered Yellow Banner, between the An-ting gate to the north and the T'ung-chih gate to the east. The district it inhabited was called the *hua-p'i ch'ang,* so named from the fact that it was the depot for shipments of birch from Manchuria from which bows were made for the bannermen. Company captain was Uruslanov, who thereby became an official of the upper-fourth grade. I-fan (Artem'ev) was made a lieutenant (*hsiao-ch'i*), with the rank of an upper-sixth grade official. Before 1684 the rank of seventh grade was given to Ao-ko-t'u and Hsi-t'u-pan (Agafon and Stepan, probably the ubiquitous interpreters Agafonko Zyrian and Stenka Verkhotur'); to Chi-li-kuo-li (Grigorii Mylnikov); and to Ma-k'o-hsi-mu (Maksim Leont'ev). Everyone received an allowance, a home, and some arable land; food and clothes; and, if desired, a wife.[36] It is upon these local women, who came from prisons or houses of detention in the capital, that later Russian missionaries found it most convenient to place the blame for the miserable conditions in which they had to work. No doubt the wives did help lead their Albazinians astray, but the matches could only have represented a Chinese estimate of what their husbands deserved.

A military company was the basic unit in the organization of the eight banners. The Russian company was not a combat arm (*wai tso-ling*) of the banner, but rather a household (*pao-i*) company, with inherited leadership. After the death of Uruslanov, which had occurred before the Nerchinsk conference, the command was given to his son, Lo-to-hun.[37] Upon the latter's death the company was entrusted to the Grand Secretary Maci, an old Russia hand (and a prominent official as well), who was undoubtedly able to turn a considerable profit from the perquisites of his captaincy. The Russian Company remained under the clan of Maci throughout the eighteenth century. Feng-shen-chi-lun, a degenerate great grandnephew of Maci and grandson of the Ch'ien-lung emperor, was captain until his death, in 1807, at which time the nominal command over a then nominal detachment passed to Prince Kung-a-la, father-in-law of the Chia-ch'ing emperor.[38]

It was the responsibility of the Russian Company to guard the northeast corner of the Tartar City wall. But not everyone in it was a soldier, for a *tso-ling* included not only the original group of warriors but also their families and their descendants. This was the case with the Russian Company. While they were plausibly able to field a guard unit of a hundred men, a better deployment for them was as bow makers for Manchu bannermen. But their numbers soon must have included just as many street vendors, restaurateurs, or simple vagabonds. When Russian caravans were in the capital, they frequently acted as dragomans, brokers, and local guides. Grigorii Mylnikov may have operated a soap-works, a flour mill, or both; in any case he appears, quite exceptionally, to have become as enterprising a businessman in Peking as he had been a collector of *iasak* on the frontier.[39]

As for Maksim Leont'ev's chapel, it was embellished in 1685 with a number of icons and church plates that had been brought from the razed Church of the Resurrection in Albazin. These included a picture of Saint Nicholas the Miracle-worker, from which the name of the Peking church was now wistfully taken. But the Nikolskii church (as it can now be called) accomplished no miracles, save that of surviving an extended period of indifference in its own parish as well as in Russia.

Of the Albazinians themselves the only possible conclusion is that none of these arrangements was capable of doing much for them. If anything, matters were worse now that their old and reckless way of life had changed, and the theory behind the Manchu formation of the Russian company could not for very long have withstood the fact of its collapse as either a military or social unit in late seventeenth-century Peking. Safely enclosed beneath the high wall of the Tartar City, idols competing with icons in their homes, overcome with ennui, the Albazinians became noticeably prone to bouts of drunkenness and public scuffling. No matter that they would soon supply the only acceptable pretext for the establishment of a Russian religious mission in Peking; missionary-historians like Adoratskii show a morbid fascination with their decadence, despising the very people whom the churchmen were trying to save. Today there are apparently a few distinguishable Albazinians still in Peking, and now it is the Soviet diplomatic mission that they pester with problems of their uncertain nationality.[40] They remain, as they always have been, a misplaced souvenir of the seventeenth century, that eventful time to which all the enduring issues of Sino-Russian relations can be traced.

The Russian Discovery of Leont'ev's Chapel

The Nikolskii church had existed since 1683, but it remained to be discovered by Russia. The discovery, when it came in 1693, occurred quite by accident, and it occurred twice. A Russian caravaneer named Basil Lobanov was the first to find it; soon afterward Izbrant Ides, a Muscovite envoy to China (who had himself come to Peking to seek permission for, among other things, an Orthodox establishment there), ran across the church while wandering through the Tartar City. Ides was unimpressed and failed to mention his discovery when he returned to Russia in 1695. Peter the Great did not learn of it until 1698, when he was on tour in western Europe. He got the word from one of his Dutch adjutants back in Moscow, where Lobanov's news of the Albazinian church had finally trickled in from Siberia.

The main purpose of Ides's much advertised but unproductive embassy was to investigate further the commercial opportunities in China now open to Russia after the treaty of Nerchinsk. It was in connection with the Russian expectation of a lively trade that the request (in article six of Ides's instructions) for a church in Peking was to be advanced. Russian merchants in China would have need of such a retreat. Lest anyone follow Barthold into the error of assuming that the proposed church was for the Albazinians, it suffices only to point out that Ides, like Lonshchakov and Plotnikov before him, had been instructed to ask the Manchus "for the release of all Russian prisoners in the Chinese empire." To this the reply of Songgotu, the Ch'ing official with whom Ides did most of his negotiating, was simply that all the Russians who had wanted to return had already been released.[41] As for the demand for a church, the Manchus properly understood that it had nothing to do with the Albazinians. Their answer to Ides, given him on February 19, 1694, held that "your Russian merchants want to build a church in Peking [asking that] a place be set aside for its construction for which, they say, 'Our Russian tsars will provide the money from their treasury.' The people of all the Latin kingdoms who have come permanently to Our Empire have only built one church. It is incredible that the people of empires far and near should all receive a place for a church in Our Empire. Furthermore, it is impossible to speak otherwise on this point."[42] A more concise expression of this precedent is found in another document, also purporting to be part of the Ch'ing reply to Ides: "the building of a church for foreigners in China is appropriate if they live here permanently, but for transients to demand a church is customarily not allowed."[43]

The paradox of demanding something that one already possessed did not end with the Ides embassy. Russian envoys continued to ask for a church in Peking as if Saint Nicholas did not exist: Izmailov did so in 1719 and Vladislavich in 1727. The Albazinian church was too much a makeshift affair, perhaps too much an ugly reminder of the 1680s as well. To be sure, the Nikolskii chapel was an improvement upon the dreadful arrangement that Spafarii had reported, in which Russians living in Peking would frequent the Jesuit church.[44] (Spafarii had therefore given Verbiest an icon of the archangel Michael, to which prayers could be better said for the tsar.) But Russia had in mind something fancier: a church not only worthy of its merchants and diplomats, but also one that stood a chance of undercutting the Jesuits' self-righteous monopoly on Peking. It was known that three shipwrecked Greeks had had their own Orthodox chapel in Peking in 1670, and Spafarii had written in 1676 that "now the Jesuits think that soon all the Chinese will be Catholic because in America too, in the New World, similar signs foreshadowed the coming of the Catholics; so too in Japan. We, however, believe that, with God's help and the tsar's happy fortune, the Chinese will ere long adopt the Orthodox Greek faith."[45] For an extravagant hope like this, the Nikolskii church would obviously never do. Ides had made an easy decision to say nothing about it.

Let us therefore take up the story of how news of the church *was* transmitted to and received by the tsar, for the details can shed a certain light on important religious and political questions of the late seventeenth century. In 1693 the caravan of Basil Lobanov had a more substantial encounter with the Nikolskii church in Peking, and upon its return to Tobolsk stirred an interest among Siberian ecclesiastics in this unexpected parish. Lobanov carried with him a request from Maksim Leont'ev for various liturgical items for his church: a tablecloth for the mass, myrrh, and some holy oils. Not only did the metropolitan of Siberia, Ignatii Rimskii-Korsakov, requisition these necessities, he also attached two clerics to the next Peking caravan, already mustering in Tobolsk, with instructions to consecrate the church in the name of Saint Sofia. The mission accomplished, they left China in 1696 with the departing caravan of Ostafii Filat'ev.[46]

Rimskii-Korsakov had, furthermore, taken the occasion to write an exhortatory letter to Leont'ev. It was dated June 16, 1695:

> To the preacher of the holy Gospel in the Chinese empire: I have learned from some honorable merchants who have visited you in China that his highness the Bodgy Khan has given you the liberty for the holy Christian Orthodox faith and a temple of his Buddhist faith [which you] have consecrated to our Saint Trinity, after having gotten rid of its Buddhist idols by throwing them all out ... Let your soul and that of all the prisoners with you not be troubled; neither take offense concerning your fate, such as it is, for who can oppose the will of God? And your imprisonment is not without advantage for the Chinese people since the light of Christ's Orthodox faith is being revealed to them by you.[47]

At last someone was taking Maksim Leont'ev seriously! Of course he had his hands quite full enough with the Albazinians and would hardly have been disposed, in any case, to pursue his missionary work into the unfamiliar alleyways beyond the *lo-ch'a* quarter; but if the price of getting some attention from the motherland was an evangelical reconstruction of his fate, and an unsolicited name for his church (the Hagia Sophia at that!), the highhandedness of Rimskii-Korsakov was undoubtedly worth it.

None of these events, however, had yet made themselves known in Moscow. During the next three years word of the Russian Orthodox church in Peking continued to travel slowly westward and finally reached the capital in 1698, at a time when Peter, now ruling alone in Russia, was himself traveling in Europe. He was therefore not on hand to get the news when it came to Andrei Andreevich Vinius, head of the Sibirskii Prikaz. But Vinius, a close friend and adviser of the tsar, and a responsible Hollander who had been Russianized "in all but his origin and superior cultivation,"[48] sent a prompt report to Peter in Vienna:

> Your lordship's continued absence saddens us above all. I announce the Siberian news: in the capital itself, in Pekin—in Europe they call it Peking—the local Orthodox Christians, those in captivity and the newcomers, founded, completely finished building, and consecrated a holy church in the name of Sophia, the wisdom of God's Word, and a great multitude of the Chinese people saw this and soon after this twenty people of the male and female sex took upon themselves holy baptism . . . To you I entrust myself, bowing with a most humble bow, I prostrate myself, Andreushka Vinius.[49]

Peter received this letter, in the center of Europe, at a time when intellectuals on the continent were experiencing a considerable titillation over China. For this the Jesuits had been largely responsible of course, but Protestant Europe had been no less affected. The Ides embassy to China, which included a number of northern Europeans in its suite, had given much hope of more information about this apparently very civilized empire which, according to Gottfried Leibniz, lacked only "the divine gift of Christian religion."[50] In 1697, soon after its return, Leibniz published in the first edition of his *Novissima Sinica* a short and thin account of the journey by the embassy secretary, Adam Brand.[51] But late-breaking news, especially when it was so incomplete, only served to quicken the need for more contact between China and the West—those two highest civilizations, Leibniz wrote, which fate had placed "at the two extremities of our continent."[52] Here Russia stood at what was presumed to be a crossroads. Geographically it would be indispensable to the reliable comings and goings of emissaries between both ends of the Eurasian land mass; and more than that it would, in what was taken as its primitive state of development, do nothing to alter the impact of one civilization on the other. The task of getting Peter to accept these arguments and throw open to Europe his underemployed Siberian land routes fell primarily to Nicolas Witsen,[53] Burgomaster of Amsterdam, who acted as the tsar's host while he was in Holland. In Vienna the Jesuits had a chance to press upon Peter the same request. They had (or so *they* thought) performed creditably as go-betweens at Nerchinsk; would he now indulge their larger purpose as international middlemen? It was at this juncture, so important to the future of such grand designs, that news of the Orthodox church in Peking arrived.

Peter was by no means the only one to receive the announcement of Vinius, for the latter had also communicated his "Siberian news" to Witsen, with whom he was well acquainted. Witsen thereupon wrote directly to Leibniz on May 22, 1698, and to Peter himself late in July: "I congratulate you on the recently gained triumph over the unbelieving enemy . . . on the persuasion of a few of the many tartars, as it has been communicated to us."[54] By this time, however, Peter had already made his answer to Vinius.

> Here you also write, your grace, that in Peking the Christians have built a church of our law and that many of the Chinese were christened. And this is a very good thing; only in the name of God act carefully and not rashly, so that you do not arouse anger in the Chinese leaders as well as in the Jesuits, who for many years have had their nest there. For this reason priests are needed there who are not so much learned as they are wise and obliging, lest because of some conceit that holy task will result in the most wicked failure, as was the case in Japan.[55]

The reply was not particularly enthusiastic, but it does appear carefully considered. At least one may infer that there was now an additional reason to protect the Russian land routes from European competitors. If it is true that Peter had given the Jesuits in Vienna his tentative permission to travel through Siberia to China, it was soon revoked upon his return to Moscow.[56] At the same time he allowed to lapse that part of his new treaty with the Elector of Brandenburg, Frederick III, which had contained a provision for the free passage of Brandenburgers across Russia to China. Even Nicholas Witsen now fell out of touch with the tsar. During his entertainment of Peter in Amsterdam in 1697 he had talked extensively with him about Siberian geography; but in 1706 Witsen wrote Leibniz that "since that time I have not heard anything from him."[57] The Orthodox church in Peking, so recently the subject of a modest celebration in Europe, was thereupon discarded from that united front toward China that Witsen had so ardently pursued. Leibniz's second edition of the *Novissima Sinica,* appearing in 1699, considered the success of the Russian mission either too much a strain on his own credulity or, if he believed it, too insignificant to report. The Roman Catholic response became openly sarcastic, one Franciscan writing from Russia this invented account of the consecration of Saint Sophia:

> Several years ago a local merchant, Filatilov [Filat'ev] delivered a priest to China, who there received permission, I don't know where, to build a church. On the very first day that the church was opened and he began to do the liturgy, twelve Chinese were joined to the Russian schism. The father of our order, upon seeing this, arranged for the church to be closed, and the priest was compelled to withdraw beyond the frontier of the state into neighboring Muscovite territory . . . such tears from here![58]

With Peter's stiffening resistance to granting what Europe wanted from Russia, there was no longer any point in disguising such malevolent prejudices.

What Peter, for his part, seemed to have taken away from his European tour was the opinion that, however bent he was on reforming his own country, it was a dubious national purpose for Russia to become a thoroughfare for Westerners whose real interests lay further to the East—the more so now that he had his own nest (as he would have said) in Peking. Protestant modernizers would be welcome in Russia, but only if they stopped there. And if in

Leibniz's fanciful prospect that everything lying in between European and Chinese civilization would be "gradually brought to a higher way of life"[59] there was a badly hidden reference to Russia, he had overestimated the Russian readiness to be influenced by a nation of *arrivés,* with which an untimely war had been fought and which still held some unfortunate men prisoners in its interior. The only Chinese influence that penetrated Petrine Russia came in the form of *chinoiserie,* and that, of course, because it was a reputable European fad which no Russian thought of tracing to its source.

Meanwhile, Peter decided to investigate the situation in Peking on his own. Far from being embarrassed by the news of his China mission,[60] he soon supplemented his jealous quarantine of the Siberian routes with a zealous ukase, in June, 1700,[61] that made a resounding appeal for the propagation of the faith in Siberia and China. As far as Siberia was concerned this edict made a lot of mundane sense: it would advance the russification of those vast territories that the tsar now ruled, and it was certainly a good outlet for a church, torn by dissension,[62] which Peter was soon to sever of its Patriarch.[63] Besides, a missionary movement was already well under way. Tobolsk, raised to the rank of a metropolitanate by the church council of 1667, had long since established itself as a center of missionary operations which, by the late seventeenth century, had touched almost every corner of its colonial domain with ever greater numbers of monks and monasteries. Even Albazin had had a cloister, built in 1671 by a monk whom Chernigovskii kidnapped in Kirensk. In 1681 two Russian missionaries penetrated into Dauria, where their metropolitan had sent them "to invite all the natives of Selenginsk and other towns and garrisons into the true Christian Orthodox faith, to instruct them and administer baptism . . . to carry on this holy work without vainglory or pride, to refrain from any violence, and to be careful lest some imprudent word chills the enthusiasm of the converts."[64] By 1695, as we have seen, Metropolitan Rimskii-Korsakov was giving orders for the consecration of the Albazinian church in Peking.

The ukase of 1700 had only to sustain the considerable momentum that missionary successes in Siberia had already gen-

erated. One of its instructions was the appointment of a new man
to the see of Tobolsk: someone "of pleasant and educated calibre"
was to be found somewhere in the Ukraine and, as metropolitan of
Siberia, it was he who was to "lead the natives in China and Siberia
to the service of the true and living God." Filofei Leshchinskii, a
native of Kiev, was chosen for the job. Leshchinskii arrived in
Tobolsk in April, 1702, and began a long and productive career of
missionizing in Siberia. Supplied by secular authorities with all
necessary funds and frequently a military escort, he made many
expeditions down the Siberian riverways, always exceeding his
assistants in the quantity of baptisms and "occasionally taking the
precaution of leaving a priest behind to watch over the newly
saved souls."[65] Filaret reports that Leshchinskii even attempted to
convert the Kalmuk Khutughtu. The failure of that effort notwithstanding, he had by the end of his life in 1721 built thirty-seven
churches and personally accounted for the baptism of forty
thousand Siberian tribesmen.[66]

None of his converts, however, were Chinese. Here the edict
of 1700 may have made good propaganda, as it were, for a Russian
monarch, but it was an impossible field assignment for Leshchinskii.
The new metropolitan was supposed "to bring with him two or
three people who could be instructed in the Chinese and Mongolian
languages, and learning their superstitions, could on the firm basis
of the holy evangelism lead many souls into the acknowledgement
of Christ our God; people who could keep the Christians living and
arriving there [in China] free from the charms of all idolatry and
who could serve mass in a Christian church in order to bring . . .
the Chinese Khan and those near him, as well as the people in general, to that holy work; and who could attend to the Russians who
come and go with the caravans and embassies."[67] Obviously a missionary movement in China required more than proclamation, more
even than Peter's "strong will in converting natives to Christianity,"
if that characterization by Slovtsov[68] can be taken seriously. What
it needed (and what, for a moment, it had appeared to possess in
1700) was a promising base of operations. It soon became clear
that this was precisely what was lacking in China.

It must be remembered that up to this point all the information that Peter had on his China mission was confined in the brief announcement sent him by Vinius in 1698. Wanting more details himself, Vinius had immediately written to the voevoda of Nerchinsk, Ivan Nikol'ev, ordering him to interrogate Russian merchants who had been to Peking, who might well have visited Saint Sophia, and therefore could supply answers to the questions of "where it is and especially at what distance from the homes of the Chinese, and whether the Chinese go to the church to look or listen, and what they say, whether they praise it or not, and what sort of jeerings and desecrations come from them, and whether they favor the Greek church or the Jesuit church, and who the priests are at that church, and his assistants, and if they live all right, and how many Russians there are, and if they have enough books and ornaments, and where the deceased Christians are buried ... and if the service is held in the open or secretly and dangerously ... and [if] there are any among the Chinese who have been baptised."[69]

Nikol'ev reported that in July of 1699 the caravan of Spiridon Liangusov had returned from Peking, and that a merchant named Ivan Savat'ev had left a deposition at the Nerchinsk town hall containing answers to the questions of Vinius. Savat'ev's testimony was then forwarded to Moscow in Nikolev's letter of December 25, 1699 to the tsar. It is the first piece of solid information on the Albazinians reaching Russia, over ten years after the signing of the treaty of Nerchinsk. Savat'ev stated:

I had been for purposes of trade to the Chinese capital with the caravan of the merchant Spiridon Liangusov, and we were in the newly consecrated church more than once and heard the sacred liturgy; and that newly consecrated church in China stood in the city of Peking, to the East, on the right-hand side at the corner of the town close to the wall, and next to that church was laid out a suburb for Russians dwelling in the Chinese capital, and that suburb communicates with the Chinese dwelling yards; and near the church are erected great earthen ramparts with facings three arshins high ... and in them they maintain the *tabun* [herd] of Russian and Mongol caravan horses; and from the embassy compound to that church by measurement it would be about two versts. And in that church the liturgy is sung by the priest Maksim; and he says that it is impossible for him to do it [properly] on account of his great age and failing eyesight, and there are no deacons there with him, only his son has learned to read and helps him in the service; and the Church-warden is Dmitri Grigor'ev, who is not married, and he bakes the wafers, but is illiterate. Spiridon Liangusov had with him the priest Vasilii Aleksandrov, who sang the liturgy more than once. And they send people to that church, to the service, from the embassy; and behind them go soldiers, three or four. The soldiers when the singing takes place come into the porch and take off their caps and stare, and from outside few other natives ever come, and there is no jeering. But to what religion they are more inclined they cannot say, though it was said that many natives come daily to the Jesuit Church ... And of our Christian religion in China, counting men, women, and children there are thirty in all.[70]

With this bleak notice, Peter had a more sober basis for judging those "triumphs" on which he had been congratulated abroad. His curiosity satisfied, there was little left to buoy an interest in the church of Saint Sophia in Peking. Although the edict of 1700 was given an occasional and perfunctory restatement—in 1703, 1706, and 1710—it had little consequence for the China mission. In 1702, late in his career, Vinius made a trip to the Sino-Russian frontier and attempted a local arrangement for getting two Russian clerics admitted to China, perhaps to redeem his first announcement of the Russian church to Europe. This effort elicited only the response from Peking that because of an improper address his letter had not been accepted (the Manchus having thought that all these niceties had been made clear to Ides), and that in the future no such indiscretions would be tolerated. Shortly afterwards Vinius's term in the Sibirskii Prikaz ended. He was now out of favor with Peter, and the ephemeral Russian missionary interest in China had lost its one staunch patron among the higher councils in Moscow.[71]

Leshchinskii, as far as it is possible to know, corresponded only once with his parishioners in Peking, who were theoretically a part of his Siberian eparchy. His long letter reproaching them for their weakening did evoke a certain amount of contrition among the Albazinians, some of whom went back to church to receive whatever religious direction was still to be found there.[72] But apart from such mail-order evangelism, Leshchinskii's missionary movement had been unexportable. In the first decade of the eighteenth century the Russian Orthodox church in Peking thereupon returned, for the time being, to the oblivion from which it had so recently risen.

The problem was that China was not Siberia and could no longer be carelessly attached to the charts of Russian eastward expansion. Russia now had the beginnings of a boundary treaty with the Manchus which limited its access to Peking and made the old Siberian dream of converting the "bogdoiskii tsar" altogether obsolete. There was nothing with which to replace it—surely no perfect certainty that missionary work across a national frontier was the thankless obligation of an advanced Russian Orthodox civilization. The church that Ides had proposed would have been a purely self-interested Russian affair, budgeted by the tsar and used by Russian merchants sojourning in Peking. The church actually discovered there was worth cautious support, but it was never able to overcome the suspicions that its external and spontaneous origins had engendered in the motherland. In fact the ukase of 1700 was devoted more to the practical question of Russian trade than to the rhetorical possibility of converting the K'ang-hsi emperor—a dream of Peter the Great that had arisen from the peculiar context of discovering his China mission while he was being hounded by European sinophiles, but a dream that soon proved unable to stand the light of day.

Europeans who were ready to build more elaborate bridges between East and West met with the same flinching mistrust in Moscow. At the turn of the seventeenth century, when the world was still large enough for Leibniz to think in terms of its "extremities," Russia had become too much the neighbor of China. Russia's intellectual horizons in the East were, quite understandably, clouded by this unpleasant fact of geography. While Europe, a safer distance away, could entertain the fantasy of cultural exchange with China, Russia was thinking more of an exchange of prisoners of war. With the Manchu empire Russia had its own scores to keep, and many still to settle. The counting would never stop, but it would always begin with the time, the place, and the circumstances in which Russia and China had first encountered each other.

Chapter II

ILARION LEZHAISKII: THE FIRST ECCLESIASTICAL
MISSION TO CHINA

Almost nothing is known about the Albazinian community in
Peking from 1699 to 1715. Sometime during this period Maksim
Leont'ev died, although the date of his death is entirely a matter of
conjecture. The only certainty is that this progenitor of the Russian
mission in China had become an unmourned and forgotten man by
the end of the first decade of the eighteenth century. After Leont'ev's
death occasional services were probably held in the Albazinian
church by priests attending the Russian caravans that continued to
arrive in Peking, as Vasilii Aleksandrov had done in 1699. Savat'ev,
for example, returned to China in 1702 and had with him a monk,
deacon, and chorister. The caravan of Grigorii Oskol'kov in 1704
included a monk named Trifil Gantimurov, grandson of Prince
Ghantimur. But none of these clerics, certainly not Gantimurov,
remained in China.[1] Among the stray notices from this dismal time
we learn that Maksim Leont'ev, late in his life, joined the Russian
Company in an expedition against the Zunghars.[2] The priest,
normally excused from such duty, was forcibly shaved in the
Manchu manner by his parishioners and then compelled to accompany them, not for the value of his services, but from their jealousy
of his privileges. And among the apostate Albazinians was Leont'ev's
own son Fedor, who refused to go to church with his father. One
generation later his grandson Zakar' was never baptized at all.[3]
    But if the church in Peking was largely defunct and surely
dilapidated, it was not yet extinct. In 1710 there were at least three
Albazinians still disposed toward their old faith—"Aleksei Staritsyn,
who upon the loss of some silver amounting to fifty rubles [later]
hanged himself in the church; Dmitri, son of the former church
elder Nestor; and someone named Savva."[4] By their very tenacity
these Manchu-Russians finally managed to arouse an interest in
their helplessness and thereby set in motion a number of events

which, however fortuitously, led to the arrival of the first Russian ecclesiastical mission to China.

In 1710 Aleksei Staritsyn and Dmitri Nestorovich wrote to Filofei Leshchinskii about their predicament of being without a priest. Leshchinskii's exhortative reply in 1711 next prompted them to write a letter to the tsar himself, an act that accomplished nothing. Then, in 1712, when Petr Khudiakov was in Peking with his caravan, they turned to him with their appeal. The intention was that he should transmit their request for a new priest to the Russian government, but Khudiakov, properly considering the Albazinians to be subjects of China, advised them to check with the Li-fan yuan first. The Manchus quickly acquiesced in this untroublesome local petition. Where else but from Russia could a new priest be obtained for "their Russians," who had so gallantly cooperated in the pacification of Albazin? Khudiakov remained in Peking until June 9, 1712, when he received a final communication from the Li-fan yuan to Prince Matvei Gagarin, governor of Siberia. He then left for the frontier with the message that not one, but several priests would be welcome in China.[5]

The Manchu Mission to Ayuki-Khan

If the Manchu conscience had indeed been touched by the Albazinians, it is also true that the international political situation suddenly made the issue of a new priest from Russia most opportune. K'ang-hsi was planning, in 1712, to dispatch an embassy to the Turghud Mongols camping on the Volga below Kazan (where they had moved from the troubled Oyirad domains in Western Mongolia a century earlier). This puzzling Manchu operation was ostensibly set in motion by the innocuous purpose of assuring the Turghud chief Ayuki that his nephew, who was passing his time in Peking as a hostage of the Manchus, was indeed alive and well. Were it not for the grave jeopardy in which his life would be placed by the Zunghars if he tried to return to his camping grounds, he would long since have been free to go—or such, at least, was the drift of what the Manchu ambassadors were to tell Ayuki when, and if, they reached him.

Of course there were ulterior motives for the expedition, which became the first of several embassies sent across Russia to the Turghud in the early Ch'ing period; what the motives were, however, is still far from clear. No Russian, then or now, could believe that the Manchus were not intent upon exciting Ayuki into an alliance against the Zunghars, although the embassy's instructions specify that no negotiations on this point were to be undertaken. From the account of his journey[6] left by its Secretary, Tulishen (which, it should be added, became almost the entire corpus of Ch'ing russology up to the mid-nineteenth century), it would appear that conversation at the two meetings between Ayuki and the Manchu delegates was utterly vacuous. Although Cahen assumed too much in equating the Manchu purpose with historical consequence—that is, with the ultimate return of the Turghud to China in the 1770s (hence the importance he attaches to the envoys' talk about all that Ayuki had in common with Manchu China),[7] there is still reason to suppose that K'ang-hsi, preparing for a new struggle with the Zunghars, was at least exploring the possibility of a more figurative rapprochement. Ayuki should be made aware of which way history was moving and of who it was that had his interests in mind.

In any event, there was no way to reach the Turghud except by going through a large slice of Russian territory—an enormous detour, to be sure, but none the less necessary as part of the Manchu preparations for clearing the direct road into Ili. The immediate problem was to get Russia to accept the itinerary. This was no mean feat; the embassy was detained at Selenginsk for six months before receiving its entree into the Siberian interior. As the Li-fan yuan was confronting the question of Russian passports, the Albazinian petition for a new priest arrived in its yamen, and it was at that moment that an otherwise minor affair became part of a much larger Manchu design in Inner Asian international relations. While no one could responsibly maintain that Russia allowed the Manchu embassy its passage through Siberia simply because of an invitation to send an ecclesiastical mission to Peking, it is certain that the tsar knew of this offer before the Manchus formally announced it to Gagarin in Tobolsk; Khudiakov, who left Peking three days before the embassy's departure in the summer of 1712, had brought back word of it.[8] Peter the Great, on learning from Gagarin (who had been informed by Khudiakov) that the Ch'ing government would now allow the residence of Russian priests in China, ordered the interim Metropolitan of Siberia, Ioann Maksimovich,[9] to find some clerics for service there. The ukase was hastily obeyed, so that when Tulishen duly made the Manchu invitation known to Gagarin in Tobolsk in August, 1713, the latter was able to reply immediately that the priests for China had already been chosen and were ready to go.[10] The Manchus then went off to have their meeting with Ayuki-Khan, returning to Tobolsk for their Russian entourage the following year. After years of uncertainty, the first ecclesiastical mission had come into being in a most methodic fashion.

This is how Tulishen recorded the conversations with Gagarin, beginning with an indirect quotation from the petition of Khudiakov and the Albazinians to the Li-fan yuan:

> In our capital there is no *lama* for carrying on the worship of God for them [the Albazinians], and there remains among the Russian people only one Dmitri, but he is so old that if he dies, no one will remain after him to direct the holy worship in their Russian faith; and Russian *lamas* would be sent if only it were granted. The ministers reported to his majesty our holy khan on this petition, and his majesty with pleasure gave his consent to the request for *lamas;* and it was also ordered to their commissar to send us a doctor skilled in the treatment of external diseases, if there was one in Russia; and it was ordered that we should take their Russian *lamas* and doctor, if they were sent with us, when we return . . .
>
> With respect to that matter Gagarin said that priests were right there in readiness, but there was not a skilled doctor to be found, although he had written about it to Moscow and hoped one would get there by the time we were returning home.[11]

The request for a doctor, which had undoubtedly been an afterthought of K'ang-hsi himself, took Gagarin completely by surprise. Although Russia in the early eighteenth century was hardly better off than China in the technology of Western medicine, the opportunity of responding to this apparently capricious appeal was too good to let pass. Peter therefore summoned one of his own foreign physicians, an English surgeon at the new hospital of St. Petersburg named Thomas Garvine, and sent him off to China half a year after the Manchu embassy had left Tobolsk on its own return. With Garvine went Lorents Lange, a Swedish engineer, who was commissioned to bring back to Russia a porcelain stove. The tsar was obviously making the most of this sudden Manchu turn of mind! Lange's trip was the first of many that he made to China in the service of Russian interests; Garvine disappears quickly from the historical record, although not before he had taken the imperial pulse in Peking. Weber intimates, probably groundlessly, that K'ang-hsi was suffering from venereal disease.[12] The inconsequential Garvine interlude does suggest the possibility, however, that K'ang-hsi was testing an alternative source of contact with the West. If maritime merchants and missionaries were beginning to cause more trouble than they were worth, perhaps their essential functions could be accomplished by others, coming from another direction. By coupling the request for a doctor with the impending arrival of foreign clergymen (as he often did with the Jesuits), K'ang-hsi may have had such expectations; but if this were so, he could not have clung to the hope for very long. When the first Russian mission arrived in 1716 it received an enthusiastic welcome; after it petered out, having amounted to nothing, none of the ensuing missions were received so well.

Lezhaiskii's Mission

The archimandrite who now became the first designated missionary to China was one of those who had accompanied Filofei Leshchinskii to Siberia in 1702. His name was Ilarion Lezhaiskii, a native of Chernigov, trained at the religious academy in Kiev. By

1709 he had become the superior of the Spasskii Monastery in Yakutsk, and in 1713 was chosen to lead the mission to Peking.[13] With Lezhaiskii went a considerable suite of clerics: a priest named Lavrentii and a deacon named Filimon; and seven clerics of lower rank—Osip D'iakonov, Nikanor Kliusov, Petr Maksimov Iakutov, Grigorii Smagin, Fedor Kolesnikov, Andrei Popov, and Iosif Afanasev. On their departure from Tobolsk the missionaries were furnished with icons, vessels, and worship books. But Metropolitan Ioann Maksimovich was reluctant to part with one of the mitres from the sacristy of the Tobolsk cathedral, considering that sacrifice too extreme. This unexpected complication was overcome by Prince Gagarin, who swiftly promised Maksimovich a new and more expensive mitre if he yielded the present one to the Peking mission. Thereupon Maksimovich gladly gave it to Lezhaiskii, only attaching the proviso that the Peking mission must pay for it if Gagarin should not make good his promise. Here the affair ended.[14]

Although the maintenance of the mission in Peking was to be a Manchu responsibility, the missionaries were given some money in Tobolsk for their journey to the frontier. Orders also went out to the Siberian monasteries that lay on the mission's path to China to give whatever was necessary, including a carefully prescribed quantity of alcohol, to sustain the missionaries up to the border. A yearly salary was also to be paid by Russia to the members of the mission after their arrival in Peking. Thus Archimandrite Ilarion was to receive a hundred rubles a year, Priest Lavrentii and Deacon Filimon, twenty rubles annually, and so forth. The money was to be sent by caravan from Irkutsk.[15] Strictly speaking this violated the self-sufficient Chinese order into which the mission was being introduced, but there is no evidence that the authorities in the Li-fan yuan objected to the sending of salaries from Russia. (Neither is there any mention that the salaries were ever sent.) Finally, Lezhaiskii was made the present of twenty-eight silver spoons, six silver cups, a tray, two cloth caftans and a brown cassock. He and his suite accompanied one contingent of the returning Manchu embassy and arrived in Peking on January 11, 1716.[16]

Not a great deal can be said about the life of this first Russian mission (for many of the documents relating to it were subsequently destroyed by fire in Tobolsk). Above all it should be observed that its life was very short—hardly more than two years. But its tenure in Peking began amid favorable conditions. Of the Russian missions to China in the eighteenth century it was perhaps one of the more advanced in its own level of preparation for what awaited it there. And certainly it arrived at a time when foreign life in Peking was not as difficult as it was to become later, after the Treaty of Kiakhta, when Russian missionaries readily retreated behind new walls that the Manchu regime was by then quite happy to build for them. Remarkably liberal provisions for its maintenance were made by the Ch'ing government. Lezhaiskii was immediately given eight hundred taels of silver with which to buy a suitable house for himself, and six hundred taels for the servants who would be tending to his ménage. Lavrentii and Filimon (the priest and deacon) were each given six hundred taels for houses, and four hundred for servants. The punctilious Manchu attention to status continued down to the lesser clerics as well, who were granted three hundred taels for houses and two hundred for servants. After three years (a tenure in Peking that most of the missionaries fell well short of) more money was to be supplied if necessary. Meanwhile a monthly salary of between four and five taels was paid to the archimandrite, priest, and deacon; the others got one and a half taels apiece. Moreover, a cart arrived at the mission every five days, loaded with food, which included sheep, geese, ducks, and chickens. And apparently an official from the Li-fan yuan regularly paid a visit, embracing Lezhaiskii and inquiring after his health, what he lacked, or who among his assistants needed anything.[17]

A final Manchu nicety was the appointment of Lezhaiskii to the rank of a fifth-grade official in the ladder of the Chinese civil service, other offices being distributed to the rest of the missionaries.[18] In Russia the newly organized Synod later reacted with horror to the news that its China mission had been swept into something that looked suspiciously close to Peter's own ranking system. That the offices were not ecclesiastical but secular was bad enough; that they were Chinese and not Russian was intolerable.

Meanwhile, however, Lezhaiskii made the most of his new importance. Frequently he employed his own clerics as mounted body-
guards (some of them had, after all, been given military rank by
the Manchus) to flank his horse-drawn carriage.[19] Perhaps one
could argue that this was not vanity but simply a necessary standard of deportment for a fifth-grade official, trying to make his
way about Peking.

The Manchu arrangements could offer hardly any grounds
for complaint, for the foreigners were being given a treatment
more reminiscent (from our point of view) of the late than the
early Ch'ing period. Because of such attention, an interest in
attending the church in the remote corner of the city was generated
for a time not only among the Albazinians living nearby, but also
over a greater distance by a number of curious Manchus and
Chinese. More worship books were therefore necessary, and the
Li-fan yuan obligingly undertook to write Gagarin (on April 23,
1717) to send them.[20] If there was any other material deficiency,
during the mission's first year in Peking, it was either not made
known, or else quickly satisfied. Yet the three Russians whom the
Li-fan yuan sent to fetch the books from Siberia never returned to
China and probably never had any intention of returning. The high
life notwithstanding, they were the first of many in the eighteenth
century to be defeated by the climate of Peking and their own
homesickness. The rest of Lezhaiskii's staff endured another year,
but before long it became apparent that even the material resources
of the mission were close to being spent. From Veselovskii we get
this description:

> To whoever among the Chinese came to his place wishing to
> meet him he gave a present, utterly generously and indis-
> criminately. The Chinese, seeing how generous the Russian
> *dalama* [archimandrite] was, began frequently either to go to
> his place, bringing some simple gift such as watermelon, fruits,
> or other little things, or to send their children with such things,
> for which they would be presented with fox furs and sables in
> exchange. It was in line with such generosity that he entrusted

the keys to his storeroom to a churchman and gave him authority over all his property. After a while, when the church-man reported to him that there were no fox furs or sables left he did not think too much of it, believing that he still had lots of silver. But when he dipped into the silver he found only a very small quantity of that left, too. Seeing how little there was he thereupon began to live very sparingly and took back authority over what was left into his own hands, in order not to cease the conversions for lack of funds. But Father Ilarion began to encounter trouble, for while the support from the Khan was very ample it was enough for household purposes only.[21]

Then an episode occurred that caused much bitterness between Archimandrite Ilarion and his mission. Lezhaiskii, in an unfortunate attempt to deal with the economic exigencies of the church, deter-mined that he alone should go to the Li-fan yuan for the full monthly salary of the mission (which would have been something in the order of twenty-four taels), and presumably serve as a less liberal paymaster for the rest of the missionaries. Through this austerity some money might still be available for the proper task of Orthodox evangelism. But the interpreter to whom Lezhaiskii discharged the task of informing the Li-fan yuan of his decision indiscreetly revealed the plan to others. If Lezhaiskii's staff was being forced to choose between spending money either on Manchu converts or on themselves, it was no choice at all. The matter was immediately appealed to the archimandrite and he was forced to retreat.[22] But the resentment surrounding the incident did not go away. Instead, the mission staff became more rebellious, causing the archimandrite to lose face among the people; the visits from attentive Manchu officials ceased; the Jesuits in Peking refused to give him refuge when he sought it among them. Lezhaiskii was left with nothing but a habit of heavy drinking, for which there always seemed to be enough money, to relieve a gnawing despondency over the collapse of his mission. Rheumatism soon set in. He died on April 26, 1718, on the road back to Peking from some warm waters where he had been seeking treatment.[23] His stay in China, begun with so much promise, lasted little more than two years.

There is no account in Chinese of the first Russian ecclesiastical mission, but Matteo Ripa, a papal envoy in Peking at the time, can provide this postscript:

> There was in Peking an abbot and twelve [*sic*] priests, who had been sent by Peter the Great to administer spiritual comfort to the families of the Russian prisoners of war. As strange things were reported concerning these ecclesiastics, I resolved to make their personal acquaintance, with a view of sending an exact account of them to the Propaganda. According to the custom of the country in which we were, I first sent a present to the abbot, then waited upon him myself. I found him courteous and dignified in his manners, and remarkably neat in his dress and furniture. Whenever he came out of his church he held a crucifix on his breast, and the pastoral in his hand. He was a schismatic [i.e., Orthodox] but with me he pretended to be a Catholic. He spoke just enough Latin to make himself understood; and as he told me that one of his priests who was ill, could also speak the language, I went to see him, but all I could get out of the man was—*intelligit, intelligit.* The abbot told me that all the Christians of his sect scarcely amounted to fifty, and were descendants of prisoners of war, one of whom still lived, though far advanced in years. I asked him whether it was true that he baptized a great number of Chinese. To this he replied that his christenings had been limited to the families of the Russian prisoners; that he did not attend to the Chinese because he was ignorant of their language, and the abandoned state of his own congregation required all his attention ... They officiate in their church without any ceremony, admitting men and women at the same time, which in China is considered nothing less than an abomination ... Although the abbot was so elegant in his dress, the priests under him had a mean and shabby appearance: and I even saw some of them at play in the public streets before the church; which in China is absolutely indecorous, and not to be done by any person of the least respectability.[24]

With the death of Ilarion Lezhaiskii the Russian ecclesiastical
mission in Peking came to an uncertain pass. Three of its members
had already returned to Russia. Two more—Deacon Filimon and
Grigorii Smagin—were now sent back by the Li-fan yuan to inform
Prince Gagarin of the death of the archimandrite. That left four
Russians in Peking: Priest Lavrentii and three of the original staff—
D'iakonov, Iakutov, and Kliusov. To them fell the task of preserving
some continuity between the first ecclesiastical mission and an as
yet unforeseeable second.

Sino-Russian Relations under K'ang-hsi and Peter
If the accomplishments of the Lezhaiskii mission were to be
judged solely in the terms set forth by the ukase of 1700, there
would be little to say except that it failed. The Albazinians were
again estranged from the religion of their motherland, while K'ang-
hsi and most other residents of Peking were probably not even aware
that one of Lezhaiskii's residual purposes had been to convert them
to his faith. As for ministering to Russian merchants who arrived
in Peking, the archimandrite remained alive and sufficiently sober
only long enough to see one caravan come and go.

But for Russia the outlook was not at all bleak. In the larger
view, the first ecclesiastical mission to Peking remained part of a
post-Nerchinsk interest in "opening" China and establishing what
might wishfully be considered the start of formal and up-to-date
relations with the Manchu state. In this sense it was the institutions
of that relationship that were important—not yet how well or how
badly they performed. Trade was of course uppermost in Russian
minds (and the caravan trade, it should be added, had been rather
promising); religious representation in Peking went along with it.
As Leibniz had said, what was needed was more international contact. Russia had set out to accomplish this in its own way with no
less than ten churchmen (two of whom knew Latin, after a fashion),
an English surgeon and a Swedish engineer! Things were moving,
not fast enough perhaps, but in the new capital of St. Petersburg
officials could still, in 1718, contemplate something like a "normalization" of Sino-Russian relations. And at a time when the Rites

Controversy was damaging Roman Catholic interests in China the
Russian position there seemed all the more competitive. Peter
added to the problems of the Jesuits by expelling them from Russia
in 1719. Soon he would try secretly to insinuate a Russian bishop
into Peking.

As far as China was concerned, perhaps K'ang-hsi was mildly
interested in learning what novelties, if any, Russia had to offer
him and his cosmopolitan capital. At least it appears that he had
no immediate objections to being "opened" by Russia if that were
the way Russia wanted to look at the situation. For K'ang-hsi, the
Russian merchants and missionaries who arrived in Peking were, in
any case, less a sign of Russian institutional penetration of China
than of Chinese ideological penetration of Russia, for they clearly
showed a desire on Russia's part to travel a long distance to par-
take in the many offerings of Chinese civilization. If the early
China trade was flattering Peter's ideas of how foreign relations
should be conducted, and if it had contributed some oriental bric-
a-brac to his new museum of curiosities in St. Petersburg, it also
added to the scope of Manchu imperial grandeur in Peking. Here
Peter and K'ang-hsi were at least agreed on the usefulness of Sino-
Russian relations to the institutional self-image of monarchy. But
what Russia hoped to find in China—namely, a monarch who shared
Peter's assumptions about foreign trade and foreign relations—was
not to be found there. Uppermost in the mind of K'ang-hsi were
not the questions of how China and Russia would relate to one
another, but rather the historical and geographical implications of
any advance on China from the direction of Inner Asia. The simple
fact that the Chinese and Russian empires had met in Inner Asia was
what gave Sino-Russian relations their great urgency to the Manchus.
The Inner Asian locus of this meeting made everything that happened between China and Russia important—as the pitiful struggle
of Albazin to defend itself against a vastly superior Manchu army
should attest. The Manchus themselves had once advanced upon
China from the north, and now Russia had come ominously close,
K'ang-hsi said before attacking Albazin, to the area "where the
ruling dynasty had its origins."[25] Whereas Russia was soon doing

its best to forget the Albazinian wars, they were for China only the beginning of a long and creative effort to deal with the new and extraordinarily difficult problems of power-relations in Inner Asia once Russia had arrived on the scene.

If the ultimate aim of Manchu policy was to keep the Russians from doing to China precisely what the Manchus themselves had done, it would also be necessary to bring as much of Mongol Inner Asia as possible under Chinese control. After Albazin the source of Manchu concern in Inner Asia therefore shifted to outer Mongolia—first to Khalkha and then further westward to Zungharia. The threat of Russian expansion had to be reckoned with no less in these areas than on the Amur. K'ang-hsi wanted at all costs to avoid fighting a simultaneous, sustained war against both Russians and Mongols, just as Russia was afraid, in the 1680s, that the Mongols and Manchus would unite to throw its settlers out of the Amur River valley once and for all.[26] Since, in either case, it was the Mongols who were the less predictable (as the case of Ghantimur amply demonstrated), the Nerchinsk negotiations at last gave Manchu China the opportunity to test Russia's willingness to agree upon a common frontier. Golovin's acceptance of this proposition was a tremendous advance, for it meant that Russia could now, in a sense, be invited to cooperate in the Manchu policy of pacifying Inner Asia. The contingent provision for extraditing fugitives (i.e. restless Mongols) across the new frontier was all that was necessary to end the possibility of sanctuary on either side. The Russians agreed, and the Ghantimur issue was therefore abandoned by the Manchus for the more important assurance that there would be no more Ghantimurs. This provision was rewritten into the treaty of Kiakhta and did not break down until the sensational escapades of Amursana in the mid-eighteenth century.[27] The treaty of Nerchinsk showed most Mongols that there was no longer any point, if there ever had been, in resisting Manchu dominion in Khalkha. Not only had the Manchus conquered China, they had now beaten Russia as well. The Tüshiyetü Khan of Khalkha and the Jebtsundamba Khutughtu made their submissions at Dolonor in 1691.

To be sure, Russia had not been conquered, and many issues remained to be negotiated. But with the treaty of Nerchinsk the Manchus had achieved the effect of putting Russia in a position that few Mongols could fail to understand: that of a submissive and compliant "outer vassal," prepared to promote, not impede, Inner Asian stabilization. And as long as Russians insisted on coming to Peking to trade and to preach, they could do little to avoid the tendentious terminology that the Li-fan yuan applied to them. Whereas Baikov, in 1656, had accidentally made China appear more Mongolian than Chinese, it was now China that was deliberately dressing Russia up in much the same way. Tulishen's reference to the Russian "lamas" who were soon brought to China with the return of the embassy to Ayuki-khan is an example of such a blurred distinction. Viewed from the windows of the Li-fan yuan Russian missionaries would become willy-nilly a part of the Inner Asian world they had to cross in order to reach Peking.

Having achieved what he wanted at Albazin, Nerchinsk, and Dolonor, K'ang-hsi was therefore encouraged in the late seventeenth century to confront the problem of the Zunghars, the most nomadic and fiercest of the Mongols who, under Galdan Boshughtu, had given every evidence that they would go down fighting. Galdan did in fact succumb after the battle of Jao Modo in 1696. Zunghar power, however, was not finally reduced in the campaigns of the 1690s, and in the early eighteenth century its destruction remained far from complete. Yet because Zungharian independence under Galdan's nephew and successor, Tsewang Arabtan, was far less menacing to China than it had been, one may well wonder why coexistence between China and Zungharia was such a troublesome issue. Not only did the Manchus now have the certain capacity to repel any Zunghar attack from the northwest, but also Tsewang Arabtan himself showed little inclination (at least until 1718, when he invaded Tibet) to try to avenge his uncle. Having reached the conclusion that economic development would favor his chances of survival far more than a stubborn devotion to warlike nomadic customs, he spent much of his time in breaking the Zunghars of their old way of life—by planting crops, mining gold,

building towns, and promoting trade relations wherever he could.
Perhaps the Manchus welcomed such changes in Zunghar society,
but they were not satisfied with them. Their ultimate aims were
more far-reaching.

Manchu claims to Khalkha rested on the premise that Manchu
China—not Russia and not the Zungharian Khanate—offered the
only legitimate source of sovereignty over the Mongol peoples.
This assumption was reinforced both by visible military prowess
and by the theatrical capacity of the Manchus, especially of K'ang-
hsi, for representing themselves as genuine Inner Asians, who shared
much in common with the Mongols: the traditional hunt, the verti-
cal alphabet, and above all, the Yellow sect of Lamaist Buddhism.
In this scheme of things there could be no contenders for primacy.
Peking alone had to become the temporal capital of Inner Asia—
an administrative center that would relieve Lhasa and Urga of the
onerous need to spend time managing the mundane details of life,
time which could otherwise be put to use in prayer. The symbolic
force of a visit by the Dalai Lama or the Urga Khutughtu to Peking
was worth more than all the cannon the Society of Jesus could
cast and in the long run, if not immediately, cost much less.
Manchu policy in Inner Asia was always intent on this kind of
showmanship; the attention of the Turghud people, far away on
the Volga, was sought just as much as that of any other Mongol
federation. The same held true for the Russian "lamas." They
traveled the road from Urga to Kalgan to Peking and prayed not
in a Christian church but in what was known in Peking as the
lo-ch'a miao or Albazinian temple. And their journeys showed that
Russian as well as Mongol clerics found it necessary to make regular
peregrinations to a city that bustled with the business of looking
after the peoples of the steppe. Inner Asia required this kind of
consistent ideological control. It had to be seen whole, and treated
the same way. The Russian mission, despite itself, became part of
the picture.

If, during the reign of K'ang-hsi, the only choice that remained
for a Mongol was between a purer form of nomadism outside of the
Ch'ing empire, and a final surrender to Manchu protection, there

would have been no problem for the imperial designs of China. The true nomads were finished. One does not need retrospect on the K'ang-hsi period to know that. The trouble was that Tsewang Arabtan himself was shifting the economic bases of Zunghar society. And behind him was Russia, beginning to show an interest in those attractive political and commercial opportunities in Ili. Left to itself, the Zunghar capital might enter a rival claim to be the polit-ical—perhaps even the religious—center of Mongol nationhood. Tsewang's invasion of Tibet in 1718, and the presence of Russian gold prospectors in his *ulus* (or nation), drew the issue with a ter-rible clarity. We must conclude, therefore, that the Manchu approach to Inner Asia could not admit the possibility of an extended and peaceful coexistence with the Zunghars, and still less of a Russo-Zunghar alliance. Lacking any means of exerting a diplomatic influence on Zungharia, the Manchus thereupon directed their efforts toward discouraging Russia, with whom a peaceful and productive relationship was well under way, from fishing in the troubled waters of Ili. Here our argument can return briefly to the question of those relations in the early eighteenth century.

To the extent that Russia believed it had begun to "open" China after Nerchinsk, the belief was nourished by Manchu policy, however ironic that may now appear. For if Russia could maintain a competitive interest in the political and commercial advantages of a peaceful coexistence with China, it might ignore the enormous potential for trouble-making in Inner Asia. This is not to say that the Manchus had completely fathomed Russian behavior or that they knew precisely, at each step of the way, what might be neces-sary to keep Russia from intriguing among the Mongol, and later the Moslem, peoples of the north and northwest. Surely they did not. On the one hand, Russian-inspired intrigue never ceased, and on the other, China was by no means ready to open itself to every-thing Russia wanted. But it is certain that by the end of the second decade of the eighteenth century, Russia was gradually becoming aware of the connection between its compliance with the principles of the border treaty—even in areas where the border

had not yet been drawn—and its access to Peking. For the Ch'ing
dynasty the stakes in this gamble were tremendous—much greater
than what is suggested by the misleading question of which side,
by the end of the eighteenth century, had gotten the better of the
Sino-Russian trade relationship. China had never profited from its
tribute-and-trade relations in the north, and had never expected to.
The more important question is to describe the means whereby
the Manchus managed to keep most of Mongol Inner Asia for themselves in the eighteenth century (or, in the euphemism of the
modern scholar Liu Ta-nien, by which they "unified China").[28]
While Soviet scholars remind us today that K'ang-hsi, Yung-cheng,
and Ch'ien-lung did, after all, undertake long and bloody expansionistic wars in Inner Asia,[29] underneath such opinions there
perhaps lies a sense that it might have been otherwise. It was not
war (which admittedly left the population of Ili decimated in the
1750s) that is alone noteworthy, but the fact that Russia itself
in the end made the Manchu campaigns easier, rather than more
difficult, by allowing nothing to undo what had already been
achieved in its relations with China.

As we have seen, one of those achievements was the ecclesiastical mission in Peking, which for Russia always had a "European"
value. Deep within the Manchu bureaucracy, however, it did not
remain European, or even distinctly Russian; neither did it become
Chinese. It was Mongolized to conform with the Inner Asian
circumstances of its origins. Here the conflicting perceptions that
underlay the history of this period may be reduced to an essential
simplicity. The Russian ecclesiastical mission, or lamasery, in
Peking, and the institutions that were to grow out of it, supplied
a common denominator by which China and Russia, working from
independent derivations and reaching different conclusions, had
already begun to confront their mutual need for contact and
coexistence.

Chapter III

IZMAILOV, LANGE, AND KUL'CHITSKII:
BACK TO THE BEGINNING

The Li-fan yuan's obituary on Ilarion Lezhaiskii was addressed to Gagarin and ran as follows:

> You [Gagarin] asked of the emperor that the Russians in our great empire be able to worship in church and ask of God eternal peace between our two countries. And to that end you sent Archimandrite Ilarion, Priest Lavrentii, Deacon Filimon, and seven Russians ... Homes, provisions—all necessities were given to them, and so that Osip [D'iakonov] and the others of the seven could get married, the emperor provided money and joined them with our Russians for prayers in church. This year young archimandrite Ilarion began ailing and died. Since from the time of the setting up of the boundaries between our countries we have lived in great harmony, we have sent Deacon Filimon and a servant, Grigorii [Smagin], who will inform you of the death of the archimandrite. Do you, Gagarin, we wondered, want to send here a second archimandrite, or do you want us to return those remaining here? Send us an answer.[1]

Filimon and Smagin arrived with this letter in Irkutsk in March, 1719, and in Yeniseisk in April, where Metropolitan Leshchinskii attached to it another of his exhortatory notes. Shortly afterwards it reached Tobolsk. Prince Gagarin was not, unfortunately, on hand to receive it. He had been cashiered, and then hanged in St. Petersburg, a result (evidently) of his entirely too self-willed administration of Siberia. The Li-fan yuan had not yet gotten wind of this turn of events, to which it had possibly contributed through its regular correspondence with Tobolsk, having found in Gagarin a man who knew his business and with whom the tasks of managing Sino-Russian relations could be responsibly undertaken. Neverthe-

52

less, the message was there for anyone—Gagarin or his successor—
to read: a new archimandrite, or *ta-lama*, would be welcome if he
were sent.

The letter which amiably makes this proposition is of great
importance. Conveying none of the mistrust that had begun to
distinguish the Li-fan yuan's attitude toward the question of Russian caravans, it is a clue to the Ch'ing opinion of what constituted
an acceptable Russian representation in Peking. By 1718 there was
no disagreement that the caravan trade had begun to dry up.
Marketing conditions in Peking were abominable, and the city was
already glutted with Siberian furs. Russian merchants were therefore staying longer, waiting for a more opportune moment to
unload their perishable cargos. And as hope turned to despair
(particularly in the hot summer of Peking), the less decently did
they behave.

The Li-fan yuan's immediate reaction to this situation was,
in 1719, to constrict it further by refusing entry to the caravan of
Istopnikov and then threatening to relegate all trade to the frontier
where it would not only be far away from Peking but, better yet,
visibly joined to the question of how well Russia was living up to
the border provisions of the Nerchinsk Treaty. But in Russia itself
precisely the opposite view was taken: the answer was to be found
in the expansion of Russian commercial opportunities, in Peking
and indeed over the whole face of the Chinese empire. This contradiction between Manchu and Russian attitudes (and more broadly,
of course, between those of China and the West), now squarely in
view, troubled Sino-Russian relations for over a century to come.
But, in an obituary of 1718, we find evidence that, however else
the treaty relationship was revised, the ecclesiastical mission would
be left undisturbed. If there had to be Russians in Peking—the Li-
fan yuan seemed to be saying—one could do worse than to harbor
these docile churchmen!

Izmailov

Well before news of either Lezhaiskii's death or the interdic-
tion of Istopnikov's caravan had reached Russia, the tsar had begun

to outfit a new embassy—the first since that of Izbrant Ides. Plans for the development of Sino-Russian relations were being written down in St. Petersburg as fast as they could be thought up. One idea, which Russia had kept alive in one form or another since Ides's trip in 1694, was to acquire a consulate in Peking and build a new church inside. This would put Russian affairs in China on a more proper institutional footing. Indeed, the Russian ambassador, Lev Vasilevich Izmailov, left St. Petersburg in July 1718 with an armload of demands for free trade in all parts of China, for Russian agents in the major Chinese cities, and for the extraterritorial privileges that would normally appertain to such people. Implicitly, as Mancall has shown,[2] Izmailov's instructions assumed complete institutional reciprocity between Russia and China. Such an assumption was fine for Russia, which was simply treating China according to the new Petrine pattern of acceptable foreign relations, but it had nothing in common with the Manchu wish to return to a strict construction of the Nerchinsk Treaty. Through no fault of his own, Izmailov was not the man to put Manchu concerns to rest when he arrived in Peking. Like Spafarii, he had with him, among his carefully paragraphed instructions, no orders that related to Inner Asian frontiers or to Mongol fugitives. How could a discussion of these distant and minor issues possibly be ranked with the higher affairs of state? For Izmailov himself, the man on the spot, matters were made worse when, on January 2, 1721, in the midst of his visit, the Li-fan yuan received news of the flight of seven hundred Mongols into Siberia. The ambassador, groping for some way out of his embarrassment, sent a soldier from his guard to the governor of Siberia with a plea to resolve the matter in all haste. For the impatient officials in the Li-fan yuan, however, this was a perfunctory and far too insubstantial treatment of a serious question. Izmailov was wasting their time. Two months later, on March 2, he was sent away from Peking.

Klaproth maintains that the Izmailov embassy had an "heureux effet,"[3] but this impression is difficult to rationalize unless it is taken to mean that Russia now had become sufficiently aware that any further progress in its relations with China could only be accompanied by a readiness to deal with the Inner Asian issues that were uppermost in Manchu minds. As if to give this helpless ambassador something to take back to Russia with him (and certainly to make clear that all was not lost in Sino-Russian relations), the Li-fan yuan allowed the Istopnikov caravan, immobilized on the frontier since 1719, to come to Peking and do its business. And in an even more seductive gesture, Lorents Lange, the redoubtable caravan agent (on the second of six trips to China that he made during his lifetime) was allowed to stay on in Peking after Istopnikov and his merchants had quit the city. Lange did not remain for long, but the year he was there gave Russia reason to conclude that it now had a "consul" in Peking. Izmailov had won his main point after all!

The matter of precisely what kind of establishment the Russian Orthodox church was to have in Peking could not be negotiated while everything else was up in the air. As we have seen, Izmailov had left St. Petersburg prepared to ask for a new church, not an entirely new mission, and was well on his way by the time word of Lezhaiskii's death arrived. Not to be outdone by the grandiose plans for China with which Izmailov had been burdened by secular officials in St. Petersburg, the ecclesiastical hierarchy set to work on plans to transform its Orthodox community in Peking into a bishopric. For the present, however, it was necessary that the more valuable materials for celebrating the mass be brought back to Russia from the Albazinian church. Where there was no longer an archimandrite, one could no longer leave behind such things as the mitre from the Tobolsk cathedral. For the purpose of repossessing these treasures, orders hastily went out to Izmailov that he should take with him to China the father-superior of the Voznesenskii monastery in Irkutsk, Antonii Platkovskii. One may be sure that this message was received and obeyed by Izmailov, although Bell never mentions Platkovskii in the course of his narration of the embassy.[4]

Platkovskii's brief mission was duly accomplished. It was an insignificant trip in every way, except that it was perhaps at this point that Antonii Platkovskii was first inspired with an ambition to lead a mission to Peking himself. Metropolitan Leshchinskii, whom Platkovskii, like Lezhaiskii, had first accompanied to Tobolsk in 1702, had been the one who suggested that Platkovskii go with Izmailov to China. When Platkovskii returned from Peking he gave a crazily optimistic report on the Albazinians to the metropolitan: "They go to the church of God and observe the rites and ritual. They have respect for church rank and have converted their heathen wives to divine Christianity."[5] Neither Platkovskii's connections nor his propaganda failed him, and he figured prominently in the course of events for the next fifteen years.

As for Izmailov, while in Peking he undertook at least two visits to the church of St. Sophia in the northeast corner of the city. One was made apparently only to satisfy his curiosity. The second occurred on Christmas eve, 1720, when a special mass was celebrated.[6] But there is no evidence that either event made him especially solicitous toward the Albazinians. At one point a number of them confronted Izmailov with the request to be taken back to Russia with him; to which he allegedly replied, in a way that departed abruptly from the common understanding of the Albazinians as prisoners of war, that "if I were in fact to take you back to Russia it would be to hang the lot of you as traitors."[7] After his departure the Albazinians were left to themselves again. Some of the relics and ornaments in the sacristy of their church had been removed for safekeeping to Siberia, undoubtedly a fair price for seeing the last of this testy man.

Lange's "Consulship"

Lange, during his extra year in Peking, had no more than anyone else to say about the church of St. Sophia. He mentioned that the parson of the church, which is to say Lavrentii, the priest in Lezhaiskii's mission, sought his help in recovering some debts that were owed to the deceased archimandrite.[8] And on January 16, 1722, Lange states that he had a *te deum* sung in the church upon hearing of the conclusion of peace between Russia and the Ottoman empire,[9] an event which, like the Christmas eve mass celebrated for Izmailov, demonstrates that the church was acceptable for the

religious purposes of visiting Russian dignitaries as well as the
Albazinians themselves. What, then, was one to make of the Russian preoccupation with building a new church in Peking? The
question had perhaps been perplexing to the Li-fan yuan until
Izmailov coupled it to the request for a permanent depot in the
city. Of course a new church would not be for the Albazinians at
all—it was for Russian merchants (and consuls), whose needs were
infinitely more important. Correct form was as important to Russia—
especially metropolitan Russia—as it was to Manchu China. On
both sides it was necessary that Sino-Russian relations look right.
The Li-fan yuan, appreciating the problem, was thereby disposed
to give Izmailov's request more attention than, on the face of it,
it deserved.[10]

The same can be said of Lorents Lange's curious consulship,
which ultimately amounted to nothing of practical importance.
The Russian idea was that Lange should have certain extraterritorial rights befitting a consular officer as, for example, jurisdiction over Russian nationals (except in cases of capital crimes
committed against subjects of China and other non-Russians). This
argument may have been more persuasive to the Manchus than
historians are generally willing to recognize, for the transactions
between Russian and Chinese merchants were often inclined to be
quarrelsome affairs. Since Izmailov himself had brought up the
question of Lange's residence in the immediate context of the
bitter disputes that had occurred in the Russian caravanserai, the
responsibility for quieting the noise might better be handled by a
Russian. Peking in this sense was no different from Macao; it
simply happened to be the Ch'ing capital. Moreover, Lange was
expected to have the power of expelling any Russian from China
who was judged guilty of an offense "such as changing his religion."[11]
As long as this did not carry an implicit reference to the Albazinians,
who were not Russian but Manchu nationals, it did not present any
problem. Yet when it came to Lange's search for that establishment
where all this trade and diplomacy could be accomplished, one that
would, as quickly as possible, replace the weatherbeaten structure
that served uncertainly as his shelter in Peking, the Li-fan yuan was

unavailing. Like almost all Russian envoys and merchants before him, Lange was put up at the old Hui-t'ung kuan. Spafarii had thought the place looked like a prison,[12] and Lange's bedroom had actually disintegrated in the course of an evening thunderstorm,[13] but it did not matter. The hostel was part of an imperial tradition into which Russians, at least while they were in Peking, were fitted.[14] In this respect the issue of form was as important to the Ch'ing dynasty, looking outward from Peking, as it was to the Russian view from St. Petersburg. Russians were required to stay in the Hui-t'ung kuan when no other tributary visitors were being billeted there; in 1724 they were given preference there, and by the end of the decade (an Orthodox church at last having been constructed inside), they had exclusive use of its premises.[15]

In 1722, when Lange abruptly left Peking, it was far from clear what form, if any, Sino-Russian relations would take. K'ang-hsi was obviously impatient to discover whether the treaty of Nerchinsk could be used as an instrument for negotiating the frontier beyond modern Outer Mongolia and the immediate issue of the seven hundred Mongol fugitives. To expedite an answer, he ordered the Tüshiyetü Khan to expel all Russian merchants from the Urga fair in the spring of 1722,[16] and on May 8 Lange was told that there would be no more trade between the two countries.[17] Then, because there was no further reason for his presence in China, Lange himself was asked to leave in August.

As in 1718, the only people who remained in Peking in mid-1722 and could, perhaps loosely, be considered Russian nationals were the old priest Lavrentii and his three assistants, leftovers from the Lezhaiskii mission. How implausible it must therefore appear that at this uneasy moment Russia attempted to transform its Orthodox toehold in China into the see of a bishop! The ludicrous events surrounding the unexpected arrival of Bishop Innokentii Kul'chitskii on the Sino-Russian frontier, just as Lange was passing in the opposite direction, were not just a consequence of bad timing. They were a caricature of the Russian expectation that China could be made to receive whatever Russia chose to offer it. After the Kul'chitskii debacle Russia at least became more interested in

ascertaining what, among the possible bases for Sino-Russian
relations, it was that China would find acceptable.

Kul'chitskii

    To trace the idea of sending a bishop to Peking it is necessary
to return to Metropolitan Leshchinskii in Tobolsk. Leshchinskii
(now tonsured, and carrying the monastic name of Feodor) had, in
1719, joined a zealous letter of his own to the Li-fan yuan's announcement of Ilarion Lezhaiskii's death. In his letter Leshchinskii wrote
that "we thank God that the Christian faith is spreading, that the
name of God is reputable among the heathens, and that hope
advances for the glorification of the name of God among the
Chinese." After suggesting that a good and wise man be chosen for
the China mission, the metropolitan went on to say that "You
might consider [someone] of the rank of a bishop, sending him
with fifteen people, because the Chinese will consider that the tsar
is sending such people for the strengthening of eternal peace."[18]
His suggestion, when it percolated upwards to St. Petersburg,
struck everyone as a good idea. Certainly there was no difficulty
in incorporating it into the Russian policy of broadening the scope
of its relations with China in every possible way. Putting a bishop
in Peking would have the further merit of testing what appeared to
be the Roman Catholic grip on that city, something which Ilarion
Lezhaiskii had failed to do. Preparations were begun, and, in due
time, the tsar was told of what his ecclesiastical minds were up to.
    Innokentii Kul'chitskii, the man to whom the see of Peking
would soon be entrusted, was born in the Ukraine about 1680.
Like Lezhaiskii and Platkovskii, he was a student in the religious
academy in Kiev; later he became a professor and prefect in the
Moscow academy. He served a short term as ober-hieromonk to the
Russian navy, and then joined the Aleksandro-Nevskii Monastery
in St. Petersburg, presumably around 1720. He was considered
"very well educated for his time, and of a strong moral and religious
fiber."[19] On July 4, 1720, while Izmailov was in Selenginsk waiting
to be admitted into China, Kul'chitskii was named Lezhaiskii's
successor. Since at that time he was only a hieromonk, it was neces-

sary to get him ordained before he could be sent on his way. By February of the following year arrangements for the appointment were complete. Two new councils—the Holy Synod[20] and the Senate[21]—jointly put the matter to Peter the Great, with the suggestion that Innokentii be made Bishop of Peking with additional administration over the Siberian cities of Irkutsk and Nerchinsk.[22] To this the tsar gave a reply which, in its cautious agreement, was reminiscent of his answer to Vinius upon hearing of the Russian church in Peking in 1698: "Ordain him as a bishop, but better without the designation of cities, at least not those bordering on China, lest the Jesuits take it otherwise and bring calamity upon us."[23] The ordination was scheduled for the next month.

Kul'chitskii himself, meanwhile, had been thinking along lines similar to those of the Synod and the Senate. In a long report to the Synod written on February 25, 1721, he also asked to be assigned the frontier cities of Irkutsk, Yakutsk, and Nerchinsk.[24] For Kul'chitskii the point of this request was that, if it were granted, he might then escape going to Peking altogether, a post for which his resolve had already begun to weaken: "According to this arrangement, if need calls, a representative might go to China with a caravan. And if this is impossible, then get me a decent salary so that I, living there [in Peking] with this rank, will not have to take favors from the Tartars and do a dishonor to Russia." But the Synod, acting on the tsar's ukase, refused the request for the Siberian towns. Instead it was determined to make Kul'chitskii nominal Bishop of the Ukrainian eparchy of Pereiaslavl', a respectable distance away, and send him to Peking with a salary of 1500 rubles *per annum* for his mission.[25] He was duly ordained on March 5,[26] by which time Izmailov's now empty-handed embassy had been three days on the road from Peking back to Selenginsk.

The Synod quickly followed with a full reply[27] to the report that the bishop-designate had made on February 25. Among other arrangements, it determined upon the needs "without which"—according to Kul'chitskii—"it would be impossible to get and live there." The Synod decided that the dress and ornaments for his service in the new bishopric should come from the Bishop of Suzdal, who had just been given some materials from the sacristy of Tambov. Anything else might be gotten from the sacristy of the now defunct patriarchate.

Responsibility was taken, either by the Synod or the Senate, to be sure that the mission was furnished with horses and boats during its trek across Siberia; that its salary was paid out of yearly Siberian revenues, to be sent to Peking by caravan; that a translator of Mongolian was provided at an appropriate point, "with whom they might traverse the steppe without difficulty or fear." Finally, the Synod agreed to conclude the arrangements swiftly, since "the winter road was breaking up and there would be no small trouble on the way"; and Kul'chitskii was promised authority independent of the metropolitan of Tobolsk, for which he had strongly petitioned. For his personnel, he had asked for a suite of fifteen people, probably basing his estimate on the suggestion of Leshchinskii in 1719. This number was reduced to twelve. To Kul'chitskii's query of where these people could be found, the Synod returned the laconic answer: "Get them wherever you can find volunteers."

Kul'chitskii worked hard to get his mission assembled before too much time was lost. Ultimately he left St. Petersburg on April 19, 1721,[28] even before receiving his final instructions and letter of accreditation to the Ch'ing authorities. Another nagging detail: he also left without one liturgical item, a *chinovnik*, or bishop's service book, that the sacristan of the Patriarchate refused to give him without a special ukase from the Synod. Failing to find another *chinovnik* anywhere, Kul'chitskii wrote to the Synod about his problem. The Synod was late in attending to this matter, and its authorization for Kul'chitskii to take the patriarchal *chinovnik* did not come until May 12. Kul'chitskii had contended that "nothing would be possible" without his service book,[29] but it is doubtful that it ever reached him since nothing, indeed, seemed possible during the course of his mission.

Not until May 12 or 13, 1721, did the Synod finally send Kul'chitskii his instructions and letter of accreditation. The Senate had drawn up the accrediting letter on April 21, but had not sent it to the Synod until April 27. The Synod forwarded the letter to Kul'chitskii, enclosing some instructions of its own, dated May 12, 1721.[30] This package must have been received by the bishop in the course of his journey across Siberia. His entourage consisted of two hieromonks, two hierodeacons, five choristers, two servants, and one cook. Their journey to Selenginsk took eleven months. On the way Kul'chitskii picked up a mitre from the bishop of Armiansk, and got another cap from the eparchy of Tobolsk that had been given formerly to Archimandrite Ilarion Lezhaiskii and which Antonii Platkovskii had recently brought back from Peking.[31] In Irkutsk, where he arrived in March, 1722, he paused long enough to denounce Metropolitan Leshchinskii to the Synod for drawing money from the salary of the deceased Ilarion Lezhaiskii.[32] The Synod had no appetite for investigating the charge. The incident was merely the first of a number of rancorous affairs in which Kul'chitskii became embroiled, damning the people who had thought up his assignment as well as those who were to stand in his way.

In a portentous afterthought, the Senate had decided that it would be more prudent if, in its introduction of Kul'chitskii to the Ch'ing officials, the fact that he was a bishop were kept secret. In the accrediting letter he was therefore announced simply as "the religious person, Mr. Innokentii Kulchitskii." Furthermore, since the Senate's decision had been made after Kul'chitskii's departure from St. Petersburg, it was necessary that he be instructed to conceal his rank from the Chinese. This was the main reason for the Senate's letter to the Synod of April 27, in which Kul'chitskii's letter of accreditation was also enclosed. The letter, addressed to the Li-fan yuan, read as follows:

> In 1719 we received a letter to Prince Gagarin on the subject of the death of Ilarion and the freedom to send another archimandrite in his place. In accordance with this the tsar had decided to send to China the religious person Mr. Innokentii Kul'chitskii, and with him two hieromonks, two deacons, and several servants . . . and we ask that he be

allowed to live freely in Peking and conduct the holy worship in church, . . . and particularly, in accordance with the friendship between both our courts, that China hold that church and bishop and all his servants and other people of the Christian faith in its protection and kindness.[33]

The Synod forwarded this letter to Kul'chitskii along with his final instructions, to be kept close to his chest:

Because the Ruling Senate has informed the head-secretary of the Holy Synod, we would in addition like to inform you that upon your arrival in China you should not dare to advertise that you hold the rank of bishop (which you might gather from the writ sent to the Chinese senators), lest some sort of opposition should arise among the enemies of our Orthodox Russian faith, and even more among the main enemies, the Jesuits, who for a long time have been accustomed to sow among the wheat of Orthodoxy the tares of strife and shame, in order to stand in the way of our good intentions. Yes, it cannot be otherwise; and here is quoted that phrase of Christ the Saviour which he said to Him who asked Him: "Lord! Have I not sown good seed, where therefore have the tares come from?" And it is said: "The foe of mankind has done this." And if by chance someone of the famous and high-ranking personalities there questions you about your rank, you can say that you have the rank of bishop so that you can ordain priests and deacons when they are needed to replace deceased ones, and for nothing else—and that with a great deal of caution.

As for the rest, from the Lord our God, and our Saviour Jesus Christ again and again we sincerely wish you, your grace, all the best for your preaching of Orthodoxy and for your beneficial success.[34]

As soon as Innokentii Kul'chitskii arrived in Irkutsk, Voevoda Poluektov sent the Senate's letter to China. Since correspondence was being channeled through the Mongol authorities in Urga, Poluektov sent the letter to the Tüshiyetü Khan, who, he had every

reason to expect, would then forward it to Peking. Kul'chitskii
went on to Selenginsk to await a reply. The twisted course of
events that followed is best described in the letters of Kul'chitskii
himself back to the Synod. On September 2, 1722, he wrote:

> The Tüshiyetü Khan did not accept the letter, sending this
> reply: "Why has the voevoda not written to me? What is that
> letter being sent to China all about?" And thereupon the
> courier returned. The same voevoda [Poluektov] sent another
> letter in April, clearly explaining to him in *his* letter on what
> business the letter was being sent, but the Tüshiyetü Khan
> did not receive it in Urga, as he had gone off with the imperial
> regiments. The voevoda sent a third letter, and although the
> messenger found the Tüshiyetü Khan in Urga, still nothing
> was done. He refused the letter written to him from the
> voevoda, threw it out, and sent back the other letters to
> Selenginsk. Finally, wanting myself to make certain whether
> the Tüshiyetü Khan had a paper written about me, and whether
> this were common knowledge in China, or whether he were
> simply refusing, I [had] translated from Russian to Mongolian
> a part of the letter, written from Peking to Gagarin on the
> other head of the mission [Lezhaiskii], and sent Filimon to
> Urga with it in the month of July. It was taken and sent to
> Peking, from where even to this day there has been no reply.
> I do not know if there will be one, and thus it is incumbent
> on me to wait in Selenginsk.[35]

Three weeks later, however, on September 24, Kul'chitskii at last
had a response. The letter of accreditation was returned to him
from Peking, with an enclosed notation from the Tüshiyetü Khan:

> According to the edict of the Bogdykhan it was ordered not
> to let Mr. Innokentii Kul'chitskii into Peking because there
> was no letter about it from the Governor of Siberia and none
> of the seals that had been given to Izmailov had been affixed;
> and especially because they did not have an answer about the
> matter of the Mongol fugitives ... And if you investigate into

the surrender of the fugitives, then will we also debate on the arrival of the above-mentioned Kul'chitskii.[36]

Kul'chitskii quoted the gist of this note in another report to the Synod written on October 6, 1722. He also wrote, "While the foxes sleep, I have had nowhere to lay my head during all this time. I stray from household to household, from home to home." And in a third report of March 8, 1723, he wrote: "With every submissiveness about my unworthiness, I am aware that I stand at the frontier neither on this side nor on that. In China they will not accept me, and not only that, neither will they allow letters from me to them or from them to me. And I am hardly able to go back without orders from you, although it is not without want that I am staying here."[37]

The drift of this correspondence at last moved Lorents Lange, who had been staying in Selenginsk since his expulsion from China the previous summer, to undertake a thorough search for those seven hundred stray Mongols about which the Tüshiyetü Khan had written. Not only had the Izmailov embassy been a casualty of this problem; Kul'chitskii was running up against it as well. When Lange's investigation was complete, all he found were twenty-six unregistered secular males and fifty-eight unaccounted for lamas. The carefully detailed survey was presented to Punchugh, the Manchu witness in Selenginsk, on February of 1724, whereupon it was forwarded to the Li-fan yuan. All the fugitives were extradited.[38]

Meanwhile, internal Russian matters could not be hurried. Kul'chitskii's report of October 6, 1722, for example, was not received by the Synod until June 22, 1723. In an answering ukase of August 5 the Synod ordered Kul'chitskii to wait in Selenginsk, to follow along behind Lange and to draw his salary from local sources. Kul'chitskii's note of March 8, 1723, did not arrive in St. Petersburg until August 19.[39] To this the Synod merely replied that it had referred the bishop's problems to the Senate.[40] It took a full year—often longer—for this correspondence to make the round trip from one end of Russia to the other, and how devoid of substance were the answers, when they finally came!

On November 18, 1723, Kul'chitskii wrote to the Synod acknowledging receipt of the ukase of August 5.[41] But—he points out—Lange was not going anywhere and thus there was no point in following him, and the voevoda of Irkutsk was refusing to pay him his salary. Then he concludes, "from all appearances only God knows how or where things are going." This letter was received by the Synod on May 15, 1724. By this time the Senate was at last taking up the problem of what to do with the marooned bishop. Enclosing a ukase, elicited from the tsar on December 17, 1722, the Senate reported (on December 18) to the Synod that Innokentii Kul'chitskii should be asked to remove himself to Irkutsk pending the outcome of the border difficulties. The transmission of this decision did not even leave the Synod until May 27, 1724.[42] On March 13, 1724, Kul'chitskii, still in Selenginsk and still without any certain source of livelihood, communicated to the Synod some new frustrations:

I received a ukase [of August 5, 1723] in which I was ordered to wait in Selenginsk until further notice, and [told] that the copy of the Tüshiyetü Khan's letter that I had enclosed had been sent on to the Senate with a detailed report, and that my salary was to be received from Siberia as already determined, on which matter a ukase had been sent. And upon receiving the tsar's ukase I sent my hierodeacon Filimon to Irkutsk to Voevoda Ivan Ivanovich Poluektov, asking for the prescribed salary, which he had not given me in 1723, and the voevoda said, "I have no orders from Tobolsk with regard to you and will not give you your salary until I receive an answer to my letter which I wrote to the governor Prince Aleksei Mikhailovich [Cherkaskii], asking whether or not to pay a salary to the bishop sent to China but not accepted there; and when an order is sent it will be necessary to deduct a quarter of your salary."[43]

The Synod turned its attention to this idiotic matter on October 7, 1724.[44]

By now, however, the pace of events on the frontier was

quickening. The Li-fan yuan had found Lange's inquiry into the question of Mongol fugitives quite acceptable, even though it had netted them a total of only eighty-four men. The point was that Lange, by his laborious effort, had acknowledged the practical need for an extension of the frontier. It was something to go on, and so the Li-fan yuan quickly dispatched two of its officials— O-lun-tai and T'e-ku-t'e[45]—to Selenginsk to reaffirm the Manchu interest in new negotiations. Here is Kul'chitskii's account of the situation:

> In this year of 1724 two [Manchu] ambassadors pleni-potentiary were sent for talks on their claims to the Mongol and other fugitives, from which agent Lange was pleased to ask about their accepting me in Peking, putting it to them that they had written to the Russian emperor about sending another head of the Russian mission in place of the deceased one, that a letter had then been sent from the Senate, that the [Russian] fugitives [in Peking] were not prepared to do the holy work, that [the Ch'ing] should not care about houses or food, that we can take care of it ... And to that they answered, "we cannot receive him [Kul'chitskii] until we report to the Bogdikhan; and when will there be some person sent from the autocrat of all the Russias having, like us, plenipotentiary powers, who will be able to conduct negoti-ations on all these things for which we were sent? At that time will we deliver ourselves on the issue of whether or not we will receive this chief of the mission."[46]

A final ukase of March 18, 1725, ordered Innokentii Kul'chitskii to take up residence in the Voznesenskii monastery in Irkutsk.[47] He complied, and it was here that the first period of his frustrated attempts to get into China closed.

The adventures of Innokentii Kul'chitskii were far from finished, but already they demonstrate the extraordinary capacity of the Russian government—including its religious hierarchy—to defeat what were presumably its own purposes in sending Kul'-

chitskii on his way. In St. Petersburg the Synod and the Senate seemed locked in a competition to escape any responsibility for tending to Kul'chitskii's problems, and the tsar himself appears soon to have lost interest in the affair. Without the spirited interference of the central administration, Kul'chitskii was bound to walk into a situation in Eastern Siberia that he could not by himself control. Here jealousies and suspicions among local officials were the rule of political life, for if everyone was free to meddle in everyone else's business, the government in St. Petersburg could at least be content that its Siberian domains would never become too strong and too independent. Until communications improved, and until Russia had a more reliable civil service, the bungling of the local administration in a town like Irkutsk was a necessary price to pay for its immense distance from the Russian capital.

Through this morass of officialdom some truths about Sino-Russian relations in the mid-1720s had, however, begun to make themselves known. Because of Kul'chitskii's problems, about which the bishop had left a labored correspondence, Russia was now more aware of the Inner Asian dimensions of Ch'ing foreign policy. If no one in Russia was yet able to appreciate Manchu sensitivities about fugitive Mongols or the status of the Urga Khutughtu, at least it was apparent that these were important issues that could no longer lie outside of any settlement that Russia and China reached. Another fact that Kul'chitskii's experience made even more clear than had Lange's impermanent consulship was the need for a Russian plenipotentiary to undertake negotiations with the Manchus, two of whom, Kul'chitskii had written, were already waiting on the frontier. No Siberian official was capable, to say nothing of being trusted by either Russia or China, to do this negotiating. Of that Kul'chitskii's letters had left no doubt at all.

It is therefore to the designation of Count Vladislavich as minister-plenipotentiary to China that we should turn. The case of the bishop, buffeted back and forth by the whims of self-important border officials and drawn out to excruciating lengths by the time it took the Synod to address itself to his cries for help, would now wait upon Vladislavich's arrival. But Innokentii Kul'chitskii, who had, in a sense, done much to expedite the appointment of Vladislavich, was wrong on one point. Not even a Russian plenipotentiary would be able, or even willing, to rescue the bishop's mission to Peking.

Chapter IV

VLADISLAVICH, PLATKOVSKII, AND THE KIAKHTA TREATY

Count Sava Vladislavich-Raguzinskii was officially named ambassador plenipotentiary to China on June 18, 1725. By now the reigns of K'ang-hsi and Peter had ended, both monarchs having left to their successors the task of sorting out the differences that had kept Sino-Russian relations from achieving what both countries had hoped. While the Mongolian frontier itself, where Kul'-chitskii was detained, was surely the most pressing issue for the Manchus, the situation further west in Zungharia remained as volatile as ever. A visit there by a Russian envoy in 1722,[1] in itself of no great consequence, at least demonstrated Russia's readiness to deal directly with Tsewang Arabtan, whose reputation in Peking as a thorn in the side of an expanding Manchu empire was already well established. The future of Russian trade with China was still entirely uncertain, since Stepan Tret'iakov's caravan of 1724, like Kul'chitskii's mission, had been turned away at the border and now joined the bishop in what must have begun to appear as an interminable wait for Sino-Russian relations to be untangled.

Preparations for the Vladislavich Embassy

In St. Petersburg the decision that some kind of an embassy to China was necessary had been made before Peter's death. Now, after the appointment of Vladislavich by the tsarina, Catherine, and his accreditation to a new ruler of China, the Yung-cheng emperor, steps were taken that caused the enterprise to surpass in size and importance anything heretofore seen in the history of Sino-Russian relations. Vladislavich received instructions in forty-five articles[2] that elaborated upon most of the demands that Izmailov had carried: free trade within China, Russian agents or consuls resident not only in Peking but also in Canton; a new entrepot for Russian wares in Peking, and the like. In addition and at last, a commission to help demarcate the Mongolian frontier was to form part of the embassy. The caravan of Stepan Tret'iakov was to accompany Vladislavich to Peking. Finally, Bishop Innokentii Kul'chitskii, passing his time at the Voznesenskii monastery in Irkutsk, was to be attached to the ambassador's suite for another try at entering China. An impression of the hopes that Russia had invested in this effort may be gotten from one interesting difference between the instructions to Izmailov and those to Vladislavich: in 1718 Izmailov was told to promise unrestricted Siberian mail routes to the Jesuits in China in exchange for their assistance in his behalf; Vladislavich was allowed to promise them their own freedom of passage through Siberia.[3] Envious of these highly placed rivals, Russia was nevertheless helpless without them. It follows, at least in Russian historiography, that for whatever went wrong in early Sino-Russian relations the Jesuits should be made to shoulder the blame.

Since Kul'chitskii would not be taken on as part of the embassy until the frontier was nearly reached, the Synod sent out word to find an attendant priest in Moscow who was "clever and had nothing to be ashamed of," and whose salary, it was carefully noted, should be paid by the College of Foreign Affairs.[4] Another of the Synod's concerns was rather more important: this was to discover some students in the Moscow Slavonic-Greek-and-Latin Academy who would willingly go to China to study the Chinese language. The decision to attach some students to the Vladislavich embassy seems almost accidental; its origins were very clouded. Yet there were plenty of recent precedents for sending youths abroad, a Petrine practice undoubtedly modeled on the European experiences of the young tsar himself in the 1690s. Modern diplomatic relations required expertise, good intelligence, and an ability to handle foreign languages. For this purpose two students were selected from the Moscow Academy, Luka Voeikov and Ivan Shestopalov-Iablontsev. The Synod again reminded the College of Foreign Affairs that the job of paying them belonged to the latter, the ecclesiastical authorities limiting their responsibility to seeing that the students went along with Vladislavich "without delay or excuses."[5] As it turned out, these men did nothing to justify either the aspirations or the costs that were invested in their trip to China; indeed, it would take another century before any appreciable results would be retrieved from Peking.

Vladislavich's instructions concerning Kul'chitskii repeated what the Synod had originally said, namely that the bishop should be allowed to make visits outside Peking, that a place should be given for the construction of a church, that he should be called not a bishop, but a "religious person," and so forth. The next paragraph, however, for the first time adds a contingency: if the Manchus were disinclined to accept the bishop, then Vladislavich should leave him at the frontier and not endanger the other purposes of the embassy by insisting on Kul'chitskii's admission.[6] On October 5, 1725, Innokentii Kul'chitskii himself was told "to conduct himself in accordance with the importance of his rank, taking advice in all matters from the ambassador, and not to interject himself into political affairs."[7] It was a hard order to follow, not because Kul'chitskii was particularly fond of politicking, but because he was already at the center of a monumental confrontation between two empires. One could not yet say with certainty that he had become more a part of the problem than the solution, but by 1725 the high ecclesiastical hopes with which he had been sent off from St. Petersburg could no longer be sustained. The possibility of replacing the bishop with Archimandrite Antonii Platkovskii was aired for the first time, before Vladislavich departed.[8]

The full embassy, amounting to about one hundred and twenty people, with military escort, left St. Petersburg on October 12, 1725. In Moscow the students and accompanying priests were taken on. The winter run to Tobolsk was done quickly, in less than a month, and Irkutsk was reached on April 5, 1726. Vladislavich, taking the time to inform himself on conditions along the Mongolian border, did not reach Selenginsk until summer. Finally he arrived at the Bura river on the frontier on August 24 where the Manchu dignitaries, Lungkodo[9] and Ssu-ko[10] were awaiting him. Here he formally requested admission of his embassy into China, together with the caravan waiting there, and the "religious person" who had been waiting permission longer than anyone else. Negotiations began at once.

The Demise of Kul'chitskii

Developments quickly made it clear that the Kul'chitskii project was doomed. Vladislavich reported the Ch'ing attitude at length in a letter to the College of Foreign Affairs on August 31, 1726, summing up the results of the first week of negotiations.

> The person of Bishop Innokentii was considered very weightily at the Chinese Court, because in the letter of the Governor of Siberia to the Mongolian tribunal [Li-fan yuan], Bishop Innokentii was termed a religious person and grand gentleman [*dukhovnaia osoba velikii gospodin*], and from this the Chinese became suspicious that he was a very important person, and their ministers said to Agent Lange that the Bogdikhan never allowed such an important person to be received, for they had a dignitary called by them the Kutukhta, and another important person like Innokentii Kul'chitskii was unnecessary to them; that when all matters with the Chinese court had been settled then perhaps an archimandrite and priests would be accepted, but a bishop never.[11]

This is only half the story (as we shall see) but it is an interesting half nevertheless. How had the Manchus discovered that Kul'-chitskii was such an important person? Had Prince Dolgorukov, governor of Siberia, betrayed his true identity? It was not he, Vladislavich later maintained, but Voevoda Poluektov of Irkutsk, Kul'chitskii's old adversary, who made the *faux pas* by inserting the word "grand" before his otherwise harmless title of "gentleman."[12] It is conceivable that Poluektov was unaware of the bishop's need for secrecy, but it is not likely. The relations between the two had never been tranquil, and Poluektov's indiscretion was probably a shrewd act of vindictiveness.

Now the time had come for Antonii Platkovskii to step forward, and he quickly put together a conspiracy of his own. Toward the end of August, as Vladislavich's preliminary talks with

Lungkodo and Ssu-ko were nearing an end, the archimandrite suddenly appeared in Selenginsk. At a moment when he knew Vladislavich was soon expected at the bishop's residence, Platkovskii presented himself to Kul'chitskii, and by talking interminably at the door, forced the bishop to invite him inside for refreshment. Platkovskii then encouraged his host to pour out for himself two rather large glasses of vodka, while he insisted, for his part, only on one very small glass. Kul'chitskii accordingly became quite drunk and soon passed out; and in less than half an hour Vladislavich obligingly arrived. Kul'chitskii lifted himself up with difficulty, but the count, "seeing that he was not himself," left the house. Now Platkovskii ran after Vladislavich and explained to him how drunk this bibulous bishop always was. The charge was supported by some of Platkovskii's seconds, who had been assembled hastily. Vladislavich accordingly became as convinced as Lungkodo and Ssu-ko that Kul'chitskii was not the man for the China assignment.[13] His letter of August 31 to the College of Foreign Affairs therefore continued:

> The bishop very much wants to return to Russia, and it would be better to do that since he is often overcome by the clamor and does little honor to the Russian empire. And if it is absolutely necessary for the sake of piety to send a religious person to Peking, then send a good and educated man under the title of archimandrite, with four to six persons, furnishing him with bishop's power by the Synod, which he would by no means divulge; and since it is difficult to send a religious person over such a distance, I suggest Antonii Platkovskii of the Voznesenskii monastery, who teaches several children the Mongolian language, who has been in Peking—a sober man of gifted mind.[14]

Platkovskii soon got himself sent to Peking, "about which he boasted and laughed."[15]

Vladislavich's letter was received in St. Petersburg on December 30. The Supreme Privy Council, acting for the tsarina, accepted the suggestion of Vladislavich, and Antonii Platkovskii was duly named to the Peking mission. This was formally decreed in a ukase from the Synod of January 9, 1727: Archimandrite Antonii Platkovskii should go to China with four to six people, and he should take with him some of the students to whom he taught Mongolian in Irkutsk so that their instruction might continue even in Peking. Salaries for the first year should come from the income of the Voznesenskii monastery. Afterwards they would be paid from the general revenues of Siberia, as well as the other local revenues and the profits of the state caravans. The Privy Council had suggested to the Synod that the archimandrite be salaried at between five hundred and six hundred rubles a year; as for the others, this was left up to the judgment of Prince Dolgorukov, but he was not encouraged to pay them more than "enough so that they may live without want." The Synod also instructed the metropolitan of Tobolsk, Antonii Stakhovskii (successor to Leshchinskii), to make the salary payments from the treasury of the Vozenesenskii monastery, and finally ordered Innokentii Kul'chitskii to stay in that monastery until an edict arrived which would command him, with the agreement of the metropolitan, "to undertake some appropriate work."[16]

On January 15, 1727, Catherine repeated the order for Kul'chitskii to remain in Irkutsk, but now he was also given that city, as well as the area of Eastern Siberia, in an independent eparchy such as he had asked for in 1721.[17] His office, however, still subordinated him to Tobolsk, and on February 17 Metropolitan Antonii entrusted to Kul'chitskii the humiliating responsibility of preparing Platkovskii's mission: the archimandrite should be given as many people as the ukase allowed; horses and fodder were to be supplied from various monasteries and the animals either sent back from Peking or sold in China, in which case the money was to be sent back. And in what must have seemed an ironic afterthought, Kul'chitskii was to make certain that no unwarranted whims were indulged.[18] He left Selenginsk for Irkutsk on July 22, 1727, arrived on August 5, and once again took up residence in the Voznesenskii monastery. On August 26 he received the ukase of July 15 entitling him to the eparchy of Irkutsk, and on December 4 the Synod officially confirmed him as "Bishop of Irkutsk and Nerchinsk."[19] Apart from one more rankling encounter with Antonii Platkovskii, Kul'chitskii's life was thereafter piously devoted to the propagation of the Orthodox faith among the native peoples of Siberia, an effort at which he excelled, as if to make up for all the time that had been lost while his case pended on the frontier. In his Eastern Siberian eparchy, in the last four years of his life, Innokentii Kul'chitskii found a place for himself between the overbearing cities of St. Petersburg and Peking. Here the clamor subsided, at least until the last year of his life, when it is not unlikely that he had the satisfaction of hearing of the noise that Platkovskii's mission was already beginning to make in Peking. He died on November 27, 1731, and was canonized in 1764. In 1804 the Synod decreed that the calendar day of November 26 should henceforth be observed as the holy day of Saint Innokentii.[20]

The Kiakhta Treaty

Since the Ch'ing regime was not party to the decision to send Platkovskii to China instead of Kul'chitskii, it remained to be seen if the archimandrite would be acceptable. Vladislavich had entered China on October 21, 1726, to begin talks in earnest in Peking. This phase of the negotiations was intended to deal with all outstanding questions apart from the problem of demarcating the Mongolian border; later the Manchu ministers and Russian envoy were to retire to the border to take up that matter on the spot. Vladislavich stayed in Peking for six months, negotiating with the Manchu officials Chabina, Tegute, and Tulishen.[21] During that time the basic points that were ultimately written into the treaty of Kiakhta were worked out: the frontier from the Ud river west would remain undefined; fugitives would be extradited; a Russian caravan of two hundred merchants would be allowed in Peking once every three years and would pay its own way in China; two trading depots would be established at the frontier for a regular and continuous trade between the two countries; passports for crossing the frontier were still required; Lange (or any other agent) could accompany the caravans, but now could not remain in Peking

past their duration there; and finally three priests in addition to
the one already resident in Peking would be accepted, and a church
would be constructed in the Russian hostel, which was to remain
the same as that in which earlier Russians had stayed.

On March 21, 1727, these agreements were drawn up in ten
points. Vladislavich had his *audience de congé* with Yung-cheng on
April 19, and left Peking for the frontier on April 23, where the
work of demarcation was next to be undertaken. On the way
through Mongolia Vladislavich received two letters from the College of Foreign Affairs. They acknowledged receiving his of
August 31, 1726, and concurred in his judgment to replace Kul'-
chitskii with Platkovskii, among other matters.[22] From Mongolia
Vladislavich wrote another letter of record to St. Petersburg,
describing what had been accomplished in Peking. In this important document, only a summary of which is available in Cahen or
Bantysh-Kamenskii,[23] Vladislavich mentioned the Ch'ing agreement to accept three more priests and to build a church. He said
nothing about the students he had brought with him, nor those
that Platkovskii would supply, but surely they had been discussed
by now as well.[24] The boundary negotiations proceeded through
the summer of 1727 and ended successfully on August 20. A Latin
draft of the general treaty was received at the frontier from Peking
on November 13, but Vladislavich found it unacceptable. On
April 3, 1728, a new text arrived by courier.[25] In this version
Vladislavich was displeased with less serious irregularities: the
treaty referred to the Russian tsarina when, in fact, Catherine had
died and the throne had passed to the new tsar, Peter II. Furthermore, the treaty did not contain the date and place of exchange.
(One might well ask how the Ch'ing officials could have known
any of these things.) A final objection was to the phraseology on
the new Russian church in Peking: the Ch'ing treaty spoke of it as
having already been built, while Vladislavich maintained that it had
not yet been begun. But here the Manchu officials were acting in
good faith, for the church had in fact been largely completed by
then. One week later Vladislavich himself received a letter from
Lorents Lange (who was once again in Peking) written on March 11,

testifying to the fact that Chinese construction materials had been brought to the Russian hostel on December 28, 1727, two days after his arrival in Peking; and that by January 12, 1728, stonemasons had arrived to lay the foundation of the church, carpenters and joiners had begun preparing the sides, "and we may hope— Lange wrote—that the church will be completed in two months, apart from its interior decoration. The model will be taken from the French church; ours will be about half its size."[26]

Vladislavich's meticulous eye could find no more grounds for complaint, and the final copies arrived at the frontier on June 14, 1728, where they were signed and exchanged. The fifth article of the treaty of Kiakhta, in its Chinese text, runs as follows:

> The *kuan* or hostel which is now used for Russians staying in Peking will henceforth also be for Russians who arrive there. Only they shall live in this hostel. And what the Russian envoy, the Illirion Count Sava Vladislavich proposed on the construction of a church has been completed in that hostel with the assistance of the ministers who supervise Russian affairs.
>
> In that hostel there will live one lama, now residing in Peking, and there will be added three more lamas, who will arrive, as decided. When they arrive, provisions will be given them, as the one who arrived earlier is being supplied, and they will be settled at the church. The Russians will not be prevented from praying and worshipping their god in their own way. In addition, four young students and two of more advanced age who know Russian and Latin, whom the Russian envoy, the Illirion Count Sava Vladislavich, wants to leave in Peking for the study of languages, will also live in that hostel, and provisions will be given to them from the stores of the tsar; and when they have completed their studies, they shall return, as they like.[27]

It remained for Vladislavich, having gotten this far, to see if the terms of the fifth article could be fulfilled from the Russian side, no small question in itself. We have already referred to the two students from the Moscow Academy, Luka Voeikov and Ivan

Shestopalov-Iablontsev, who had formed part of the Russian embassy from the very beginning. But when Vladislavich arrived in Moscow in December, 1725, to pick them up, he was annoyed to find that they were already rather advanced in years, and therefore made Voeikov the Latin translator for his boundary commissioner, Stepan Koluchov, replacing him with a younger man from his own suite, Stepan Pisarev. Iablontsev was retained. By the time the embassy reached the Chinese frontier, however, Pisarev had become one of Vladislavich's personal scribes (*pod'iachii*) and was therefore unavailable for service in China as a student. He was then replaced by Vladislavich's page, Ivan Pukhort, who also knew Latin. Meanwhile Ivan Shestopalov-Iablontsev was wounded in an unrecorded fracas on the border (and later died on December 24, 1727); he was in turn replaced by his old schoolmate, Voeikov. This change guaranteed that the two students now intended for Peking—Pukhort and Voeikov—still knew Latin, conforming to the emerging terms of the treaty.[28] A third student was now also added. This was Feodot Tret'iakov, the sixteen-year-old son of one of the few available Russian translators of Mongolian, Aleksei Tret'iakov. The younger Tret'iakov had made a strong plea on September 5, 1727, to be taken to Peking as a student, and his uncommon initiative was rewarded.[29] These three students, half the number allowed by the provisional agreements, were to go to Peking with the caravan that had been waiting for four years at the frontier. The original commissar of the caravan, Stepan Tret'iakov, had since died, and Dmitri Molokov had been appointed in his place. After the successful conclusion of the frontier treaty, or the "treaty of Bura" on August 20, 1727, the caravan was at last permitted to enter China. It departed from Selenginsk on September 13, 1727, nine months before the formal exchange of the general treaty of Kiakhta; with it went Lorents Lange, the caravan priest Ilarion Trusov, some two hundred merchants, and the three students: Voeikov, Pukhort, and Tret'iakov.[30]

Platkovskii's Mission

Vladislavich had intended that Antonii Platkovskii, with his own group of clerics and students, should also enter China at this

opportune moment. On June 14, 1727, upon Vladislavich's return
to the frontier from Peking, he had summoned Platkovskii to
Selenginsk, and no doubt informed him of the Ch'ing agreement
to accept three more priests. On August 4, when the treaty of Bura
was nearing conclusion, Platkovskii left Selenginsk for the frontier.
A week later he informed the embassy that of his eight students in
Irkutsk, four had been judged ready for language study in Peking.
He also asked for himself a regular salary so as not to be reduced
to the charity of the Ch'ing emperor. Accordingly, Vladislavich
followed the prescription of the Synod and gave Platkovskii an
annual salary of 550 rubles; the remaining members of his suite
were given 130 rubles each.[31] Everything was ready by August 22.
Platkovskii was sent back to Irkutsk to get his money from the
Voznesenskii monastery as quickly as possible, but here Vladislavich's plenipotentiary powers were inadequate to stave off
another contretemps. Foreseeing trouble, the archimandrite
arranged for a military officer to accompany him in order to exe-
cute the orders of the ambassador, because, as he said, "neither
the bishop [Kul'chitskii] nor the brothers of the Voznesenskii
monastery listen to me and they will give me nothing." With his
escort Platkovskii succeeded in taking from the treasury of the
monastery three quarters of its holdings. Kul'chitskii thereupon
denounced him to Vladislavich, saying that Platkovskii had
devastated Voznesenskii. Lange, meanwhile, implored Platkovskii
to hurry, as the caravan was about to depart; but his plea was
unheard, Platkovskii insisting on staying in Russia to retrieve his
honor. The caravan left without him.[32]

Neither was any member of his group taken with Lange's
caravan. In fact, it is uncertain at this point where Platkovskii's
suite was, and of whom it consisted. Vladislavich had informed
St. Petersburg only that "Archimandrite Antonii Platkovskii . . .
arrived at Selenginsk after the caravan had already left, and with
him he brought only one priest, and he a drunkard." Then Vladislavich went on to report about the affair with Kul'chitskii: "The
archimandrite strenuously asked me not to send him to Peking
now, lest in his absence his enemies violate his honor, since he was

guilty of nothing against the monastery, and wants to return to the monastery himself and reply to the points of Bishop Innokentii, and when he is vindicated he will, in the spring, willingly and in an orderly fashion go to Peking."[33] Vladislavich was helpless to solve this problem quickly. He wrote to the Ch'ing officials the invention that Platkovskii had become shipwrecked on Lake Baikal and would join later the others who had already departed.[34] When the caravan reached Urga Lange was told by Tulishen of this letter from the count with the news of Platkovskii's "shipwreck," which Lange, lacking any alternative information, no doubt believed and perhaps even welcomed. But at least the caravan was now free to hasten its pace to Peking which, after a difficult crossing of the steppe, was reached on December 26, 1727.

What awaited Lange in Peking neither justified his anticipation nor required any hurry in getting there, for as soon as his caravan arrived, a Manchu guard of seven hundred and fifty soldiers deployed themselves, day and night, around the Russian hostel. Under these oppressive conditions the Russian merchants had difficulty selling any of their furs, and through the winter of 1728 almost no business was done. Not only that; the hostel itself was, as usual, badly in need of repairs; the entry in Lange's diary for March 9 notes that the Li-fan yuan refused either to take the responsibility for mending the roofs or to allow him to repair them.[35] Was this the price of the frontier negotiations—that Russians would no longer be welcome in Peking? Not at all, for two days later, on March 11, Lange wrote to Vladislavich that construction of the new church (which, as we have seen, had begun soon after the caravan's arrival) was progressing smoothly[36]—in the very hostel whose roofs were in studied disrepair. His diary also reveals that the three students who had accompanied the caravan were being well cared for by the Li-fan yuan, having received the necessary facilities for their studies as well as a mace of silver and a measure of flour every day.[37] How eloquently does Lange attest to the Manchu interest in reducing Russian business in Peking merely to the ecclesiastical mission and its students!

With the timely intercession of a group of second- and third-generation Albazinian brokers (who also appear to have been Manchu double-agents), the caravan of 1727–1728 was finally able to manage a considerable trade. But before Lange left Peking in July he was assured by the Li-fan yuan only as to its good will toward Russian missionaries and Russian students.[38] It showed no enthusiasm for the caravans. Caravans, by treaty, were still allowed to go to Peking, but their success or failure as business ventures would obviously depend upon "Oriental whims" which Russia found so hard to comprehend. The ideological value to China of the Peking caravan appears, in fact, to have shifted. No longer content to find in the caravan trade itself a mark of Russian submission to China, and no longer, therefore, content to subsidize it, the Li-fan yuan was more interested in showing that those Russian merchants who came to Peking were dependent upon trading conditions that the Ch'ing government could manipulate as capriciously as it chose. But the caravan merchants who did arrive, when faced with the obstructions that were supposed to keep them in their place, became more restless and less submissive. If the obvious answer to this problem lay ultimately in amputating altogether that part of the caravan trade that brought Russian merchants to Peking, how would the Russian need for representation in the Ch'ing capital, and the Manchu need for dependent Russians inside of China, be satisfied? The point to return to is that the Russian ecclesiastical mission became increasingly useful to both Russia and China—in 1728 and later—as an indication that losing the caravan trade in Peking would not mean losing everything there.

While the caravan of 1727–1728 was in Peking, Sava Vladislavich remained at the frontier waiting for the arrival from China of an acceptable form of the general treaty. During this time the dispute between Platkovskii and Kul'chitskii had failed to quiet down. When the treaty of Kiakhta was at length signed and exchanged on June 14, 1728, the two ecclesiastics were still bickering. At length Vladislavich himself went to Irkutsk in July to reconcile this absurd and tiresome affair. He seemed to favor

Platkovskii, but no doubt only for practical purposes.[39] The archimandrite had, after all, been officially designated for Peking, and Vladislavich had already made rather extensive preparations for his admission, being assured by Chabina at their final meeting that Platkovskii, along with two priests, three students, and two servants, was still welcome in China.[40] Getting him packed off now remained the last order of business before the work of Vladislavich's embassy could be considered finished. What kind of settlement was made with the Voznesenskii monastery is unknown, but Vladislavich wrote to the frontier commissioner, Bukholts, on July 14 that Platkovskii at last had his passport and was on his way.[41] Bukholts was needlessly cautioned against revealing Platkovskii's ecclesiastical rank to the Urga authorities, for here China was surely under no misapprehension. Platkovskii was neither the bishop nor the "grand gentleman" that Kul'chitskii had been (as the Li-fan yuan would soon have occasion to realize). An archimandrite was being acceptably translated as *"ta-lama"*—a proper functional equivalent, inasmuch as both ranks designated monastic superiors, and a term that carried no threat to the status of the Khutughtu. Far from resisting the arrival of an archimandrite, the Manchus expected one; indeed, the Russian lamasery in Peking needed him!

The personnel for the ecclesiastical mission had been selected by a ukase of January 18, 1727.[42] Ioann Filipov Filimonov, the father-superior of the Treskovskaia-Arkhangel'skaia church on Lake Baikal, was named as Platkovskii's chief assistant; the other cleric was hierodeacon Ioasaf Ivanovskii. Because the treaty of Kiakhta called for only four Russian clerics to reside in Peking, and since one—Hieromonk Lavrentii—was already there, only three more, including Platkovskii himself, could be added. The students accompanying the mission were Gerasim Shulgin, Mikhail Afanas'ev Ponomarev, and Ilarion Rossokhin. All three had begun studying at Platkovskii's Mongolian school in Irkutsk after its opening in 1725. Shulgin was an orphan in a Siberian monastery; Ponomarev was of ecclesiastical birth, from the settlement of Ialutorskii-Rogatorsk in Siberia; and Rossokhin was from Selenginsk, also the son of a priest. In due time these three students would join the other three that had long since entered with Lange's caravan: Tret'iakov, Pukhort, and Voeikov.[43]

On July 15, 1728, while Vladislavich began his westward return to St. Petersburg, Platkovskii and his suite left Irkutsk. They arrived in Selenginsk about August 9, where they awaited a Ch'ing official to escort them to Peking. Bukholts solicited the Urga authorities three times before the answer finally came back that a courier had arrived there on December 25 to escort the archimandrite and his group.[44] Vladislavich had, meanwhile, left behind instructions to Lorents Lange (who himself had returned from Peking on October 4, 1728) to provide the mission with a salary for two years in advance, to be taken from the treasury of the town of Selenginsk. No doubt sensing the advantage of Vladislavich's absence, Lange refused to surrender this money. Platkovskii complained loudly and once again his voice did not fail him: the money was handed over, in the amount of 2660 rubles.[45] The mission thereupon left Selenginsk for Kiakhta on February 20, 1729, and crossed the frontier on March 17. Supplied by its Manchu escort with the necessary carts (which must by then have appeared more like tumbrils) for its onward journey, the second ecclesiastical mission finally reached Peking on June 16, 1729, a year after the treaty of Kiakhta had been concluded.

Sino-Russian Relations under Yung-cheng and Peter's Successors

For Vladislavich there was little to cheer about in the Kiakhta treaty: no Russian consuls, no free trade inside China, no access to other cities, no bishop, and no certainty that even the caravan trade to Peking would work out as advantageously as had been hoped. To be sure, great progress had been made in surveying the frontier and then extending it over much of the old Khalkha domains. But what Petrine man of the world (as Vladislavich undoubtedly thought of himself) could take comfort only in such insignificant gains? Boundaries between states were taken for granted; the more important question was how states related to each other across their frontiers, from one metropolitan center to another. The entire Russian effort in China since Izmailov had been to carry the "Europeanization" of its relations to a logical end: first, by removing powerful Siberians like Gagarin, and then by putting into practice a variety of principles roughly equivalent to what Peter had personally learned about the way modern governments expressed their own power as well as their interaction in a wider world. During this time the city of St. Petersburg had appeared on the map of Russia and then new offices in it—the Holy Synod, the Senate, the College of Commerce, the College of Foreign Affairs. All of these organs were products of Peter's reforms, and they carried within their own chanceries an inclination to rationalize the conduct of their business. But in what the Russians took to be proposals for order and organization in Sino-Russian relations, Manchu China saw only chaos. This point has been too well explored by Mancall to require any further treatment here; let it suffice to say that Vladislavich, a man of Russia's European world, had come back to it badly bruised by his negotiations with the Manchus. How ironic that he, who had achieved a stable treaty relationship that was to last well over a century, should have raised the question of a general war against China upon his return to St. Petersburg.[46]

The view from Peter's capital was not, however, quite so troubled. Had not the treaty provided for a regular correspondence between the Senate and the Li-fan yuan? Were not embassies still able to make their passage between Russia and China (a provision of which the Manchus were the first to avail themselves)? Was not the Russian ecclesiastical mission, now with students, firmly established in the center of Peking? China, no one needed to be told, remained a long way away from St. Petersburg. War might be difficult, but other things could be rendered easier by the distance—especially the desire to see in the Kiakhta treaty some provisions that resembled the way Russia carried on its foreign relations elsewhere. To be sure, no one was any longer under the illusion that the Russian and Chinese empires had much to share in their views on international affairs. The "normalization" of Russian approaches to Peking, it had turned out, meant something entirely different to

the Manchus. But in St. Petersburg the inclination was to find in
the Kiakhta settlement an instrument of peace, almost as if a war
had been brought to an end. Vladislavich's plan for renewing the
conflict, drafted by a man who had been too much in the thick of
things, was therefore shelved.

What, meanwhile, did Kiakhta mean in Peking? It would
appear that the treaty was taken not as something that signified
the end of conflict, but as an expedient for permitting the Yung-
cheng emperor to pursue his goal of conquering Ili, a plan with
which this monarch, like his father, was consumed. For an undertaking of such enormity the Kiakhta treaty served only as a new
beginning. It was soon supplemented by Manchu embassies to
Russia; by the founding of a Latin school in Peking (in addition to
the already existing, and failing, Russian school) whose students
could serve as interlocutors between Manchu and Russian diplomats; by an insistent quizzing of Jesuits like Antoine Gaubil on the
nature of Russian relations with Europe, Persia, and Turkey, as
well as Zungharia; and then, in 1731, by the first campaign against
the new Zunghar *kontaisha* (imperial prince), Goldan Tsereng.
Manchu concerns, in other words, remained located in the wider
geopolitical environment of Inner Asia, and in the tasks of conquest that still lay ahead.

This steppe land was far from being a historical desert, and
Manchu policy could not, at least not yet, deal with Russians as if
they were arriving from across the sea. Kul'chitskii, for example,
had expected to find his competition in the Roman Catholic
establishment in Peking, not in the Jebtsundamba Khutughtu of
Urga. And he had to be sacrificed not because China was unable
to accept the idea of a bishop in Peking (the Franciscans could
date their see in the Chinese capital back to the early fourteenth
century), but because there was no room for two prestigious
clerics, with lamaist nomenclature, in, or near, Mongolia. And
Vladislavich, who had wanted to secure competitive Russian trading rights at Canton, found that Russia, according to the Manchu
compass, was locked in the northern quadrant, where all Inner
Asian barbarians belonged.

Ultimately the problem of Sino-Russian relations in the eighteenth century lay in the fact that Russians and Manchus were being tugged in opposite directions by the more mature institutions of Europe and China which they, respectively, were in the process of making their own. The more one searched for common grounds of contact, the fewer there were to be found. Such a painful discovery had been implicit in the consternation of Vladislavich, and was confirmed in the 1750s, when Manchu China, its conquests in Ili completed, at last began to treat Russia like the European powers it was trying its hardest to emulate: that is, with arrogance and contempt. We will return to this history, but it is necessary first to look at the ramifying institution of the Russian ecclesiastical mission itself, upon which the burden of Sino-Russian relations was now to weigh so heavily.

Chapter V

THE INSTITUTIONS OF THE RUSSIAN MISSION

In eighteenth-century Peking there were five institutions, connected and often confused with one another, that functioned as
part of the Russian ecclesiastical mission. Meng Ssu-ming[1] distin-
guishes four establishments which have been variously labeled
"O-lo-ssu kuan" (Russian hostel) in Chinese sources: these were
the Russian hostel proper; the Nikolskii church, or in Chinese, the
O-lo-ssu pei kuan in the north of the city; the O-lo-ssu hsueh (Russian school of Chinese and Manchu studies); and the O-lo-ssu wen
kuan (the Manchu school of Russian studies). For our purposes,
however, one should also differentiate the Russian mission itself
from the larger Russian hostel within which it was situated. In
neither Chinese nor Russian texts is this done very frequently, a
fact which is itself of historical interest. Together the Russian
hostel and mission were often called the O-lo-ssu nan kuan or the
southern hostel, not to be confused with the pei kuan in the
north.

The O-lo-ssu kuan

The institution in Peking most essential to the ambivalent
Manchu-Russian view of the ecclesiastical mission in particular,
and of Sino-Russian relations in general, was the O-lo-ssu kuan,
the Russian hostel. This compound, which enclosed the mission on
its western side, was originally the Hui-t'ung kuan, an important
tribute-caravanserai in Ming and early Ch'ing history. In 1441,
under the reign of the Cheng-t'ung emperor, two Hui-t'ung kuan
had been constructed in Peking.[2] It was the southern one, located
on the north side of Tung-chiang-mi street, and east of the Jade
canal,[3] that became the Russian hostel in the Ch'ing dynasty. It
was refurbished in 1492 to contain three hundred and eighty-
seven rooms, three courts, an idol-house, and at some time shortly
before or after, a banquet room.[4] After 1644 the Ch'ing dynasty

continued to use the Hui-t'ung kuan as a caravanserai for visiting embassies. It was large enough to permit a lively trade after the tributary offerings had been made, and thus of course to make profitable the system of sending tribute to Peking.[5] Although the Hui-t'ung kuan was under the administration of the Board of Rites, tribute missions from all points of origin, including those overseen by the Li-fan yuan, were put up there.[6]

The provisions for receiving these missions, inherited by the Ch'ing at the beginning of the dynasty, are rather carefully documented in the early editions of the *Hui-tien*.[7] One Manchu and one Chinese were deputed by the Reception Department (Chu-k'o-ssu) of the Board of Rites to manage the affairs of the Hui-t'ung kuan. In addition the Hui-t'ung kuan had a local supervisor (*t'i-tu*) who was instructed to report to the Reception Department after tributary envoys had arrived. At that point consultations were also to take place with the Boards of Works, Revenue, and War on the matters of how much straw to provide, how to distribute soldiers for keeping watch, how the mission was to be fed, how many banquets the envoy was permitted, and so forth. In the event that the Hui-t'ung kuan was already being occupied, the Board of Works was supposed to produce other quarters. Stables for horses and camels were to be carefully assigned. Some fifty servants were made available to the tributaries, as well as interpreters (who held the rank of second-class secretaries). After the tributary envoys read their memorials and bestowed their gifts, they could commence trading at the market that was opened inside the Hui-t'ung kuan. They were not allowed to purchase history books, weapons, or other contraband.

It was in this context that the early Russian envoys to China in the later seventeenth century were frequently assigned to the southern Hui-t'ung kuan. Evidently in 1656 Ivan Baikov did not stay there because it was being used by the Dutch.[8] Spafarii, however, as well as later envoys like Ides, Plotnikov, and Izmailov, all stayed at the Hui-t'ung kuan.[9] The same appears to be true of all of the Russian caravans visiting Peking before the treaty of Kiakhta. The process by which the Hui-t'ung kuan became the

O-lo-ssu kuan is not entirely clear, but it had begun by 1693 when the Manchus first expounded the rules for Russian trade in the capital; it is at this time, in any event, that the term "O-lo-ssu kuan" first appears.[10] Lange confirmed this in his journal of 1722, writing that his residence was called the "Urussa Coanne . . . when occupied by the people of that nation."[11] Still, the Hui-t'ung kuan was not yet exclusively the premises of the Russians. Lange mentions that "when there is no Russian caravan, nor any of that nation at Peking, they quarter those of Korea in the habitation appointed for the Russes; but when there are Russes in this city they give the Koreans other quarters; for this reason the Chinese call this house Couly Coanne [Kao-li kuan], or magazine of the Koreans, when it is occupied by the Koreans."[12] Lange's statement is borne out in Chinese sources, which hold that "the first to arrive should stay at the Hui-t'ung kuan; the others shall be assigned to the Korean house."[13] This policy obviously needed elucidation, however, since it was difficult to imagine the Russians staying at the Korean house if some Koreans happened to be in Peking before they arrived. The Ch'ien-lung *Statutes* therefore specify that: "From the second year of Yung-cheng [1724] it has been settled that when Russia comes to the capital they will be assigned the Hui-t'ung kuan. Since that time, therefore, when Russia has come they have necessarily stayed at the Hui-t'ung kuan, following upon the established practice. Since there is now a temple [there] for their religion, the envoys of other countries may no longer stay there."[14] It was the ecclesiastical mission that caused this statutory cession to Russia of the Hui-t'ung kuan, and it is from this disposition of its buildings that Russians in turn acquired the habit of referring to the hostel, at least for their own purposes, as their "embassy" (*posol'skii dvor*) in Peking long before the establishment of formal diplomatic relations in 1861.[15]

From the perspective of Ch'ing China, however, nothing at all had been conceded. Certainly Russia did not own its lodgings in downtown Peking. Turning the Hui-t'ung kuan over to Russia was simply a means of putting order into a system of foreign relations that required order. Visitors from abroad had to be carefully monitored, and their stays in China carefully programmed, if the "tribute system" (however inadequate the term) was to function smoothly. This was particularly true in the imperial capital, where the consequences of any malfunction in the system were much more serious than on the frontiers of China. It made sense to establish a place in Peking where visiting Russians would always be located; the alternative was an ambiguous situation in which troublesome people like Lorents Lange would cause a disturbance by looking for other quarters.

There were, furthermore, larger Manchu concerns beyond the procedural question of where Russians in Peking would reside. In taking power in China the Manchus had created institutions and policies that drew upon the entire Chinese tradition of government, inherited most recently from the Yuan and Ming dynasties. External affairs under the Ch'ing continued to be managed on the principle that the foreign potentate was inferior, that his envoy was a guest, and that his country, being marginal to the center of civilization, was greatly in need of the many gifts which his tribute missions were given in Peking. It was a part of the "tribute system" to have a hostel in the Ch'ing capital for delegations from abroad, where they would be housed and fed at state expense. It was often a part of the system to have a school for handling the requisite language, because the burden of translating into and out of Manchu and Chinese belonged to China. Foreigners in Peking were subordinate and dependent. They were allowed in the capital on the sufferance of the emperor. And when they came they were, like giraffes, curiosities which added to the imperial scope and grandeur of the dynastic house.

If Russians needed to believe that they had managed, through the provisions of the Nerchinsk and Kiakhta treaties, to circumvent the nefarious practices of Chinese diplomacy, the Manchus equally needed to demonstrate that Chinese traditions had not been violated. What was necessary was obviously an institutionalized point of contact that could mean different things to different people. For Manchu China the Hui-t'ung kuan served this purpose as well as it served Russia. Its name and its history bespoke a veneration for proper tributary rites. Any Russian who set foot inside was crossing into a world in which past and present combined to make him an upholder of the very traditions he abhorred. While the establishment of the ecclesiastical mission within the Hui-t'ung kuan may have confirmed an exclusively Russian use of these premises, the presence of Russian priests and students in Peking gave the eighteenth-century emperors of China a continuing means of doling out imperial largesse. The essential point, and one that was made regularly to the members of the ecclesiastical mission, was that they were receiving their livelihood from the Chinese state. When rice was delivered to the courtyard of the Hui-t'ung kuan, or better, when the emperor thought of sending over something from his own table, no one could doubt who it was that was superior and who inferior. This was how the rulers of China took in the Russians.

Of the Hui-t'ung kuan Spafarii reported that "the courtyard is spacious, but the buildings are old and many of them in ruins . . . there are no gardens or wild growth of any kind, and the whole place is most gloomy—like a prison."[16] Occasionally the Li-fan yuan would attempt to make superficial repairs to the hostel before the arrival of a caravan or embassy from Russia. Done in the traditional Chinese wattle-and-plaster style, these did not hold up for long, and throughout the eighteenth century the old Hui-t'ung kuan elicited a variety of opinions from its guests. John Bell, upon arriving there in 1720, described it in good condition, "of a quality to last ages" (as indeed, whether he knew it or not, it already had).[17] Only a year later, on the other hand, Lorents Lange wanted to rent another house for his consulship in Peking after the departure of Izmailov. "The Coanne is in ruins," he wrote, "and might well not survive another rainy season."[18] But Lange remained in the hostel, and his doubts were confirmed (as we have seen) on May 1, 1722, when he suffered through a severe rainstorm: "All the wall of one side of my chamber fell, about midnight, into the courtyard, which made me very apprehensive for what remained."[19] Back again in Peking in 1727, he complained about being brought to "a cold and badly arranged room" in the

Russian hostel.[20] In 1756 Vasilii Bratishchev reported that "in the hostel I did not find one chamber suitable for habitation—the ceilings were falling down, the windows were broken, and everywhere only ravage was visible."[21]

There was one other difficulty, and that had to do with the Buddhist prayer house between the second and third gates of the hostel, fifty yards away from the Russian church. Russian missionaries were never comfortable with its presence inside their domain. Sophronii Gribovskii, archimandrite of the eighth mission (1794–1807) put it this way:

> The idol house is quite undignified of Russians living as people of Christian law in the khui-tun' [Hui-t'ung kuan] and is utterly incompatible with a house of God. For it often happens that on the first and fifteenth of the Chinese month, which is often a holiday for both them and us, when we ring the bells for lunch or dinner they also ring the bells in their idol-house. Therefore, I found it necessary to propose to the head of the foreign tribunal [Li-fan yuan] that he might consider quieting the sounds from the idol-house in the Russian embassy, for the preservation and integrity of Christian honor.[22]

But Gribovskii, like so many before him, was caught in the middle of a situation that was more properly seen from a distance. At least from the Li-fan yuan, around the corner and up the street a short ways, the efforts of two bell ringers to drown each other out, however dissonant the peals, were no doubt pleasantly audible evidence that the Hui-t'ung kuan was continuing to function as an excellent theater for Sino-Russian relations. And the scene at New Year's was even better than this bi-monthly competition, for then crowds of Mongols would descend on their camping grounds in Peking,[23] just beyond the northern wall of the Russian hostel. While Russian missionaries were always instructed to avoid taking part in this heathen celebration,[24] from the Manchu point of view it was as if all the tributary niceties of their Inner Asian affairs were being observed within one square block of the city.

When Egor Petrovich Timkovskii arrived in 1820 to replace

the ecclesiastical mission of Iakinf Bichurin (1807–1820) he
provided this suddenly agreeable picture of the Russian hostel:
"This establishment, called in Chinese the Hoei thoung kouan,
contains everything calculated to render it an agreeable abode.
More than fifty persons may be accommodated very conveniently;
there are fine gardens and orchards. A person fond of study will
find his time pass very pleasantly at Peking. He may always find
objects worthy of attentive investigation, and sufficient opportunities for relaxation and amusements."[25] By Timkovskii's time,
however, it was perhaps not so much the Hui-t'ung kuan that had
changed, but the tastes of the Russians who were coming to
Peking.

The O-lo-ssu pei kuan
    The first institution to emerge from the seventeenth-century
encounter between China and Russia was the Nikolskii church, or
the O-lo-ssu pei kuan. The origin of this chapel may be dated in
1683, and its location was in the northeast corner of the Tartar
city, as already noted. Its Russian name had soon changed to the
church of St. Sophia, and later, to Our Lady of the Assumption
(Uspeniia Bogoroditsa),[26] but neither caught on and for most Russians it remained sentimentally known as the Nikolskii chapel. After
Maksim Leont'ev it had housed the entire first mission of Ilarion
Lezhaiskii in 1716, two decades before the official consecration of
a new church within the Russian hostel six versts (or four miles)
to the south. In the eighteenth century its importance for Russia
waned, yet it continued as a parish church, maintaining its claim
as the religious center for the "Albazinians"—that community of
emotionally and economically depressed Orthodox Christians in
the midst of which it was located. After the treaty of Kiakhta the
pei kuan was visited by the Russian archimandrite scarcely once a
month. Occasionally it had no resident Russian cleric of any
description; but usually a hieromonk and an assistant would be
assigned there to tend its ducks and vineyards, and to conduct
weekly services. For the most part the Russian missionaries preferred the protection afforded by the compound to the south.

Apart from the chapel itself, three other houses were in the possession of the pei kuan. One had been acquired by an Albazinian, Gavril Savin, in 1716; another by Hieromonk Lavrentii, of the first mission, in 1734. The third came out of the bequest of Dmitri Nestorovich, who died in Peking during the fourth mission (1745–1755).[27] The chapel was once, in 1730, demolished by an earthquake that rocked all of the capital. Most of its ornaments and vessels were thereupon moved to the new church in the nan kuan.[28] With money from the Yung-cheng emperor, and without any help from the Russian mission, the Albazinians rebuilt their church.[29] When Archimandrite Ilarion Trusov was in Peking (1736–1741) he reported that the sacred icon of St. Nicholas, taken from Albazin, was still in the pei kuan.[30] Later it also was removed to the nan kuan, perhaps by Amvrosii Yumatov during the fifth mission (1755–1771).[31] Until Yumatov arrived, the pei kuan had been under the administration of the Albazinians. Now, however, Archimandrite Amvrosii took a fresh interest in it, perhaps noticing the anomaly of its miserable existence alongside the better-financed mission church. Forty taels were given to the church elder, Fedor Iakovlev, for repair of the walls.[32] Nine years later, in 1764, a bell tower was added, a fence was constructed, and five cells in which the hieromonk and his staff were supposed to dwell. In 1765 the roof was recovered and a ceiling added. Four grape vines and several trees were planted in front of the church.[33] Later, Archimandrite Nikolai Tsvet (1771–1781) caused a new west wall to be built, and the roof to be painted.[34]

Despite these efforts there were nothing but grim reports of the state of the pei kuan in the late eighteenth century. Ioakim Shishkovskii (1781–1794) found that "the Nikolskii church, inside and out, had completely decayed."[35] In 1796 Anton Vladykin added that it was "run down and squalid and, besides, is nothing like a Russian chapel."[36] When Timkovskii arrived in Peking in 1820 he reported that the pei kuan was in a very poor quarter of Peking and in very bad condition; it was guarded by a Manchu soldier whose house next door to the church was surrounded by a large stagnant pool in the rainy season.[37] Later he wrote that "the church was in such a ruinous state that it seemed ready to fall."[38]

Nevertheless, the chapel carried on until the mid-nineteenth century when, after the signing of the treaty of Peking in 1860, the first Russian diplomatic mission in China installed itself at the Russian hostel. Then Russian missionaries were once again obliged to live in the pei kuan, as they had under Ilarion Lezhaiskii. In the late nineteenth century it was greatly elaborated, with additional buildings, a new cathedral, a library, mills, beehives, and a printing press. As an institution it survived the Boxer Rebellion, the fall of the Ch'ing dynasty, and the end of the Romanovs. Still going strong in the years of the Chinese Republic, its splendid Easter service was something that a foreign resident of Peking would not want to miss. Although it had served as a refugee center for Russian emigres after the October Revolution in 1917, the pei kuan itself had no refuge from the revolutionary events of 1949. Soon afterwards it was leveled and became merely the site upon which a new Soviet embassy was constructed—an enormous concrete edifice that Izmailov, Lange, or Vladislavich would have greatly admired. Perhaps, however, what one once took for progress has become more a process of historical reversion. According to Nagel's guide of the city,[39] a new Orthodox chapel has been built nearby the old grounds, almost three hundred years after Maksim Leontev's arrival. It would be worth the trouble to inquire whether the icon of St. Nicholas is inside.

The "Sretenskii" Monastery (O-lo-ssu nan kuan)

With the exception of Hieromonk Lavrentii, the entire Russian mission moved to the nan kuan after the treaty of Kiakhta. Here within the walls of the Russian hostel the ecclesiastical mission was housed for more than a century. Even before the final exchange of the Kiakhta Treaty China had begun the construction of the church, depositing a pile of bricks and wood inside the Russian hostel on the morning of December 28, 1727.[40] By the time Archimandrite Antonii Platkovskii reached Peking with the second ecclesiastical mission in 1729, the outside of the church had been completed. There were not, however, any habitable monastic quarters, so that

Platkovskii took up his residence in a vacant hall-way, while the students lived in the commissary.[41] All helped with the interior decorations of the church, but the necessary icons and antimins (altar cloth) could only be obtained in Russia. These were delivered with Platkovskii's successor, Trusov, and the church was finally consecrated in the name of the Meeting of the Lord (*sretenie gospodina*) on December 20, 1736, in the presence of Trusov, the Russian agent Lorents Lange, and the assembled Russian missionaries with the sole exception of Platkovskii who, although still in Peking, had been incarcerated for misbehavior.[42] Acting upon Lange's suggestion, the Synod also gave Trusov money with which to buy or build three apartments adjoining the mission.[43] Soon these were constructed.

By the time of Trusov, then, the basic requirements for a functional church and monastery in Peking had been met. The mission was lacking only in a well-defined sense of why it was in a place like Peking, or, once there, what its mission really amounted to. Throughout the eighteenth century an air of impermanence hung over the buildings of the nan kuan, which the missionaries left unattended except when it was necessary to patch up walls and plug up leaks. When Gervasii Lintsevskii arrived in Peking (1745) the monastic cells were found to be without stoves or roofs; no special chamber for the archimandrite existed; there was not enough water for watering the vineyard. The church had been "indecorously pasted over with paper, the iconastasis was completely decayed, the mitre was in poor condition, the vessels and dishes were broken, as was the archimandrite's crozier; the church was decrepit and dark, and the little court in front was all cracked. There was no bell tower, only posts with bells on them."[44] Amvrosii Yumatov also complained about the degeneration of the church: "In the Sretenskii church the wall at the southern side of the altar has collapsed from top to bottom, and a corner of the altar itself has not inconsiderably caved in. The roof as well as the other side of the church, and the bins around it, are all fallen into decay."[45] Yumatov did cause several repairs to be made. He also built himself a separate chamber, befitting the father-superior of a Russian monastery. A bell tower was constructed with six new bells cast in Peking, a German clock, and "two large copper pans." Ceilings, floors, and stoves were installed in the monks' quarters. Five new cells were built. A deep well was dug near the bell tower in 1757. In 1760 two kitchens were added, along with a large oven for baking bread, and finally, a bath, dressing room, stable, and a large barn. Fences were erected here and there, bricks and stones were laid for paths, and the garden was planted with thirty-seven grapevines trellised on seventeen frames.[46]

By the late 1760s the mission thus appears suddenly at a high stage of development. It abutted on the Russian hostel, which was about twice as large, on its north and east sides. The church stood roughly in the center, with the archimandrite's quarters to the southeast, facing the hostel to the east. To the west lay the garden and vineyards. South of this were the barn, bath, kitchen, and a cellar. Along the northern wall were situated the monastic quarters, nine cells in all, facing south in the Chinese manner. A gate to the Russian hostel was located in the east wall; otherwise there was no egress. The students lived in the adjacent hostel, in a special building along its north wall. With the passage of another ten years, however, this idyllic picture had greatly faded. The churchman Stepan Zimin, sole survivor of the fifth mission, reported that "on top of the church was a wooden cupola so decayed that the nails were already unable to hold it up. It had fallen to one side so that in times of heavy rain there was a big leak."[47] About the same time it was further reported that the wall around the church had collapsed in two places. Another leak on top of the church had been puttied over. The students' chambers, according to Nikolai Tsvet, archimandrite of the sixth mission, were in ruins and the Li-fan yuan refused to fix them.[48] During the following mission Ioakim Shishkovskii observed that "in the Sretenskii church, because of the decrepitude of the roof, the paper ceiling was sagging from the leaks and in several places had even caved in ... The north wall of the mission had fallen away here and there and the monastic cells, because of the disrepair of their roofs, were in a dangerous condition."[49] Lacking incentive to make necessary repairs, many missionaries in the late eighteenth century soon lost the incentive to continue living in uninhabitable surroundings.

Apart from its two churches, the Russian mission had title to a variety of other holdings in or near Peking. Most important was its cemetery, lying slightly to the northeast of the Tartar City, a short distance beyond the An-ting gate. This piece of land had come into the estate of the mission from a bequest of Luka Voeikov in 1734, who, shortly before he died in Peking, had purchased the tract with the intention of building a dacha on it.[50] The cemetery quickly became too crowded. Ten years later the grave of Ilarion Trusov extended beyond the boundary.[51] After another decade Amvrosii Yumatov wrote that there was no place to bury his missionaries.[52] A nearby piece of land was probably purchased during the fifth mission, for most of the Russian missionaries, including Yumatov himself, continued to die and be buried in Peking. Although a fence was built around the graveyard in 1774,[53] some of the land was lost during the mission of Shishkovskii. In 1820 Timkovskii, after visiting the cemetery, wrote that "we cannot but regret that, under the archimandrite Schisch Rofski [sic]... a large piece of ground was ceded by a member of the mission to a Chinese, by which it was much diminished."[54]

The mission owned five additional pieces of arable land, from which it realized a small rental income.[55] By the latter eighteenth century it also owned a dozen houses in Peking, most of which were rented to Chinese. But this was a precarious business. Zimin explained in 1773: "It often happens that a tenant, not paying his rent for three or five months, will depart in the middle of the night with his family and belongings, leaving the house ravaged. According to their barbarous habits they tear down the shelves, pull up the floor and stove, pull out the windows, and occasionally escape with the torn off articles."[56] Shishkovskii reported to the Synod that "the twelve houses belonging to the monastery which were leased to Chinese, having gone without repair all these years, were falling into decay."[57] The archimandrite had no money for making repairs, but he did ask the Synod to annul the bad debts of some of the tenants. Soon after Shishkovskii, in the early nineteenth century, the mission mortgaged most of its real estate holdings, not because they were such a headache, but because it was now plunged into debt itself. The reason, it appears, was Napoleon's invasion of Russia in 1812. For eight years thereafter no one in Moscow or St. Petersburg seemed to remember that there were Russian missionaries in Peking, let alone that they required an annual salary from the motherland.

Because Russian missionaries and students in China remained Russians and, unlike most other foreigners in the eighteenth century, were allowed to leave the country at the end of their service there, an early task of the Li-fan yuan was to establish a number of permanent offices and administrative practices that would outlast these irregular comings and goings. A superintendant (*chien-tu*) of the mission was therefore appointed,[58] and with him two porters (*kuan-fu*) to guard the gates of the hostel.[59] John Dudgeon, writing in the late nineteenth century, verifies this reasonable arrangement (without explaining why he found it necessary to use an exclamation point): "Up to 1860 the Nankwan . . . was honoured with a white buttoned official sent by the Board of Foreign Colonies (Li-fan-yuen). He had a special house assigned to him, although he did not dwell here. He kept a porter, but came frequently himself to the Nankwan. A little Yamen was even erected in the neighbourhood for the benefit and oversight of the Mission!"[60] In addition, a censor (*yü-shih*) was delegated to review the activities of the mission and, one assumes, to ascertain whether its members were engaged in any sort of espionage.[61] At least once in the mission's history the superintendant also held the office of censor.[62]

Although the Ch'ing government had, since the early 1720s, stopped paying the traveling expenses of the Russian caravans that came to Peking,[63] after the Kiakhta Treaty it continued to insist on subsidizing the Russian ecclesiastical mission. The costs were not great: the equivalent of one thousand rubles, and nine thousand catties of rice, every year.[64] The point of these modest arrangements was, however, of great importance, for only by paying for the Russian mission could the government establish the fact, at least as it appeared in Peking, that proper tributary etiquette was being practiced in its relations with Russia. Every three years, furthermore, the mission was given the equivalent of six hundred rubles for clothes.[65] This sum enabled the missionaries to dress in Chinese fashion, something it is quite possible they would have found the means to do anyway, since they were always sensitive to the antiforeign sneers of the people.[66] Until the protest of Lorents Lange prevailed in 1737,[67] the missionaries were also given rank in the ladder of Ch'ing officialdom, as Maksim Leont'ev and Ilarion Lezhaiskii had been. The well of the Li-fan yuan, reputedly containing the best water in the neighborhood, was also used by the Russian mission, although later it acquired one of its own.[68]

In short the lifelines of the mission, with or without a well, ran directly to the Li-fan yuan. No missionary was ever given an opportunity to overlook the utter dependency of his fragile institution on the munificence of the Manchu bureaucracy. The Russian government did try to observe the sovereign nicety of paying for its missionaries in Peking as well as for the students, but often during the eighteenth century the salaries sent to China were not accepted at the border. This happened in 1731, for example, when Vladislavich's deputy, Ivan Bukholts, tried to persuade the Mongol authorities to transmit to the mission in Peking the rubles he had put aside in Selenginsk. The reply was simply that "the Russian priests and students in Peking are quite content with their allowances and consequently it is impossible to accept the money and send it to Peking."[69] In a sense this was true. The circumstances of its existence in mid-eighteenth century Peking gave the Russian mission little chance to spend its subsidy from abroad, whenever the money did manage to arrive. Permission to leave the Russian hostel was not easily obtained. The superintendent often saw his job as merely to keep the missionaries and students in their compound. He memorialized in 1737 that "the [Russian] students who study in the capital should not be allowed to go freely anywhere that will enable them to learn the secrets of the Interior. Maps and atlases of the Interior and other contraband should not be sold to them."[70] Letters leaving the mission for Russia were collected by the Li-fan yuan, regularly opened, and possibly even comprehended.[71] During the mission of Archimandrite Gervasii Lintsevskii (1745–1755) it was reported that the missionaries were allowed to leave the hostel only in summertime, and then usually for the funerals of their fallen comrades.[72]

The method of managing the mission with which the Ch'ien-lung emperor experimented briefly in 1759—when the members of Amvrosii Yumatov's fifth mission were all locked inside the Russian hostel—was the farthest any emperor seemed prepared to go. Russia protested his action, eliciting this angry reply from the Li-fan yuan:

> We have shown your note to his most august majesty, who has instructed as follows: "How extravagantly those Russians write! For as much as a year their lamas have been living here as before—on an adequate subsistence, with every charity, and without the least oppression—and they are so stirred up over them! They might well consider that if we did not desire to maintain their lamas here we would long ago have driven them out. And what use is it to us to wear down such people? ... Let them [the Russians] come straight to Peking with their own people and inform themselves as to the condition of the lamas: are they being oppressed or not? Convey this to them clearly." In consequence of this edict we inform you of the following: whether to observe a peaceful accord or to destroy one point or another of our treaty, that is your business. Only from now on do not fictionalize with such foul and dissolute perorations.[73]

Neither now, nor ever, was the Russian mission expelled from China, and during its eighteenth-century history the Manchus did not provide it with even one martyr. The many premature deaths among the missionaries and students stemmed from much more prosaic causes.

By the late eighteenth century the situation had much improved. Resourceful members of the mission wandered more freely about

Peking and even visited the warm waters in its outskirts,[74] as
Ilarion Lezhaiskii had once done in 1718. It also became easier to
acquire Chinese books, maps, and gazetteers to add to the holdings
in the St. Petersburg Academy of Sciences, earlier assembled
mainly as presents from Jesuits in Peking. What made the debt-
ridden mission of Iakinf Bichurin (1807–1820) different from that
of Platkovskii in 1731, when the Russian subsidy had also failed
to materialize, was not only that its nineteenth-century tastes were
more expensive, but also that it now had access to restaurants,
night spots, tourism, and bookstores. When Bichurin at last left
Peking in 1821, fifteen camels were required to transport all the
books he had collected there.[75] Unfortunately, there was still no
one in Russia who was prepared to take the view that this was a
fair return for the shambles in which he had left his mission, and
he was promptly arrested.

The O-lo-ssu wen kuan

The linguistic problems that accompanied the early contact
between Russia and China in the seventeenth century were themselves so much a part of the history of the time, and indeed had
such an impact on the course that events had taken, that they soon
led to the establishment of two exceptional eighteenth-century
institutions for language study, the O-lo-ssu wen kuan and the
O-lo-ssu hsueh. Both schools were located in Peking. In the former,
Manchu students would try to learn Russian, and in the latter,
Russians would study Chinese and Manchu.

We have already seen, in the first chapter of this volume, how
pitifully deficient seventeenth-century Russia was in its capacity
either to handle the languages of China or to do anything about
learning them. Russians were forced to depend completely, and
precariously, on Jesuits in Peking, Mongols on the frontier, or
those treacherous Albazinians who were the least trustworthy of
all. Milovanov, Spafarii, and Ides had all been badly in need of
better interpreters during their visits to China. For example, when
Spafarii went to Peking in 1676 he took with him four letters that
had been sent from China to the tsar in the course of the seven-

teenth century, one of them dating from 1619. None of these letters, which represented the entire correspondence from Peking to Moscow up to that time, had the Russian government been able to translate. It was Spafarii's responsibility, among other things, to have them translated in Peking.[76] The first two points of his instructions also dealt with the language problem: he was to ask that all letters written by the Manchus to Russia be translated before being sent, and that a definite language for further communications be agreed on.[77] Throughout his embassy to China, furthermore, Spafarii suffered from both incompetent interpreters as well as a fear of being betrayed by the Russian "traitors" in Peking, to whom he was occasionally obliged to turn.[78] No improvement had taken place by the time of Golovin's mission to the frontier in 1688. Golovin complained about the Mongol interpreters and was suspicious of the Jesuits.[79] Several embassies and caravans later, the situation was still unchanged.[80] A letter to Russia from the Li-fan yuan, received in St. Petersburg on March 3, 1725, had to be sent back to Selenginsk for translation; it was another year before a translated copy was finally received.[81] And when Lange's secretary, David Grave, was in Peking in 1726 to announce the coming of Vladislavich, he requested the Manchus to send all letters to Russia in Latin, as at that time there were no translators, not even on the frontier.[82]

At the turn of the seventeenth century Russia had begun to interest itself, although in a most tentative fashion, in investigating the languages of East Asia. In 1697 the first shipwrecked Japanese to be taken off the Kuriles was sent to Moscow, persuaded to convert himself to Orthodoxy, given a Russian name in the process, and then assigned to teach his language to Russian students.[83] Somewhat later, in 1707, two students attempted (evidently without success) to learn Mongolian when they went with Ilarion Lezhaiskii on a mission into Outer Mongolia,[84] nine years before he arrived in Peking. China, however, was still closed to this kind of enterprise, and there was as yet no means of initiating the study of Chinese and Manchu within Russia, for there were no teachers to be found.[85] Out of this predicament came, ultimately, the idea of attaching a language school, or what became the O-lo-ssu hsueh, to the Russian ecclesiastical mission.

Manchu China, meanwhile, had exhibited a much more energetic approach to the problem of managing Russian, or at least of having available people who could read and speak it. Of course this was in part because previous Chinese dynasties, the early Ming in particular, had demonstrated a patronizing interest in learning the languages of their loyal tributaries.[86] But Manchu strategies in Inner Asia also demanded a knowledge of Russian, and much was therefore made, as we have seen, of the opportunity of seizing stray Cossacks on the frontier. But since almost all of them were uneducated, it was obviously going to be hard for the Ch'ing to maintain any ability at all in Russian, which appears to have depended entirely on one or two men.[87] When Veniukov and Favorov were in Peking before the Nerchinsk negotiations began they were told that henceforth Russian notes to China should be written in Mongolian and Latin.[88] And at Nerchinsk in 1689 both sides were dependent on the Jesuits. Although the papers of Isbrandt Ides, composed only in Russian, were translated by the Manchus in 1693,[89] by the beginning of the eighteenth century it is probable that the Ch'ing dynasty had lost much of its modest capacity for dealing with the written language. Illiterate interpreters still existed among the Albazinians (the members of the Izmailov embassy, for example, were given a guided tour of Peking by some of them)[90] but all the precise, official negotiating was done through the Jesuits. Bell states that Tulishen knew Russian, but apparently could not read or write it.[91]

In order to achieve a self-sufficient literacy, the Manchus therefore established a Russian language school, the O-lo-ssu wen kuan, for their own bannermen. Historically the O-lo-ssu wen kuan is an elusive institution, but its existence cannot be doubted. The *Jih-hsia chiu-wen k'ao* gives its location as the west side of the Pei-ch'ih-tzu street, across from the Tung-hua men, the eastern gate of the Forbidden City,[92] and the *Ch'ien-lung hui-tien tse-li* mentions how much it cost to support the school.[93] The practical tasks of operation were undertaken by two proctors (*t'i-t'iao*); teaching was done by two professors (*chu-chiao*) and several assistant professors (*fu-chiao-hsi*). Students for the school were chosen from among the eight banners; no more than twenty-four were to be enrolled at a given time. Examinations were given periodically, the most important of which occurred every fifth year. Successful students were admitted into Ch'ing officialdom at a level that was determined by their examination grades.[94] The connection between the O-lo-ssu wen kuan and the Russian ecclesiastical mission was close, especially as the school lost touch with that spirit of self-reliance that had prompted its founding. In the mid-eighteenth century the Russian students Ilarion Rossokhin and Aleksei Vladykin were members of its faculty. Timkovskii states that the Manchu professor at the school in 1821, embarrassingly deficient in Russian, frequently sought the help of the ecclesiastical mission in meeting the demands of his job.[95]

What is missing from the surviving descriptions of the O-lo-ssu wen kuan is any feeling for its institutional life.[96] For that matter, one searches in vain for any text, Russian or Chinese, that gives a credible date of origin. Timkovskii, without any evidence, suggests that the school began shortly after the treaty of Nerchinsk, which is possible.[97] Meng agrees with him, but on the basis of circumstantial evidence that must now be dismissed.[98] Korsak also concurs in an early origin. He writes that "in Peking the Chinese government employed the Albazinians for teaching the Russian language to the Manchus in a special school where the children of the best families studied, but soon after a violent uproar they [the Albazinians] were converted to soldiers."[99] No authority is cited. P. E. Skachkov gives 1725, or the third year of Yung-cheng, for the beginning of the school.[100] Adoratskii supplies two different dates in two different parts of his work, one during the time of the third ecclesiastical mission (1736–1745) and one in 1758.[101] On the basis of a cloudy record, the last word must be left for Ho Ch'ui-t'ao. He does not attempt an estimate, but simply notes that "it is not known when the school originated."[102] Let us, however, at least attempt to narrow down the possibilities.

Although neither the K'ang-hsi nor Yung-cheng editions of

the *Collected Statutes* (the *Hui-tien*) mentions the school, the *Ch'ien-lung shih-lu* does state definitely that it was established during the reign of K'ang-hsi. The notice reads as follows: "A Russian school was established in the K'ang-hsi reign. K'u-hsi-ma and Ya-kao of the Russian company were appointed professors, and twenty-four students were enrolled from the Eight Banners. Later, no one in the Russian company was able to become a professor, and the graduated students were entrusted with the management of the school."[103] Lo-shu Fu, who has translated this passage,[104] notes that the Russians K'u-hsi-ma and Ya-kao were "two of the forty-five Russians who had surrendered to China in the first Albazin campaign." Meng Ssu-ming does not attempt an identification beyond approximating their names in Russian: "Kuzma? [or] Kosima? [and] Yakov."[105] Who then were these first professors at the O-lo-ssu wen kuan? It is only in Veselovskii that two such names appear together again: then it is with respect to the indiscretions of Hieromonk Lavrentii of the first ecclesiastical mission, who had allegedly appropriated mission funds for his own use after the death of Ilarion Lezhaiskii. At that time, according to the Veselovskii account, "Kozma and Iakov Savin began to make approaches to him [Lavrentii], to the effect that he give the silver back to the church; but he disagreed with them, and so they went to the Mongolian Department [Li-fan yuan] to report."[106]

At one point in Veselovskii, Kozma and Iakov Savin are mentioned together: Feodosii Smorzhenskii, in compiling a list of the few baptized Albazinians remaining in Peking when he was there with the mission of Gervasii Lintsevskii (1745–1755), includes the two sons of Savin, Fedor and Dmitri, together with "the grandson of Kozmin, who used to be in the Russian company."[107] If "Kozma" and "Kozmin" are interchangeable, as the Veselovskii account seems to suggest, then it may well be that K'u-hsi-ma was Stenka Kozmin, a Russian captured in the Spring of 1685, and a man whose relative youth and literacy is attested to by the fact that he wrote a letter to his father and mother in the summer of that year.[108] It would therefore have been possible for Kozmin to survive the remainder of the K'ang-hsi reign and to have attained a

certain stature by the time that the new Russian school needed a
professor or that Hieromonk Lavrentii needed questioning about
the Nikolskii church's silver. By this reckoning, K'u-hsi-ma would
not have been among the first group of refugees from Albazin, as
Lo-shu Fu states; he would already have been in China several
months by the time they arrived.

Neither would Iakov Savin—if we may now reasonably
hypothesize that he is the Ya-kao referred to in the *Shih-lu*—have
been among those refugees, for Lorents Lange explicitly mentions
that he was born in Peking of Russian parents.[109] Smorzhenskii
indirectly gives support to Lange by revealing that he dealt with
Savin's sons and with Kozmin's grandson. As a second-generation
Albazinian Iakov Savin must have moved rapidly into a position of
influence. Not only was he fluent in Chinese, but literate in Russian,[110] a fact which was soon brought to the attention of the
O-lo-ssu wen kuan. He was, furthermore, able to deal in a broker's
mathematics with Lange in 1727–1728.[111] By that time, if one may
judge from the amount of money he earned simply in finding
customers for the Russian caravan, he had indeed achieved social
distinction within the Russian community and a variety of connections that might have come from professorial status in a banner
school. Two members of the first ecclesiastical mission are also
mentioned in Russian materials as being teachers (presumably
assistant professors) in the O-lo-ssu wen kuan. These were Hieromonk Lavrentii and Osip D'iakonov, both of whom had remained
behind in Peking after Lezhaiskii's death. Of Lavrentii, Smorzhenskii simply recounts that he was given the rank of an eighth-grade
official for teaching in the Russian school.[112] As for D'iakonov,
P. E. Skachkov states that he was on the faculty of the school.[113]
According to Bantysh-Kamenskii he was also employed by the
Li-fan yuan to translate letters arriving from, and being sent to,
Russia.[114]

All these details help narrow somewhat the possibilities of
when the O-lo-ssu wen kuan was first established. Kozmin and
Savin might well have been teaching at any point from about 1715
to the treaty of Kiakhta; after that Kozmin would have been quite

old, while before 1715 Savin would have been too young. Lavrentii and D'iakonov would have been available any time after 1718 or 1719. The K'ang-hsi reign ended in 1722. Is there any reason to accept the statement in the *Veritable Records* of the Ch'ien-lung reign (the *Ch'ien-lung shih-lu*) that the school was set up in the K'ang-hsi period? If so, it would probably limit the date of origin to the six-year period from 1715–1722. Only one external shred of evidence can be cited for support; it is a curious episode reported by Lange during his residency in Peking after the departure of Izmailov.[115] In the spring of 1722 Lange received a letter from Selenginsk. The president of the Li-fan yuan, showing a great deal of interest in it, told Lange that he could not open the envelope unless he made known its contents. At his side the official had ready two "translators" to copy it. Lange complied, opened the letter, and the translators sat down beside him and evidently proceeded to make their copy. All this episode is capable of suggesting is that there were in Peking in the spring of 1722 some Chinese or Manchus who were able to copy a letter written in Russian. Nothing was said about making a translation; it is quite possible that the translators were barely able to copy the letters of the Cyrillic alphabet. But surely Lange would have informed us if they had been Albazinians, or Russian missionaries. If, as it appears, they were Manchus, then it would constitute an important indirect piece of evidence that some instruction in Russian had begun, or that the O-lo-ssu wen kuan had indeed been established in the K'ang-hsi period, probably not long before the emperor's death.

One reason that the O-lo-ssu wen kuan defies an attempt to pin down the date of its beginning is that it never flourished and therefore never excited a look into its past until it was too late to find anything there. It could not have been much of a success—even in its early days—because soon, in March, 1729, the Ch'ing dynasty established a school of Latin for Manchu youths, the aim of which was to train interpreters for Sino-Russian relations.[116] The rector of the school was Dominique Parrenin, the superior of the Jesuit mission in Peking. Its second regent was Antoine Gaubil, who succeeded to the rectorate after Parrenin's death in 1741. In

1732 Gaubil wrote that "la classe latine va bien; plusiers écoliers parlent assez bien Latin."[117] Two years later the Russian courier Semen Petrov acknowledged that Parrenin was teaching Latin to twenty-four "Chinese."[118] It is impossible to attest any immediate connection between the Latin school and the O-lo-ssu wen kuan, although they were quite alike. The *Yung-cheng shih-lu* for 1729 does not mention either school. Although the Latin school lasted fifteen years, until 1744, none of its graduates appear to have been employed in the business for which they were being trained. During the Yung-cheng period, Parennin himself did most of the translating work for the Li-fan yuan's incoming correspondence from the Russian Senate. By Ch'ien-lung times he had simply been replaced by Gaubil.[119] These Jesuits were, of course, translating from Latin copies of the Russian originals. When the supply of reliable Latinists began to dwindle in the latter eighteenth century, Russian students would be summoned to the Li-fan yuan instead, to make translations from the Russian. Meanwhile, the Li-fan yuan continued to take responsibility for translating its own letters to the Senate before they left Peking, a practice that would again bring its officials around to the doors of the ecclesiastical mission looking for someone to translate back into Russian.

And what of the O-lo-ssu wen kuan? If the school was not a total failure in the eighteenth century, it could not have provided the Nei-ko and the Li-fan yuan with more than a few translators capable of reading and writing Russian.[120] An edict to the Grand Council from 1791 offers evidence of the existence of one such person, a Chinese bannerman:

> The newly appointed Department Magistrate of Chihli-chou, Yuan Ch'eng-ning, is familiar with the Russian language. In all Russian affairs he has carefully and properly translated all documents. We should keep Yuan Ch'eng-ning in Peking so that whenever we are confronted with this kind of affair he can be our expert. We order that Yuan Ch'eng-ning be removed from his present position as a magistrate and stay in Peking as a candidate for the office of second-class secre-

tary of the Board [the Li-fan yuan]. However, we remember that he has had difficulty supporting his family; he may have the same difficulty while fulfilling this office. We bestow upon him a special favor; he is ordered to be sent to the Board of Civil Appointments. Whenever there is a vacancy in the position of second secretary in the various treasuries or of superintendent of the mint, the Board should present Yuan Ch'eng-ning as a candidate to fill that post. Yuan Ch'eng-ning should hereafter know how to be grateful and do his duty more prudently. He should carefully train the students who are studying the Russian language.[121]

By the nineteenth century, however, the school was virtually defunct. The invested Mongol *wang* (prince) of Urga, Yung-tung-to-erh-chi, had asked for translators from the O-lo-ssu wen kuan at the time of the Golovkin embassy to China in 1805. But, according to Timkovskii, "the Mantchoo interpreters candidly confessed that they did not understand a word of what the Russians said. The following morning the Vang sent them back to Peking."[122] Yung-tung-to-erh-chi suggested that the school be moved to Urga, but nothing apparently was done. Instead Russians were increasingly counted on in Peking to make the necessary translations for the Li-fan yuan, while on the frontier the more resourceful Chinese merchants had invented a pidgin-Russian that was proving quite adequate to their needs; Timkovskii further tells of one merchant from Shansi who was able to speak an uncorrupted Russian.[123] In Peking the official papers of the new mission (which Timkovskii was conducting) were brought privately to a Russian student in the old mission to be translated into Manchu. "The masters of the Russian school at Peking [he writes], not being sufficiently versed in the Russian language, were obliged to have recourse to our assistance." Later a man named Shou Ming, "professor of the Russian language to the school at Peking," came to the mission to request a translation into Russian of the return letter from the Li-fan yuan to the Senate acknowledging the change of mission. The document had already been rendered into Latin by Father Gau, a

Portuguese. Shou Ming also asked Archimandrite Petr Kamenskii, who had earlier been a student in Peking, to translate into Russian some Chinese dialogues "for the use of his scholars in the Mantchoo school"; and he admitted, quite understandably, that he could not have retained his position without the help of the Russians.[124]

In this useless condition the O-lo-ssu wen kuan maintained its place in Ch'ing bureaucracy. If nothing else, it continued to provide an annual stipend for the Manchu banner families who registered their children there and for the professors of its vestigial faculty. John Dudgeon visited the location of the school in the late nineteenth century and wrote that: "The houses are of the most humble and limited description. Over the outside door is a tablet with the characters *nei-ko o-lo-sz-wen-kwan,* the only thing by which it can now be recognized."[125]

The O-lo-ssu hsueh

Having followed the dismal history of the O-lo-ssu wen kuan, let us return to its counterpart, the Manchu and Chinese language school for Russian students in Peking, or the O-lo-ssu hsueh. Vladislavich's proposition for such a school had been accepted, without any visible reluctance, by the Manchus, to whom it must have been clear already in 1727 that learning Russian in the O-lo-ssu wen kuan was no easy matter. The school was located inside the Russian hostel. Its association with the ecclesiastical mission was, of course, very close; both institutions had their formal charter in the fifth article of the Kiakhta treaty. Thereafter students and missionaries lived, ate, and fought together, came to China and, if they survived, left together.

The Russian students, upon their arrival in Peking, were admitted into the Academy of Learning (Kuo-tzu-chien), although classes were held in the Russian hostel.[126] They were assigned teachers of Manchu and Chinese as well as a monthly stipend.[127] They were expected to wear Chinese clothes and observe Chinese customs.[128] The Ch'ing, quite properly, imagined these students to have come to China for a kind of "vocational training."[129] But it should be pointed out that their school, the O-lo-ssu hsueh, was

always listed in the statutes of the Ch'ing dynasty along with the
special school in Peking for students from Liu-ch'iu, who were in
fact studying there in faithful acknowledgment that China was the
source and remained the center of Confucian civilization.[130] The
Ch'ing gazetteer, after mentioning the Liu-ch'iu school, exclaims
that "even Russia sends youths to study in the Kuo-tzu-chien."[131]
As far as the catalogue of the university was concerned, foreign
students who came to Peking to pursue their education—whether
from Russia or Liu-ch'iu—were obviously being very submissive,
for they are listed in the section on "external vassals who come to
study."[132] No Confucian ideologue, however, had to concern himself with the behavior of the Russian students in more than a
theoretical sense. The thankless task of looking after them, which
encouraged anything but a picture of submissiveness, belonged to
the Manchu superintendant of the hostel.

In the mid-eighteenth century the O-lo-ssu wen kuan and the
O-lo-ssu hsueh were roughly comparable institutions, neither one
doing much to justify the reasons for its existence. A laconic
Soviet contention that it was during this time that the "indispensable
base"[133] of Russian sinology was laid is about the most anyone can
say. There is a point, however, in looking at the relative strength of
these schools over the broader sweep of the Ch'ing dynasty, for in
the attention, or lack of it, that was paid by Russia and China to
the problems of language learning from one historical period to the
next, one has a symbol of the enormous differences that separate
the nineteenth century from the seventeenth. In the early Ch'ing
period the momentum had been all with the Manchus: they had
been the ones to send translated letters to Russia, to found a Russian school in Peking, and to form a cadre of "Russian experts"
capable of managing the delicate, complex, and hugely important
tasks of Sino-Russian relations. In them there was no hysteria over
the "unfathomability of the barbarian mind," quite the contrary.
It was Russia, slow to face up to the possibilities as well as the
problems of its relations with China, that had put itself in the position of being manipulated by a country whose languages and

customs it did not understand and of which it therefore formed
the impression of perverse inscrutability. But by the latter part of
the eighteenth century things had begun to change. Manchu China,
exhausted by its own successes in Inner Asia, no longer had the
interest or the energy to keep alive its capacity for teaching Russian to its banner youths. By the mid-nineteenth century the
government in Peking was dependent on the ecclesiastical mission
for its view not only of Russia but of that larger Western world by
which it was now being engulfed.[134] The O-lo-ssu wen kuan, hope-
lessly defunct, could provide nothing but a feeble precedent for
new foreign language schools after the prostrating treaties of
Peking had been signed in 1860.

The history of the O-lo-ssu hsueh ran in the other direction.
Its few successes in the eighteenth century had gone largely
unnoticed in Moscow and St. Petersburg. Not until the return of
Iakinf Bichurin from Peking in 1821 did it even occur to the
Academy of Sciences that Russia might have, among its own
closeted sinologues, people who knew China better than the French
school. Bichurin's tempestuous career, and in particular his
impertinent letters to Julien Klaproth in Paris, had the monumental
effect of causing a new generation of Russians to see opportunity,
not exile, in Peking. By the 1850s, the O-lo-ssu hsueh had at last a
coherent sense of its own mission, at once tackling textual antiqui-
ties and thereby preparing to translate into Manchu and Chinese
the onslaught of Russian imperialism in Asia. In its readiness to
respond to the needs of the time the school had become, in other
words, exactly what the O-lo-ssu wen kuan once was in the early
eighteenth century.

Chapter VI

THE MISSIONARY LIFE IN EIGHTEENTH-CENTURY PEKING

What was going on inside this hodge-podge of buildings that echoed such different histories and yet clung together as parts of the Russian ecclesiastical mission in Peking? The question begs to be answered, although answering it will perhaps accomplish little except to satisfy a gruesome sense of curiosity. The second ecclesiastical mission, that which was led by Antonii Platkovskii into Peking in 1729, is a good place to begin.

Platkovskii's Mission in Peking

Having at last overcome the difficulties in reaching its destination, Platkovskii's mission appeared on paper to be a strong contingent. The archimandrite himself was an old hand in Siberian Russia and had been to Peking once already. One of his priests, Ivan Filimonov, had had experience on the Sino-Russian border ever since 1721 and the abortive mission of Innokentii Kul'chitskii. Hieromonk Lavrentii, a holdover from the first ecclesiastical mission of Lezhaiskii, had been living in China continuously since 1716, a record that few other missionaries in China at that time, Roman or Orthodox, could equal. Little is known about the background of Ioasaf Ivanovskii, hierodeacon of the mission, but it is likely that he also had been in the Kul'chitskii suite earlier. As for the students, the fact that two of them came from the Moscow Academy testifies to a national investment in this mission's opportunities. And three others had already been subjected to one Oriental language in Platkovskii's Mongolian school in Irkutsk. But as subsequent events will show, this group, as competent as it seemed, was unable to meet the test of a decade in Peking. Its fate, like that of all the other missions in the eighteenth century, suggests that Russia was not ready to exercise usefully the advantages it had struggled so long and persistently to win in the Kiakhta treaty.

At the beginning prospects were far from bleak. When Lorents

115

Lange returned to St. Petersburg in 1730 he reported that the mission was settled in the Russian hostel.[1] Soon afterward Platkovskii wrote to the Synod that he counted more than fifty baptized souls among the Chinese and Manchus, women not included.[2] Although this number was considerably reduced in a report of the following year, Platkovskii mentioned that he had just baptized nine Chinese, that another eight were about to be converted, and that he anticipated an average conversion rate of two natives a month.[3] Among the Albazinians, furthermore, a certain spiritual ardor was evident, although their numbers appeared to be dwindling. When the Nikolskii church was entirely razed by the great earthquake of 1730, it was resurrected by its parishioners instead of being left to die a natural death. To this effort the Yung-cheng emperor, like his father, lent a hand by contributing money for its restoration.[4]

Platkovskii was a well-organized man, and took an interest in trying to equip the mission with materials that would help sustain a high performance. He tried hard, for example, to have a complete set of church books delivered to Peking, as well as some Slavonic grammars with which communicants would be instructed in the language of the ritual to which they had committed themselves. Such basic materials as these did not yet form part of the inventory of the church. Again, it was Platkovskii who, soon after his arrival in Peking, sent to the Synod a simple Chinese character text, asking that the Manchu emperor be approached from St. Petersburg with the request that the book be translated. Nothing came of this venture, but the effort made by the archimandrite is itself noteworthy.[5] Meanwhile the missals that were so desperately needed were never sent because Platkovskii, in his haste to get them, had apparently applied to Irkutsk instead of to the Synod in St. Petersburg, exciting old jealousies between the metropolis and its Siberian possessions. Thus only simple prayers could be said in the nan kuan. Masses were not introduced until 1735,[6] and the church itself not consecrated until the following year.

For other necessities Platkovskii wrote frequently back to Russia. On January 16, 1731, he gave a note[7] to the Russian courier in Peking, Solov'ev, which was to be delivered to Sava Vladislavich, seeking his intervention in sending ecclesiastical garments, vessels, books, and other things about which he had already written three times (he said) to the Synod. He also tried to persuade Vladislavich of the need of designating an additional sum of money for operational expenses, saying that the Chinese were pilfering more than ever from the mission. When he had complained about this to the Li-fan yuan—so he wrote—he had been thrown out by the scruff of his neck. Either the few books that the mission possessed had been stolen—he continued—or else the Chinese had torn the pages out of them for toilet paper. Furthermore, bells and a bell-tower were necessary, and a new gate. The iconastasis in the new church was still unfinished. And not only in this letter, but in others as well, Platkovskii recurrently asked for candlesticks, incense burners, chandeliers, wax, communion bread, wine, coal, a sexton, a candle-maker, a breadbaker and warden (*trapeznik*), three complete changes of ecclesiastical vestments for all the mission, socks, shoes, shirts, and pants for the baptized people, five hundred silver crosses to be given out to future converts, just as many "sacred images of the Savior," and more money. From this list it is clear that Platkovskii intended to make the ecclesiastical mission in Peking a serious enterprise, something that evidently rather surprised officials in both Russia and China.

As far as it is possible to tell, not many of these things reached Peking during the time of the second mission. Steps were taken to send some painters to do the iconastasis; more money was eventually sent. But in impatiently waiting for deliveries from Russia that never came, Platkovskii resolved to go again to the Li-fan yuan for help. This time the Ch'ing ministers compliantly told him to make out a list of what was needed for his church. Platkovskii's itemization, however, now included a complete set of church plates and goblets, and amounted altogether to over five thousand taels silver. The Li-fan yuan was patient with his requests. Platkovskii was asked to supply some pictures of the clerical robes that he had requested, so that they could be reproduced by a Chinese tailor. He then served personally as a model at the Li-fan yuan, in full ecclesiastical dress, and the clothes were ordered. But when he next asked for a diamond ring and croziers of expensive stone or gold, "without which," he claimed, "it is impossible for me, an archimandrite, to live,"[8] the Li-fan yuan had had enough and again showed him to the door. There was nothing wrong with Platkovskii's interest in bettering the material condition of his church, and even his attempt to wheedle a diamond ring out of the Li-fan yuan he would have justified as a necessary means of establishing respect for his authority over the mission. After all, survival in Peking required disciplined obedience, and that would scarcely be achieved if a fussy archimandrite, having spent a great deal of time primping in front of his mirror, was still not content with his appearance. Platkovskii's problems lay, instead, with those lesser human beings over whom he was trying to impose himself, for no one was able to get along with him, or worse, to take him very seriously. This, more than anything else, explains the failure of the second mission to live up to its promise.

The first person to run afoul of the archimandrite was Hieromonk Lavrentii. Lavrentii and his three assistants, Osip D'iakonov, Nikanor Kliusov, and Petr Iakutov, had been living in the Nikolskii church since accompanying Ilarion Lezhaiskii to China in 1716. Before the arrival of Platkovskii, Lavrentii had gone for years without his salary from Russia. The assistants, even after Platkovskii's arrival, were paid only ten rubles a year. Living on the local economy, at first a necessity, had no doubt by now become something of an amenity. Lavrentii's simple life among Manchus, Chinese, and Albazinians was unlike that led by the newly arrived missionaries to the south. When Platkovskii had first arrived in Peking Lavrentii suggested, perhaps impudently, that the archimandrite should live in the Nikolskii church, as the first mission had, among the Albazinians. To this Platkovskii had replied, biliously, that he would not move from the nan kuan "without a ukase from Her Imperial Majesty and the blessings of the Holy Synod." After the earthquake of 1730, he did nothing to assist in the reconstruction of the pei kuan.[9] And then, two years later, he attempted to wrest the old monk from his corner of the city, now going so far as to take the matter up with the College of Foreign Affairs. Lavrentii

had refused to move south, Platkovskii wrote, and even Lorents
Lange "by himself and without any ukase from the Imperial
Majesty" had said that Lavrentii could go on living in the Nikolskii
church.[10] Whatever the College of Foreign Affairs may have replied,
Platkovskii had managed not only to trouble it with a problem it no
doubt considered trivial, but also to make life more difficult than
necessary for everyone in Peking. Lavrentii, who had wanted only
to keep clear of the new and self-important missionaries to the
south, was allowed to remain in the Nikolskii church. In fact, out
of this episode originated the practice of assigning one member of
each new mission to residence in the pei kuan, but it was hard to
get anyone to take up service there since it was considered rather
like banishment into a dark, forbidding, and after Lavrentii's return
to Russia, perhaps haunted quarter of Peking.

Other members of the mission got on just as badly with the
archimandrite. According to his diary, which was subsequently
stolen by Ilarion Rossokhin and Feodot Tret'iakov, the Jesuits in
Peking had been approached by two of the students in the mission,
Luka Voeikov and Ivan Pukhort, during the holy week of Easter,
1730. They were asked to use their influence to arrange the expulsion of Platkovskii from China.[11] Because of such outrages Platkovskii himself went to the Li-fan yuan at least five times[12] to make
known his wish to return to Russia at once. But while nothing was
done, the archimandrite's chain of command was breaking, and
life at the mission was becoming more precarious. In a letter of
January 14, 1731 (this time to the Synod), Platkovskii stated that
his priest, Ivan Filimonov, and Deacon Ioasaf had already made
four separate attempts on his life.[13] The Li-fan yuan became mildly
interested in these varying efforts to expedite Platkovskii's departure from the scene, and on September 6, 1731, sent a note to the
Senate stating that "Priest Ivan and the students are unable to live
peaceably in our country, so that disagreements and great quarrels
have taken place. He [Ivan] brutally wounded Priest Antonii in the
hand, and for that Priest Ivan is being expelled to the frontier
authorities."[14] In a letter of July 25 to the College of Foreign
Affairs the archimandrite gave a fuller account of this incident:

On June 22 the priest [Ivan], indecorously drunk and running around the embassy with the students, first spit in my eye—at me, the archimandrite—and then threw a brick that hit me in the shoulder and gravely wounded me. At suppertime in the middle of the embassy he practically stabbed me to death, running me through the left hand with his knife and making me permanently disabled. And when this priest Ivan came after me again, if he had not stumbled and fallen he would have cut me, the archimandrite, and my intestines into pieces and would have killed me.[15]

Ivan Filimonov was put into chains after this episode and incarcerated for three months in a Chinese jail before being returned to Russia.

Platkovskii had also lost the services of Hierodeacon Ioasaf temporarily. On September 20, 1730, having drunk a great deal, Ioasaf set out for the imperial palace and, in his position as an official of the seventh grade, managed to gain entry into the outer buildings. Here he began causing an uproar, and even accosted a group of ministers. For this transgression he was punished by a twenty-four hour confinement.[16] Platkovskii also reported that Ioasaf spent his days playing checkers, cards, and dice with the students, and his nights in getting drunk. In a later report Platkovskii states that at a procession (presumably to the Nikolskii church) on May 25, 1732, Ioasaf was drunk and Lavrentii insulted him.[17] A report of January 16, 1733, reveals that his diary had been stolen (Platkovskii erroneously attributes the theft to Ioasaf) and states that Ioasaf had tried to strike him with a boar-spear.

Lavrentii was also continuing to behave badly. He is said to have concealed his clerical status, engaged in a local slave-trade, and kept two servants, a couple whose names are recorded only as Simeon and Feodosia. Feodosia became his own wife, more or less—living nearby, receiving guests, and seeing to his domestic affairs. This thinly disguised liaison was a source of amusement for the people of the community, some of whom, it is reported, would steal up to Lavrentii's house in the middle of the night and in a whisper ask to be let in. With Feodosia, Lavrentii had two sons whom he baptized and named Ivan and Ilarion. He raised them, taught them some Russian, got them both married, bought them a piece of property, and baptized their wives, who came from the country. As for Lavrentii himself, he is said always to have been niggardly, going to the market on foot, wearing an undershirt and straw hat, and carrying his purchases home himself.[18] After Ilarion Lezhaiskii died and the deacon of the first mission, Filimon, returned to Russia to announce the news, Lavrentii was entrusted with custody of what remained of the mission's supply of silver. But learning that Filimon was not returning to China, and no longer receiving a salary, Lavrentii took the silver for himself. From Irkutsk, Innokentii Kul'chitskii and Filimon wrote to Lavrentii that he should send the silver back to Russia. Instead Lavrentii simply sent Filimon's clothes, adding that the mice and rats had eaten all the chasubles. Two Albazinians, Stenka Kozmin and Iakov Savin (whom we have already met), asked him to return the silver to the church, and finally asked for the intervention of the Li-fan yuan. The outcome of this affair is unknown. When the caravan of 1732 arrived in Peking Lavrentii was seen drying bread crusts in the sun and selling them. Four years later when Lange arrived with the caravan of 1736 he had instructions to take the old monk back to Russia. Even then Platkovskii tried to discredit Lavrentii, accusing him, on the grounds of testimony from Ioasaf, of living with a wife and having children. But in the caravan council which, under the jurisdiction of Lange, conducted an inquiry into the doings of the Russian mission in Peking, Ioasaf reversed himself and stated that he had actually never seen Lavrentii lying with a woman. Lavrentii was taken back to Russia in 1737, his reputation still intact, but without the family he had sired. What became of him in the fatherland, after an absence of twenty-two years, remains a mystery.[19]

Meanwhile, the deterioration of the second ecclesiastical mission continued. Soon the Li-fan yuan became as interested as Platkovskii himself in putting an end to his service in China, and agreeably forwarded to Russia his appeals to return. Pending a hurried deliberation by the Synod on the matter of Platkovskii's return, it was decided at least to furnish him with new assistants.

Here, however, unexpected difficulties were encountered in getting
clerics in Russia to accept the call to missionary work in Peking. In
September, 1732, when a priest named Semenov was appointed, he
refused to go, pointing out that he had already had his fill of missionary work among the Kalmuks, as a result of which he was now
suffering from scurvy and shingles. Furthermore, were he to depart
for Peking, there would be no one to look after his seven-year old
daughter. The Synod then turned up a priest named Ioannov, saying
that "no negative representations would be accepted from him."
But Ioannov asked his superiors to excuse him from the journey
because of a "belly complaint." And another cleric called upon by
the Synod, a deacon named Grigor'ev, also pleaded, "belly and
epileptic illnesses" and the more compelling excuse that he had an
old mother to support.[20] But at length, by the end of 1732, a new
group of five missionaries had been put together, and they all
arrived in Irkutsk in 1733. In 1734 they were sent on to the frontier
where, after expending all this time and effort, they were found by
the Mongolians to be wanting in the proper credentials.[21] Thus
they faced a wait in Irkutsk of two more years until they could
proceed to Peking with the third mission.

The problems with the clerics, whether already in China, or
trying either to get to China, or avoid getting there, form only one
part of the history of the second ecclesiastical mission. The Russian
students, who outnumbered the missionaries six to four, not only
contributed importantly to the troubles of the archimandrite; most
of them failed either to survive in China or to learn anything while
they were there. It is known that upon the arrival of the final
contingent of students in 1729 a teacher of Manchu and Chinese
was assigned to them.[22] Perhaps it is also true that these first students managed collectively to compile a simple lexicon in four
languages—Russian, Latin, Manchu, and Chinese.[23] But as far as
Antonii Platkovskii was concerned, the only activities they engaged
in with any ardor were heavy drinking, arguments, and often fisti-
cuffs.[24] When Lange was in Peking in 1732 he advised the students
to get down to work, and prohibited them from going about the
city in search of good restaurants. Delinquents would be subjected

to the knout.[25] In 1734 Captain Semen Petrov of the Tobolsk garrison arrived in Peking, bringing, among other things, a ukase to Platkovskii directing him to continue his strong supervision over the students, as he had been told in 1730, and to punish them for any disobedience; an additional ukase was presented to the students, exhorting them to be obedient to their archimandrite and to pursue assiduously their language study.[26] But in the same year Platkovskii again reported that they were continuing to drink outrageously, were not listening to him, and in their constant drunkenness were wasting time and money; he concluded that there was nothing to hope for from them as far as any service to the state was concerned.[27] For their part, the students all petitioned against Platkovskii that he was the one confirmed in vice and in intolerable manners, that he insulted them, and had withheld their salaries.[28]

Luka Voeikov and Gerasim Shulgin led the most dissolute lives, and not surprisingly, they were also the first to die, both in Peking, in 1734 and 1735 respectively. As we have noticed it was Voeikov's dacha, a retreat outside the city where he could drink in peace, that became the site of his own grave and subsequently the burial ground for other members of the mission who died in Peking. Apart from Voeikov and Shulgin, the remaining four students—Tret'iakov, Pukhort, Rossokhin, and Ponomarev—gave some cause for more hope. When the Russian courier, Solov'ev, was in Peking in 1732, he reported that Voeikov and Shulgin were constantly drunk; he did state, however, that the other four "were fit for studying." Following Solov'ev's judgment, Lange took Tret'iakov and Pukhort back to Russia with him when he left Peking on September 8, 1732. Why Rossokhin and Ponomarev were left behind is unclear, for Lange had brought four students to Peking with his caravan. Only two of them—Aleksei Vladykin and Ivan Bykov—were acceptable; otherwise the quota prescribed by the treaty of Kiakhta would have been exceeded. Thus the two other students, named Pozniakov and Barshchenkov, who had accompanied Lange all the way to Peking, presumably turned around and went all the way back with him.

In 1735 Lange left again with a caravan for China. The death of the Yung-cheng emperor on September 27 forced the caravan to pause a long time on the frontier, and it was during this delay that news reached Lange of Voeikov's death in Peking the preceding year. When the caravan was finally able to continue its way to Peking Lange wrote from Mongolia to the College of Foreign Affairs that he had taken on a student named Ivan Shikhirev to replace Voeikov. Shikhirev was accepted by the Li-fan yuan. In 1740, another courier, Mikhail Shokurov, was sent ahead to Peking to announce the fourth post-Kiakhta caravan that had begun organizing a year earlier; he was also instructed to request the agreement of the Li-fan yuan to the return to Russia of the two students who had been in China the longest, Rossokhin and Ponomarev. But again the rapid mortality of the Russians in Peking did not wait upon the painfully slow communications of the time, and Ponomarev was found to have died before Shokurov's arrival.[29] Ilarion Rossokhin did return and on March 19, 1741, began an unnoticed but productive career at the Academy of Sciences. Even so, his return had been justified to the Li-fan yuan by the need in Russia for translators to facilitate the diplomatic correspondence with China; with Rossokhin back in St. Petersburg only a short distance from the College of Foreign Affairs, this need inexplicably went unfulfilled for a considerable time.

The Third Ecclesiastical Mission: Ilarion Trusov

As early as 1732 the Synod had begun its search for Platkovskii's replacement. Notwithstanding its failure to find any-one immediately, the other preparations for a new mission were painstakingly thorough. The Synod proceeded with a slow and meticulous investigation of the accusations and counteraccusations being made by the missionaries already in Peking. Lorents Lange was brought into the Synod chambers to give his own testimony after his return with the caravan of 1732–1733, and was commissioned to conduct a local inquest in Peking when he returned there with the next caravan. An enormous list of new instructions was prepared, and at last a new archimandrite was found. His name was Ilarion Trusov and he, like Platkovskii before him, was no stranger to China and the Siberian service. He had been priest to the China caravans of 1727 and 1732. Earlier he had been part of the first Bering expedition to Kamchatka, and reportedly almost froze to death there. When not on the road he served in the bishop's rectory in Tobolsk.[30]

Trusov's career was almost ruined by an encounter he had had with Platkovskii during his second visit to Peking in 1732. Platkovskii accused him of deliberately spilling the contents of a bottle of ink onto a placard carrying the names of the imperial family nailed on the altar of the new church. This was a serious indiscretion, for which Trusov was arrested when he crossed the frontier to Russia the following year. Brought back to St. Petersburg, by all accounts he argued his case before the Synod so eloquently that it was he who was finally chosen to lead the next mission. At the same time, Lange presented testimony against Platkovskii and suggested that he be recalled forthwith, which, coupled with the identical opinion of the Li-fan yuan, sealed the fate of this man who seemed variously to cause or court nothing but trouble throughout his life.

The edict of the tsarina appointing Trusov to the Peking mission dates from September 9, 1734. It was during the preceding summer that Trusov had been interrogated closely by Feofan Prokopovich, Archbishop of Novgorod and Lutsk; at the end of this investigation into his alleged desecration of the church altar, the bishop took him into his home, judged him innocent, saw "some promise" in him, and thought him worthy of being an "archimandrite and ambassador" to Peking.[31] On September 10, 1734, the Synod amplified the tsarina's edict of appointment of the previous day: Trusov was to be raised from his rank of hieromonk to archimandrite by Bishop Gavril of Suzdal and Iurevsk, who was also to administer the oath of allegiance to the throne; he was to be issued a passport to Irkutsk; Bishop Innokentii Nerunovich of Irkutsk and Nerchinsk[32] was to be informed of Trusov's appointment and arrival in his eparchy; the brethren and secular servants at the Preobrazhenskii monastery (near Irkutsk), of which Trusov was also appointed father-superior, were to obey him "without any contradiction whatever"; when the next caravan was en route to Peking Trusov should go with it, as Her Majesty had instructed, and replace Platkovskii; and finally, he should stay there without so much as moving until further word from the Synod arrived.[33]

A week later Ilarion Trusov received his promotion. He was at once ordered to inform the Synod of what he took to be the needs of the mission. His proposals[34] were presented on September 30, 1734—a quick piece of research that bears in many places the unmistakable imprint of the vain requests that Platkovskii had been making up to that time. He began by supplying information on the Russian religious establishments in Peking that apparently was still only faintly known in St. Petersburg, although thirty-five years earlier answers to these questions had been given to Andrei Vinius, and Platkovskii himself had written on the subject as recently as 1732. The rest of the document simply enumerates the chasubles, incense burners, prayer books, and so forth, that were deemed vital to the functioning of the mission. Bells were necessary, especially since "both the Catholics and the heathens have them"; shirts, stockings, sacred icons, and crosses should be available as presents to make easier the job of converting. A hundred rubles were requested for the purchase of wax, incense, coal, millet, treacle, honey, communion bread, and wine. Trusov made two final requests: he asked for permission to take along to Peking his adopted son from Kamchatka, a Kuril native now named Iakov Ivanov, as a salaried assistant; and he asked for the advance of a year's salary, as he had accumulated a rather heavy debt since the affair of his arrest and incarceration in Irkutsk. Such a debt, he pointed out, certainly did not become an archimandrite.

It took the Synod a little more than a month to produce the final ukase,[35] incorporating all the details leading up to the appointment of Trusov and the recall of Platkovskii. Dated November 6, 1734, it begins abruptly as follows: "Place Archimandrite Antonii Platkovskii under arrest, and bring him back to Russia, at his own expense, to the Holy Synod in St. Petersburg. And in his place, in accordance with Her Imperial Majesty's ukase of September 9

which was based on the report of Bishop Feofan with the agreement of the other members of the Synod, dispatch Archimandrite
Ilarion at once." The ukase goes on to specify that Trusov will be
given a complete set of church books and he should put them all
carefully in a trunk and transport them safely to Peking; he is to
make an inventory of all the properties of the Russian mission in
Peking, itemizing everything separately; he is to keep a journal in
which he is to write down information on the people accompanying him; it should be stored in the box of books; if he is suspicious
of anyone he should leave them behind in Irkutsk and find new
people there. And as for Deacon Ioasaf, still in Peking, since Lange
defended him, since he is well known and liked by the Chinese,
and is of good manners, "since his impertinence in entering the
imperial court and interrupting the ministers was a piece of fun
and of no consequence," and since Platkovskii's suspicions of him
turned out to be unfounded, therefore he is not to be taken from
Peking but left there with Ilarion Trusov as a deacon in the embassy
church, as before. "As for the fact, reported by agent Lange, that
Ioasaf now and then takes liquor, the archimandrite is to tell him
that, by imperial ukase, if he does not abstain and in a state of
intoxication engages in some audacious act, he will be returned to
Russia, deprived of his rank and defrocked, and cruelly tortured—
nothing being omitted."

Trusov and Lange are next ordered to make a thorough investigation of the financial situation of the mission; in particular they
are to audit the accounts of Platkovskii and hieromonk Lavrentii.
Trusov should make a full account of his own expenses and send
copies to the Synod, the College of Foreign Affairs, and the
Sibirskii Prikaz, as usual. Lange should judge upon the complaints
made by the students against Platkovskii for withholding their
salaries, and other purported offenses; he should also investigate
both the affair between Platkovskii and Ivan Filimonov and the
allegedly lustful behavior of Lavrentii at the Nikolskii church. The
information gathered by Lange and Trusov should be kept in some
secret place in the "embassy," out of sight of the Chinese. Lange
should take away Platkovskii's mitre and give it to Trusov; Trusov

should be sure to take from Platkovskii and Lavrentii whatever other church properties they had arrogated for themselves. While the investigation is proceeding Platkovskii is to be detained at the embassy and is never to go out. Upon completion of the investigation Lange is to send Platkovskii and Lavrentii back to Russia in all haste; they shall be placed under arrest in the provincial chancellery in Irkutsk, and, from there, sent to the Synod in St. Petersburg at their own expense; the soldiers who guard them should be instructed to follow the main roads and neither turn off anywhere for anything nor tarry at any point on the way.

Moreover, Trusov should take the sacred antimins to Peking and upon his arrival consecrate the church in the name of "the Meeting of the Lord" (*Sretenie Gospodina*),[36] provided that the iconastasis and other decorations have been finished. One thousand rubles are authorized for church vessels, chasubles, other clothing for all occasions, and for a bell tower and bells "with a passable sound." Two thousand rubles are allocated for buying or building additional houses, for decorating the church in a way that would not be "dishonorable or infamous" by local standards; and for handouts to the people who come to be converted. More money shall be given to the mission every year for incidental necessities. The salaries of all the members of the mission shall be paid every three years. The archimandrite shall issue vouchers that are redeemable from Lange when a caravan is in Peking.[37] It is agreed to advance Trusov his first year's salary, as requested.

The College of Foreign Affairs should be informed as usual that a clerical party is leaving for China, and is in need of a passport for their passage to Peking.[38] The college should also send a letter to the Chinese tribunal (i.e. the Li-fan yuan) soliciting its attention and assistance to the priests "if from the part of the local population something contemptuous or insulting (more than expected) is done to these clergymen." The college should also be informed that Archimandrite Ilarion will have supervision over the students so that they will not drink heavily, spend their days idly without studying, or commit outrages. Lange should also be given a ukase empowering him to make his inquiries; it would not be suitable to entrust the investigation to Trusov, since he and Plat-kovskii are of the same rank and are not on good terms. At the new church shall serve the archimandrite, one hieromonk, one hiero-deacon, two assistants, the Kurile orphan Iakov Ivanov, the Chinese who is now serving at the Nikolskii church as a psalmreader, and a *trapeznik* to keep watch. At the old church shall serve one hiero-monk and two assistants. On feast days the mass shall be said for the whole community at the Sretenskii church. The students shall always be in attendance, and the Chinese of Russian faith as well as the newly baptized shall also be summoned. Only do not force them to come, but exhort them gently, lest some suspicions are engendered among them. And finally, Trusov should be supplied with traveling money, a suitable number of coaches, as well as boats with rowers and ruddermen, and, where necessary, guides.

At this point the instructions, having gotten Trusov to China, go on to supply in twelve verbose articles every conceivable pre-scription for the maintenance of proper relations with the Alba-zinians, with the Jesuits or other Roman Catholics, with the people of Peking, and among the Russians themselves. This extraordinary document must have left the impression that there was practically nothing a Russian missionary could do in China that would not be subverted by the problem of *double entendre*. Such at least was the case in February. Among the endless number of nocturnal vigils and divine liturgies that had to be undertaken for the various members of the imperial family was the celebration of the name-day of Her Imperial Highness, Tsarina Anna, which happened to fall close to the Chinese new year. Trusov was therefore instructed to make this unfortunate coincidence clear in a special sermon, lest anyone should think it was the latter, not the former, that was being observed by the Russian mission. Peking demanded not only vigils but vigilance. When all else failed, an ostrich-like defense was to be taken against the dangers of the city, on the principle that what one did not see or hear did not exist. Converts, for example, were not to be accepted for confession through an interpreter, an injunction that left Russian missionary work with an untroubled sense of a job well done, since no archimandrite in the eighteenth century learned enough Chinese or Manchu to manage the kind of vocabulary that a local confessional was likely to generate. The instructions to Trusov close with stern provisions for dealing with members of the mission who would predictably find their own salvation in being drunk and disobedient. To each succeeding archimandrite this document was reiterated with little change.

Because the other members of his suite were already in Irkutsk waiting for him, Trusov left St. Petersburg with only his adopted son Iakov Ivanov. He carried the credentials necessary to get him to the border and then past it into China: a passport from the College of Foreign Affairs and a letter from the Senate to the Li-fan yuan. This note reminded the Li-fan yuan that of the previous four priests in Peking Ivan Filimonov had already been taken back to Russia; now Antonii Platkovskii and Hieromonk Lavrentii were being recalled "in recognition of their long service in China." Therefore three additional priests were being sent to replace them— Ilarion Trusov, Lavrentii Uvarov, and Antonii L'khovskii, with three servants. The contradictory demands for protection from the people of Peking and for freedom to move among them were repeated.[39] Trusov safely reached Irkutsk in the train of a caravan being led by Lorents Lange and Commissar Erofei Firsov. Here the rest of the mission was taken on, including the student Ivan Shikhirev as well as two additional priests, reputed to be experts at iconastasis, who were to do the painting in the new church. Following the mourning for the Yung-cheng emperor in China, the caravan passed the frontier on July 9, 1736. Peking was reached on November 10.

The gathering effort of the past two years to get Platkovskii removed from Peking and Trusov installed there was now at the moment of trial. Platkovskii had heard in 1735 that he was going to be replaced by the very man who had, as he put it, wanted to kill him during the visit of the previous caravan, and that the new archimandrite was already on his way. He quickly sent off a letter to Bishop Innokentii in Irkutsk, asking him to write a letter to the Synod in which it would be stated that he, Platkovskii, was resigning of his own choice, and that Trusov was rude and ignorant. When the caravan arrived in Peking Platkovskii continued to hold the initiative by accosting Lange and accusing him, unbeliever[40] that he was, of undermining the church altar and using it as a vault, after which the wall of the new church had caved in. After this Lange presented to Platkovskii his sealed ukase from the Synod. Taking it, Platkovskii threw it on the ground and demanded to know how an unbeliever was entitled to deliver a ukase to him. Lange complied with his instructions and, no doubt, his own feelings of the moment, and had the archimandrite arrested and put under solitary detention in the nan kuan. Just as Platkovskii was once preferred to Kul'chitskii, there was never any doubt that the predispositions of Lange, Trusov, and the Synod would return a guilty verdict against him in Peking. Even as his case was being studied Platkovskii was subjected to whippings and other corporal punishments, and then hobbled in chains. Sick from his beatings, he was ordered to confess his crimes to the caravan priest.[41]

While Platkovskii was being confined, Trusov was attending to some of the details of his instructions. On December 20, 1736, in the company of all the clerics save Platkovskii himself, the new church was consecrated. Although the icons had been botched by the two professionals whom Lange had brought along, there was time to have them repainted before the caravan left Peking. Arrangements were made to start the building of new cells for quartering the missionaries. A new cross of guilded iron was put on top of the new church, and the Chinese paper windows were replaced with new ones made of mica. As the caravan began making preparations to leave the city in April, 1737, Lange asked the Li-fan yuan, among other things, that he be allowed to make the changes in the personnel of the mission, for which he had permission from the tsarina. He also stated the hope that the ecclesiastical mission would continue to be under the patronage and supervision of the Li-fan yuan and no other department (what forbearance it had shown with Platkovskii!), and that the Russian clerics would no longer be given rank, either in the Russian company or as regular officials, since "in Christendom" no church people were ever allowed to hold rank. The Li-fan yuan assented orally on April 26.[42] Lange's *audience de congé* took place on May 9, and the caravan departed the next day. From Selenginsk Lange wrote to the College of Foreign Affairs (on September 1) that he had Platkovskii with him, having concluded an investigation into his violent behavior in Peking. Back in St. Petersburg Platkovskii was tried again, found guilty, deprived of his rank, and sent as a hieromonk to live under surveillance in the Troitse-Sergiev Monastery nineteen versts outside of St. Petersburg. His fate dramatically changed only a few years later. In 1742 Tsarina Elizabeth Petrovna happened to be paying a visit to the monastery, and after all the monks were assembled and presented to her it was on Platkovskii that her glance rested. When she inquired about him, the archimandrite of the monastery, Amvrosii Dubnevich, replied with a brief résumé of Platkovskii's checkered past, adding that he had since undergone a thorough reform. Platkovskii was thereupon pardoned by the tsarina, quickly became paymaster of the monastery, later was restored to his former rank of archimandrite, and finally became father-superior of the Troitskii Danilov monastery in Pereslavl'-Zaleskii. He died there on June 15, 1746.[43]

In Peking the third ecclesiastical mission, like the second before it, functioned smoothly for a brief period. Financially the situation was much improved. The two thousand rubles worth of various goods, mostly furs, that had been given to Trusov for buying or building new houses were exchanged on the Peking market very favorably, returning to the mission an amount more than twice their original value. To this sum of almost four thousand five hundred rubles was added almost twelve hundred collected variously from the estates of Ilarion Lezhaiskii, the old Albazinian Dmitrii Nestorovich, scattered Manchu promissory notes, and unexplained sources. With other money provided by the Synod, church vessels had been purchased en route in Moscow, Tobolsk, and Irkutsk. Three hundred rubles were later paid to a Chinese icon-painter; and fourteen hundred were spent on building a house next to the new church. It was badly constructed and for seven years water ran through the roof, but at length the Chinese contractor agreed to mend it. In any case, things were not as bad as they had been. In 1737, furthermore, Trusov filed a report on the good behavior of the students.[44]

Among the clerical staff the problems that arose at first seemed to stem from natural causes. On July 7, 1740, Lavrentii Uvarov, who was serving at the Nikolskii church, asked that he be allowed to return to Russia because of an illness. On April 20, 1742, Hieromonk Antonii L'khovskii also claimed to have become ill from the summer air in Peking and asked to be replaced.[45] Trusov's ward Iakov Ivanov died in 1738, but was apparently replaced in 1742.[46] Of the three assistants who worked at the Nikolskii church—the old members of the first mission—Osip D'iakonov had probably died before 1736; Peter Iakutov and Nikanor Kliusov died in 1737. Deacon Ioasaf, who had come with Platkovskii and whom Lange had so stoutly defended, remained sober and survived the third mission, while playing an important role in representing its interests at the Li-fan yuan.[47]

But what of Trusov himself? It was not long before he was undone by his own inability to live up to the standard of behavior which his instructions assumed he would be imposing on the others. In 1740 Trusov's inferiors suddenly wrote to the Synod that, "the archimandrite, not preserving the dignity of his calling as his instructions say he should, and oblivious of any fear of God, constantly turns to endless drunken sprees and seldom directs the church service. We often informed him about his lack of service, to which he replied, 'I was not sent here for that,' and often he begged off because of illness."[48] The missionaries accused Trusov of drunkenly reeling about the grounds of the monastery in female dress, by which he excited the laughter of the Chinese; and also of squandering over one hundred and fifty-eight taels of silver from the treasury of the Nikolskii church. In addition to this, one of the students, Aleksei Vladkykin, reported that Trusov had stolen the silver from the Sretenskii church and had even torn the silver trimmings off the icons.

In a later message which Rossokhin brought back to Russia when he returned in 1741, Vladykin charged that not only was the archimandrite not paying any attention to the students, but he himself had sunk into drunkenness and blasphemy, dressing up in female clothing and occasionally entering the church in such attire, not fulfilling his duties even on days of high fasting, delivering

many insults to Chinese subordinates and thereby bringing about
the rapid decline of all the Russian clergy with him. The Synod
reacted on March 11, 1741, by ordering that Trusov be suspended
from all his duties as archimandrite of the Peking mission.[49] No
longer, apparently, would any time be wasted with a long inquiry
like that which preceded the recall of the second mission. Erofei
Firsov was already en route with the next caravan to China, and
he was given the responsibility of investigating the allegations of
Vladykin and the others. This was to be accomplished with the
help of a specially appointed hieromonk named Lavrentii
Bobrovnikov.

Actually it had been Firsov himself who had suggested the
appointment of Bobrovnikov when, meeting Rossokhin on the
way back to St. Petersburg in 1740, he had been told of Trusov's
insalubrious conduct. At this time Bobrovnikov was the acting
superior of the Posol'skii-Preobrazhenskii monastery, lying on the
road to China beyond Irkutsk, over which Trusov was still the
titular head. He had joined the Firsov caravan to Peking as its
attendant priest. The orders from the Synod must have reached
the caravan on the frontier, where it waited for over a year before
being able to cross into China. Finally it reached Peking on September 24, 1741. But here the anticipated trial of Ilarion Trusov
was suddenly made quite unnecessary by the fact that he had
already died, on April 22, 1741. Nevertheless a posthumous
inquest was organized, and all the charges against him were,
expectably, upheld. As to the surviving members of the mission,
their conduct was found to be uniformly exemplary, notwithstanding a deposition from the Li-fan yuan that all the Russian
clergy had spent much of its time in Peking in a state of drunkenness, in quarreling among themselves, and in generally wanton
behavior.[50]

When Firsov left China,[51] Bobrovnikov remained behind to
oversee the affairs of the mission until a new archimandrite could
be appointed. Antonii L'khovskii also remained in Peking; Lavrentii
Uvarov returned to Irkutsk. As for the students, only three now
remained: Aleksei Vladykin, Ivan Bykov and Ivan Shikhirev.

Shikhirev soon died in the summer of 1742. In November of the same year three more students were sent with courier Mikhail Shokurov to Peking, who was on his way to announce the belated news of the accession to the throne of Elizabeth Petrovna. These were all from the Moscow Academy: Aleksei Leont'ev, Andrei Kanaev, and Nikita Chekanov. They were the last to enter Peking until the arrival of the sixth ecclesiastical mission in 1771. During Bobrovnikov's brief tenure difficulties were only compounded. The Russian mission unexplainably advised Shokurov not to accept the gifts from the Ch'ien-lung emperor that were intended for the new tsarina, and this solecism greatly annoyed the Manchus, who had not completely abandoned the hope that Russians could learn and apply the lessons of protocol in Peking. Admittedly, it was a very hot summer (the hottest, Shokurov noted, that anyone could remember), and tempers were no doubt short. If Shokurov's account can be trusted, people were dropping in the streets and "even in the tribunal [the Li-fan yuan] itself, the ministers sat stark naked before me."[52] Perhaps because he was facing a rank of unrobed officials, Shokurov could bring himself to genuflect with only one knee when he paid his last visit to the Li-fan yuan before leaving Peking—a final affront from which he was probably lucky to escape. Meanwhile, within the mission Bobrovnikov himself had very quickly begun to drift from his responsibilities. Soon he earned a reputation, like Trusov, for playing out transvestite fantasies—in his case, trying to seduce his brethren with the announcement that he was an "untried virgin."[53] Again, he was typically careless with money and was reduced to thieving from the church and pawning church properties. Once, when he was apprehended in the act of committing a robbery, he would have been sent back to Russia forthwith had it not been for the fact that, as he said, "he had not finished his investigation of Trusov."[54] For the most part, however, Bobrovnikov simply remained in his monastic cell, hating his solitude but lacking the incentive to go outside. Ultimately he requested the Synod to give him his release, which was granted. Yet he also failed to survive until the arrival of his replacement, dying of complications from alcoholism in 1744 or 1745. His one constructive act had been to suggest to the Synod that in the future more educated personnel were necessary for the Peking mission, but in eighteenth-century Russia this advice was not easy to heed.

The Fourth Mission: Gervasii Lintsevskii

On March 15, 1742, the Synod, acting upon instructions from the College of Foreign Affairs, had set out to find a replacement for the third mission. Bishop Rafail of Kiev, who happened to be in Moscow at the time, was commissioned to find suitable candidates to be the new archimandrite. To any prospects that were found, China was advertised by the Synod as follows: "Although the Asian country is quite far away and lives in almost complete idolatry, the people there—as is known to the Synod—are all gentle and pleasant and of not bad manners, and all the more so inasmuch as the word of God is propagated there freely, without any fear or prohibition whatever. The Khan himself as well as his ministers treat the word of God with fair esteem."[55] At the end of this piece the candidates are promised, along with an augmented salary, other tangible rewards, and finally, an intangible but immortal glory upon their return to Russia. Rafail presented seven candidates to the Synod. All of them refused to go to Peking. The job thus fell by lot to one of them, the deputy superior of the Zlatoverkhii monastery in Kiev, Gervasii Lintsevskii.

It took almost a year for the full mission to be organized.[56] On January 20, 1743, the Synod reported to the College of Foreign Affairs that the mission was ready and in need of a passport, letters to the Li-fan yuan, a traveling allowance, and instructions. These were provided. In addition the missionaries were given a translator, the students were exhorted to try to learn Japanese and the attention of the archimandrite was again needlessly called to the fifth article of the Kiakhta treaty in which there was no mention of the imposing title of "archimandrite" so that he should not call himself one. Lintsevskii was also advised to give his letter of recommendation to the Li-fan yuan "in the appropriate manner," according to the suggestion of Deacon Ioasaf, who had already been in Peking for a long time, who knew Chinese, and who was well-connected; and finally, the term of residence in Peking was set at seven years, not counting the time it took to make the trip in either direction. The fourth mission probably left Moscow in March, 1743. There had been trouble over the passport since, as it turned out, the Moscow office of the College of Foreign Affairs did not have a seal big enough to impress the Manchus. Then, in Tobolsk, the passport was sent back because it failed to mention the servants of the archimandrite and others. Lintsevskii nevertheless did manage to reach Irkutsk, on October 12, 1743. The Tüshiyetü Khan in Urga was notified of the arrival, but in a letter that reached Selenginsk on December 1 he replied that the mission could enter China only with a caravan and not by itself; therefore it must be delayed.[57]

The organization of the fifth state caravan to China had been initiated by the Sibirskii Prikaz on March 5, 1744. Chosen as the director of this caravan was Gerasim Lebratovskii, a man who had risen from his early life as a choir boy in Irkutsk through a series of adventures. When Innokentii Kul'chitskii arrived in Irkutsk in 1721, Lebratovskii was taken on as a chorister in his suite, and after Kul'chitskii failed to get into China Lebratovskii remained with him to manage the clerical land holdings in the eparchy of Irkutsk and Nerchinsk. He remained in this position, plundering the church properties freely, until the death of his patron in 1731. Kul'chitskii's successor, Innokentii Nerunovich, immediately put Lebratovskii in irons, but he was soon released because of good connections with the vice-governor in Irkutsk, Andrei Pleshcheev. Under the protection of Pleshcheev, Lebratovskii was, for the moment, safe from Nerunovich, who could only order all churches in the eparchy to refuse him entry and all priests to deny him rites. The bishop also put a curse on him, which was a more serious affair. Lebratovskii went to the Synod office in Moscow, asking for the removal of the imprecation. Apparently this was done; in any event it was while he was in Moscow that Lebratovskii was introduced to Count Aleksei Grigor'evich Razumovskii, who in turn recommended him to the tsarina herself. Thus he quickly became a college assessor by imperial appointment and, in 1744, director of the caravan to China.[58]

Lebratovskii received his credentials from the College of
Foreign Affairs on March 27, 1744. On April 9 he was ordered to
take with him to China the missionaries who were waiting in Irkutsk.
This was accomplished, and the combined suites reached the frontier
on September 1, 1745. The journey across the Mongolian steppe
was slow and arduous, not only because the horses were in poor
shape, but also because Lebratovskii, with unhappy memories of
Russian clergymen, treated Archimandrite Gervasii very badly,
refusing him carts and servants. Peking was finally reached on
November 27, 1745, and on December 15 the papers of the entire
company were presented to the Li-fan yuan. The caravan remained
in Peking until June 6, 1746. The trade was very bad, and Lintsevskii
reported that Lebratovskii spent the greater part of his time occupy-
ing himself with various amusements which included singing and
banqueting at the expense of the caravan merchants. He was also,
said Lintsevskii, distracting the students from their studies and
from obedience to him. Possibly finding the caravan funds insufficient for his style of living, Lebratovskii also borrowed 1400 rubles
from the Catholic Bishop Polycarp,[59] which was not paid back
before the caravan quietly slipped out of Peking. Two students
returned to Russia with the caravan, Aleksei Vladykin and Ivan
Bykov. Both were said to have completed their studies and were
now "idling," and, furthermore, had "discovered several important
secrets useful to the Russian empire."[60]

In Peking Gervasii Lintsevskii found the mission buildings in
a state of collapse and the Albazinian flock, under heathen influences,
in lamentable condition. He also soon complained about the impudent
behavior of the missionaries, especially Feodosii Smorzhenskii, who
had accused him of contemptuous treatment of the hieromonks,
and of weak administration of the students, who had become quite
unruly. "They fired at each other with rifles, pistols, and harquebuses, played on balalaikas, fiddles and bandores, and danced and
whistled, not only inside, but out in the compound."[61] After the
departure of Vladykin and Bykov there remained four students in
Peking: Aleksei Leont'ev, Andrei Kanaev, Nikita Chekanov, and
Efim Sakhnovskii. Chekanov died of consumption in 1752. Not-

withstanding his earlier criticisms, Lintsevskii reported in 1753 that the three surviving students had been successful in their studies. Leont'ev and Sakhnovskii returned to Russia two years later with the rest of the mission, but Kanaev died shortly before the departure from China. Of the thirteen students who had thus far been sent to Peking, six had died there.

The Fifth Mission: Amvrosii Yumatov

The fourth mission remained in Peking for ten years. When the next caravan to China was being contemplated in 1751, the Synod suggested that it was also time to begin casting about for a new mission and thus avoid the previous difficulties of an uncoordinated attempt at entering China. Not until March 8, 1753, however, was Metropolitan Timofei of Kiev given the order to begin looking for an archimandrite for the Peking mission. The metropolitan's search turned up a teacher in the Moscow Academy named Amvrosii Yumatov. Invited to choose his own staff, Yumatov found everyone he needed, including a hieromonk named Sofronii Argievskii who had actually come forward and volunteered for the China service.[62] On June 11 was issued the Synodical ukase on the change of the mission; Yumatov was raised to the rank of archimandrite on June 13, and on the following day the entire mission was assembled in the offices of the Holy Synod in St. Petersburg. Although Yumatov's request for a raise in salary was turned down, he was provided with a four-wheeled carriage (*koliaska*), two horses, and a groom from the Synod's estates for the journey to China. He also received a large cross from the Synod sacristy, and some new prayer books. The suite left Moscow on August 24, 1753. The winter road had already set in by the time Eastern Siberia was reached, making it necessary for the wheels on the archimandrite's carriage to be replaced with runners. At the Mongolian frontier this process was reversed for the crossing of the steppe. Other resources were also added, in particular thirty-seven horses, six Cossacks, ten camels, and yokes, bridles, more wheels, riders, saddles, and one hundred feet of rope. The border was passed on September 15, 1754, and Peking was reached on December 23. The credentials of the mission which asked, among other things, for "protection against insults," were presented to the Li-fan yuan. Of the fourth mission only two priests were still alive: Archimandrite Gervasii, and Hieromonk Feodosii Smorzhenskii.[63]

The residence of the Yumatov mission in Peking was the longest of any in the eighteenth century. And this one had to endure its stint there at half-size, for the Manchu government had suddenly refused to admit the students whom Yumatov had brought with him to the frontier. After the caravan of 1755 took back to Russia the two remaining students from the previous mission (Leont'ev and Sakhnovskii), sixteen years were to pass before the O-lo-ssu hsueh held another class.[64] During this time Sino-Russian relations were undergoing another upheaval,[65] but the mission was touched by these extramural affairs only once, in the fall of 1759, when it was impounded by the Li-fan yuan. Otherwise the problems it faced were no different. A year after arriving Yumatov sent his first report back to the Synod.[66] It contained the familiar complaint about the run-down state of the buildings and an inventory of what few properties there were of value. As for the Albazinians in the Russian Company, most of them were unbaptized. They no longer spoke Russian, and an interpreter had to be employed in order to talk to them. But then, Amvrosii continues, "without gratuities they do not want to be baptized, and admonishments and exhortations have no effect."

At the outset the mission was probably in a position to meet the financial strain of carrying on its work in Peking; there was also money for repairs, for casting and recasting of bells, and for buying land for a new graveyard. A modest income also came from selling candles and incense. Among the listed expenses of the mission was the money required for the travels of the archimandrite around the city, which included the purchase and upkeep of horses and camels. These beasts were especially necessary for the trip to and from the Albazinian community. It was impossible to go this distance on foot, Yumatov explained, all the more so because "the Chinese, seeing the foreigners, even wearing their kind of clothes, would swear, laugh, and spit." And according to another notice, "whenever he [Yumatov] allows someone to leave [the mission] he always sends out two at a time . . . and in order to escape the abusive derision of the Chinese he and his whole suite wear Manchu or Chinese dress."[67] The archimandrite himself was tall and wore a long beard, which made his incognito quite pointless.

But Yumatov refused to allow these embarrassments to dampen his spirits. Safely back within the walls of the mission he planted an orchard and caused new outhouses to be built. He ate common meals with the rest of his mission, held church services every day, and maintained friendly relations with most of the Roman Catholics, conducting with them monthly ecumenical meetings at which collective blessings were asked.[68] Among the Russian emissaries[69] who visited Peking in the mid-eighteenth century, Vasilli Bratishchev reported (in 1757) that "Archimandrite Yumatov and his suite are well and have no complaints. They are orderly and obedient."[70] The Manchus concurred, informing Bratishchev of the mission's good behavior up to that time.[71] And this archimandrite, unlike Platkovskii, seemed to have a sense of how to steer among the Chinese elite, if not the masses. His assistant, Stepan Zimin, wrote that "In Peking there was no resident Russian [official], but instead the archimandrite had a relationship with the tribunal from where—as from other departments—officials often arrived at the Russian embassy on high feast days and on holidays, in order to observe the ceremony and decoration. The archimandrite, to the great glory and joy of Russia, treated them with dinner at his own expense, and to the most necessary persons he presented Russian things for any eventualities. Such visits and such presents cost the archimandrite a not inconsiderable sum every year, the more so as at that time in Peking everything was expensive."[72]

In 1763 new salaries arrived from Russia, there being no objection from the Li-fan yuan to the way Yumatov had been spending his money. What the archimandrite had wanted, however, was to return to Russia. In 1764 the Manchu government made it clear that a new mission could not be admitted until border troubles were settled. This did not happen until 1768, when a protocol to the Kiakhta treaty was signed.[73] Then three more years passed before the next ecclesiastical mission crossed the frontier. It reached Peking in the summer of 1771 to discover that Amvrosii Yumatov, after sixteen and a half years in the city, had died shortly before its arrival. He was buried in the old Russian cemetery beyond the An-ting gate, where there was now barely enough room for him.

The Sixth and Seventh Missions: Nikolai Tsvet and Ioakim Shishkovskii

Yumatov's fate was shared by every other member of the fifth mission but one. Such a high rate of mortality created problems in continuity between missions that were hard to overcome. The Synod, mindful of this problem, had tried for a long time to organize a new mission, but it was only in 1767 that the College of Foreign Affairs agreed, expecting the imminent improvement of border relations with China. After a search of three months the Synod selected a teacher of French and German at the Troitse-Sergiev Monastery, Hierodeacon Nikolai Tsvet, to be the next archimandrite.[74] Tsvet was occasioned an unexpected delay when no one could find the exhortatory instructions (unrevised since Trusov's time) for the Russian mission;[75] but at length everything was ready and the Synod sent the archimandrite off with a valedictory ukase making the same provisions for carts, boats with helmsmen and oarsmen, furs for salaries, and so forth. The sixth mission left for China in fourteen carts at the beginning of 1768. It arrived in Irkutsk safely enough, but still had to face a two-year wait pending a final decision on its entry into China; customarily, as we have seen, a mission was supposed to be escorted to China by a caravan, but in this instance, the caravan which it was accompanying sold most of its goods on the frontier and decided not to go on to Peking. Then, when it was discovered that by the agreement of 1768 Russian students would once more be permitted to study in Peking, more time was lost in finding a suitable group. None could be located in Irkutsk; instead three were commandeered from the seminary in Tobolsk, and a fourth was taken on in Kiakhta.[76] On the border several more months were spent in replacing Hieromonk Ioannikii, who had died suddenly of fever, and two servants who had turned out to be "unfit for service." At length all was ready, and the mission, chaperoned by Vasilii Igumnov and a small coterie of three Cossacks and twelve servants, crossed the frontier on September 4, 1771 and arrived in Peking on November 8th.

The discovery that only Stepan Zimin of the preceding mission was still alive infected the new mission with a sense of morbidity that lasted throughout its time in Peking. After five years had passed Tsvet wrote back to Russia asking to be relieved of his post; he also complained that the mission was in terrible shape, that no one had received their salaries for 1777, that some of his subordinates were in advanced states of destitution, while others had already expired.[77] One episode in the life of this entirely undistinguished mission may suffice to dramatize the great yearning to return to Russia that almost all missionaries felt in the eighteenth century. On September 28, 1774, ostensibly suffering from delirium tremens, the clerical servant Ivan Grebeshkov appeared at the Li-fan yuan and made a number of incoherent charges against Archimandrite Tsvet. The Li-fan yuan was assured by others in the mission that Grebeshkov had, for several days, been insane. Afterwards he confessed that there was method in his madness: he had purposely caused this incident in the hope that the whole mission might be sent back to Russia as quickly as possible. He was arrested and put into chains, and died three years later. A baptized Chinese servant at the mission was also implicated in this incident; after the investigation he hanged himself on the wall of the compound.[78]

After a decade had finally passed, a new mission, the seventh to be sent to Peking, arrived to ransom Tsvet and those who had managed to survive along with him.[79] Characteristically, this mission had no small amount of trouble in getting to China. None of the several candidates proposed for the job of archimandrite would accept and Metropolitan Veniamin of Kazan even refused, when asked, to help in the search. Finally Ioakim Shishkovskii was recruited and appointed as head of the mission on February 17, 1780. By the following summer the other members had been chosen.[80] Peltry was provided as usual, to be picked up in the

provincial chancellery in Irkutsk and exchanged for silver on the
Peking market. The mission was directed to observe Ch'ing ritual
in presenting its credentials, and it was given new chasubles, books,
and a new mitre for the archimandrite. Shishkovskii's supplementary
instructions also carried this injunction:

> While in Peking, when the proper occasions present themselves,
> but without arousing suspicions on the Chinese side or giving
> them grounds for finding in you any purposive examination
> into their affairs, gather information on whatever events are
> taking place in that remote empire which affect the thinking,
> behavior, and activities of the government, and keep a secret
> account for presentation, upon your return, to the College of
> Foreign Affairs, who would not be uninterested in having
> some reliable news of local occurrences.

And Shishkovskii was also reminded to behave well in a foreign
country: "Sufficient to say that your rank and title demand of you
the responsibility of addressing yourself not only to the acquisition
of souls in Christ, but equally to the honor of the sovereign."[81]

The mission left Moscow, "because of various delays," only on
October 14, 1780, but made a fast passage to Irkutsk, arriving on
January 5, 1781. Here its furs were picked up, Bishop Mikhail made
a present of myrrh and two antiminsia, and Vasilii Igumnov appeared to take the group beyond the frontier. But final departure
was again delayed by the exhaustion of the beasts of burden and
the oncoming summer heat. In addition, Hieromonk Antonii had
"behaved badly" on the frontier, and more time was taken in trying to extract an apology from him to the border commandant,
Vlasov. Then fresh horses were supplied by a local merchant,
Andrei Ikonnikov, and after waiting out the summer, the frontier
was passed on August 23, 1781.

The seventh mission entered Peking on November 2, and four
days later presented its papers at the Li-fan yuan. Both churches
were found in pitiful condition, causing Shishkovskii to doubt the
value of the inventory that Tsvet had compiled as his last act in
Peking. The new archimandrite also reported that "at the Nikolskii

church on holidays of the Lord I habitually saw only twelve men and two women; even they had grown out of the habit of going to confession and receiving the eucharist, and it is impossible to incline them to it ... And apart from the four houses in which Orthodox Christians are known to reside it is unknown how the others live, unknown when they die, or whether they are buried according to Chinese custom." Twelve years later Shishkovskii reported a total of thirty-five adherents in Peking: twenty-one Albazinian males, four females, and "ten natives."[82]

Although there were, during the time of the seventh mission in Peking, recurrent difficulties on the Sino-Russian border that led the Manchus to interrupt trade between the two countries, life in Peking itself was generally tranquil. The Li-fan yuan was punctilious in bringing the missionaries and students their monthly salaries. The Russians were free, furthermore, to walk around Peking and to visit the warm waters in the suburbs. Several times, it is noted, the students were summoned to the palace to translate foreign documents.[83] The only problem on record came from an intractable cleric named Ivan Orlov, a church servant who had been only fifteen years old when he joined the mission on its way to China. Orlov, in his rambunctious adolescence, tried the patience of everyone during the journey from Moscow to Peking, and possibly for that reason, was appointed to the more remote Nikolskii Church. There his responsibilities were simply to maintain the supply of communion bread and wine, but he refused to undertake this assignment from the archimandrite, causing services to stop indefinitely. During this time Orlov lived alone in the Albazinian chapel, busying himself by tending to the vineyard, ducks, chickens, and songbirds. Holding a grudge against Shishkovskii he twice complained to the Li-fan yuan about the archimandrite and asked to be sent back to Russia. Shishkovskii admonished him, to which he answered in rude language. He was thereupon beaten and arrested by the missionaries and finally sent back to Russia at the end of 1787.[84]

For the other members of the mission, however, there was no fixed equation between good behavior and survival. Death overtook many of them prematurely. Hieromonk Antonii died in 1782; Ivan Filonov, a student, died of unknown causes in 1792; Hierodeacon Israil died in the early part of 1795. Of the three students only Anton Vladykin lived to return to Russia, where he served as a dragoman at the College of Foreign Affairs. On May 21, 1795, Archimandrite Ioakim, seated Christ-like on a mule, led the remaining members of his mission out of Peking on the return road to Russia. At the third post-station on the outskirts of Kalgan he became ill and succumbed the following day. Shishkovskii was buried hurriedly, for nothing would now be allowed to slow the race of his survivors back to the motherland. Soon afterwards the site of his grave eroded tracelessly into the steppe.[85]

The eighteenth-century history of the Russian ecclesiastical mission, unlike that of the Jesuits, does not submit easily to a recapitulation of high points and low points, or of rise and decline. Almost as soon as its existence was formalized by the treaty of Kiakhta the mission encountered difficulties which kept it from attaining any notable heights. And because these difficulties were largely self-imposed, they cannot be used as a standard of how well, or how badly, the Manchu government received Russian missionaries in Peking. On the whole it appears that the Manchus were tolerant. Their policy, after all, had been not merely to tolerate, but to patronize the Russian "lamas" who visited Peking. Sustained by the support, and the good humor, of the Li-fan yuan, the Russian mission therefore came out of the eighteenth century more or less as it had started in 1728. If there had been no high points from which to fall, neither was the Russian mission threatened with the extinction of its work in China, as were the Roman Catholic missions at the turn of the century.

Manchu tolerance in Peking did not, however, mean that Russian missionaries would be tolerant of the fate that put them where they were, or of the conditions that they found there. Few of them had any sense of how to take advantage of ten years in the capital of China: they did not try to learn the Chinese and Manchu languages, they did not try to proselytize among the population of the city, they did not even try very hard to keep the mission buildings in decent shape. Instead they tried an imaginative assortment of means to shorten their tenure in Peking. They would ask to be returned to the motherland prematurely; they would commit crimes, or behave in a variety of deviant ways, and thereby hope to be expelled; they would get sick and blame it on the intolerable climate of northern China; they would drink; and they would die. Certainly these eighteenth-century missionaries should not be ridiculed for their failures. They appear rather heroic in their attempts to outlast a situation which they were hardly prepared to endure, and into which they carried little enlightenment and sympathy from their superiors in Russia.

Chapter VII

THE ECCLESIASTICAL MISSION AND THE PROBLEM OF
"CHINA" IN EIGHTEENTH-CENTURY RUSSIA

If we are to conclude, on the basis of its performance in the eighteenth century, that the Russian ecclesiastical mission functioned very imperfectly, and that no one seemed to care enough to correct its flaws, how can its institutional survival be explained? Once in Peking Russian missionaries told us little. They tried to withstand the city simply out of an instinct for self-preservation, making the best of their bad luck. Neither can the Li-fan yuan's treatment of the mission attest to more than the fact that it discharged its responsibilities rather matter-of-factly, taking only the precaution of applying an Inner Asian terminology to what it was doing. Since the authority for dispatching and recalling each mission belonged to Russia, it is in Russia that a better answer to the question of why it continued to exist, and what it was expected to accomplish, should be found. But even here it would be a mistake to subject the purposes of the mission to a hypothesis that assumed more than a casual relationship between fact and value.

Russian Missions at Home and Abroad
What were the compelling ecclesiastical bases of the mission in Peking? Inasmuch as the Russian mission was part of an eighteenth-century Orthodox missionary movement (and here our argument will be carefully qualified), it must be compared to the missionary work that was being conducted, at the same time, in remote areas within Russia. In 1725, for example, a mission was dispatched to Astrakhan that was quite similar, in its constitution, to the one already being contemplated by Vladislavich: it consisted of an archimandrite, a hieromonk, a priest, two deacons, six students, and a cook. At the same time the Synod began a quest for people who knew the Kalmuk language, since the grandson of Ayuki Khan, Petr Petrovich Taishin, had been converted in the early 1720s.

148

Later, in 1744, a mission was dispatched still further south, to the central Caucasus. Missionary efforts in the east were mostly concentrated around Kazan and Tobolsk, where new churches and new schools were being built for converted Tatars, but following the explorations of the Bering expedition of 1725–1730, church building picked up speed in remotest Eastern Siberia as well. And in 1742 a mission was sent to Kamchatka that again was similar to the mission in Peking, consisting of Archimandrite Ioasaf Khotutsevich, two hieromonks, two hierodeacons, and several students from the Moscow Academy.[1]

In eighteenth-century Siberia the political and ecclesiastical powers of the Russian state operated in a neatly leap-frogging manner, each giving to the other a *point d'appui* from which to continue the process of russifying the empire. Even in Kamchatka, as untamed as it still was, Russian missionaries had no doubt that they were in Russia. The only problem was to persuade the native peoples of it by causing them to be baptized and to accept new names. But as we have already had occasion to note, the convenience of this position ended in China, and the effect was confusing. Were Chinese and Manchu communicants, who were instructed to pray for the tsar, to be taken as subjects of Russia? This would have been very impractical. Indeed, the possibility of a Russian rites controversy seemed to have a withering effect on the interest that the Synod took in its China mission, and as a result, the trivial statistical accomplishments in China can stand no comparison with the exploits of the Siberian missions, where concepts of universality and nationality went happily hand in hand. Worse, the narrows of Orthodox dogma through which Russian missionaries approached their work in China helped make them narrow men as well. None of these people showed any interest in trying to learn Chinese or Manchu. (They relied, ironically, on Roman Catholic translations of basic catechisms throughout the eighteenth century.) Aleksei Vladykin, a student in the mission of Gervasii Lintsevskii, put the problem clearly to the Synod in 1753:

Archimandrite Gervasii [he wrote] and the other clerics do

not know Chinese. For them to know it—or for anyone who spends only seven years in Peking—is impossible. Because they do not know the language, it is difficult, even impossible, to carry on preachings and baptisms among the Chinese people. No religious person has had any success. Even though Chinese people are occasionally (but seldom) baptized and delivered of their baseness, they only receive it for one reason: it is because they are given clothes. But not knowing anything about the Christian faith they cannot adhere to it, and after selling the clothes they remain in their former condition. Thus the religious personnel only direct masses at the two churches, and there is no other work for them.[2]

Unable to make their proposition understood, missionaries had to depend on the persuasiveness of alms, which converts were given in order to buy underwear and charcoal. In general these proved insufficient to excite a durable faith. Amvrosii Yumatov complained that "without gratuities they do not wish to be baptized," and that "exhortations have no effect." Yumatov purportedly accomplished sixty-three conversions during his fifteen years in Peking, and his successor, Nikolai Tsvet, accounted for twenty-four. But by the arrival of Sofronii Gribovskii in 1794 only ten non-Albazinian natives were seen among the local adherents.[3]

Timkovskii confirms what is perfectly obvious, that by the turn of the century Russian archimandrites had acquired a substantial fear of converting Chinese and Manchus.[4] The source of this fear he prefers to assign to the troubles that were befalling the Roman Catholics at the time, which the Russian mission had no desire to share. Although it is hard to imagine that there would not always be something that Russian missionaries were afraid of in Peking, Timkovskii's explanation is helpful, for no discussion of the motive power, such as it was, behind the ecclesiastical mission in Peking should proceed without taking into account the curious competition between the Roman Catholic and Orthodox churches in China. Late in the seventeenth century the Jesuit presence in Peking had helped to excite in Russia a stubborn wish to have a mission there as well—a wish that antedated the discovery of the

Nikolskii church, and was by no means satisfied by it alone. In the early eighteenth century the Jesuits had two churches in Peking; after Kiakhta Russia also had two, the latter of which was more or less a copy of the French church inside the imperial city. Subsequently Russian archimandrites were instructed to maintain only the most proper relations with Jesuits and other Roman Catholics in Peking, if indeed any contact with them was necessary. One should not forget—not even in China—that it was impossible to reconcile the mortal divisions between the two churches. Of course in practice Russian missionaries like Amvrosii Yumatov had quickly discovered that the distinguishing characteristic of the Roman Catholics in Peking was that they were not Chinese, and therefore their company could be rather pleasant. But in St. Petersburg the Holy Synod nourished its fantasy of a silent struggle for survival in a place where there was little to lose. That, in fact, was the point: the competition, it turned out, was not for fame, or power, or influence, and certainly not for conversions. It was for survivial itself. Ever since Peter's first comment on the matter, in 1698, Russian missionaries had been advised not to press their advantage by being too zealous in the pursuit of their professions. The ukase of 1700, which instructed such a zeal, was an aberration and quickly gave way to more sober thinking. If only the members of the ecclesiastical mission were careful not to behave too much like missionaries, the chances of survival might yet favor the least fit to survive. The Jesuits, who did not appreciate the peculiarity of this Russian approach to its China mission, had lost to the Franciscans by the late eighteenth century; and when the Russian mission buried the last Franciscan in Peking in 1827[5] a historical game of some sort had been won, although the Synod had as little to show for its victory as it had had a century earlier.

Saving the Albazinians

Apart from its unannounced competition with the Roman Catholic church, the Russian ecclesiastical mission had a more immediate battle to fight, and it was a losing one. This was the struggle against the complete acculturation of the Albazinians. If the ruse

employed by the Manchus to capture Maksim Leont'ev, along with
Grigorii Mylnik and the others, had not succeeded; or if no attempt
had then been made by the Albazinians to continue their Orthodox
practices in China, there is little doubt that they would all have
simply been called "traitors," excommunicated perhaps, but in any
case forgotten. But this was impossible as long as they remained disposed toward their old religion. Of course it followed that Russia
should take an interest in maintaining their religious connections
with the homeland, where the ideas of sovereignty, nationality,
and religion were still very much confused in the eighteenth century. Exception should therefore be taken to Pavlovsky's judgment
that the Albazinians "were no longer needed, even as a pretext"
after the treaty of Kiakhta, and "were abandoned to their fate."[6]
Throughout the eighteenth century the Albazinians, far from being
a pretext, or being abandoned, continued to be a theoretical concern not only of the missionaries in Peking, but of the higher secular
and ecclesiastical powers in St. Petersburg. In the Orthodox view,
after all, it was much more important to keep the communicants
one already had than to risk their allegiance in an attempt to enlarge
the flock. Members of the Russian Orthodox Church were not
allowed to deny their faith and under most circumstances were not
supposed to leave Russia. But whenever it happened, as it had
happened in China, that a Russian Orthodox community existed
outside the territorial limits of the country, a responsibility was
felt, and usually taken, by the church to meet their religious needs.
For example, at the same time ecclesiastical missions were being
sent to Peking the Synod was taking measures for the "defense of
Orthodoxy" against Roman Catholics and Uniats in Poland. And
in 1733 a priest and four assistants were sent to Potsdam to attend
to the Orthodox Christians serving in the Prussian army, much like
the first mission to Peking in 1715. In 1768 the Synod indignantly
refused the suggestion of the Swedish ambassador that Lutheran
pastors conduct the religious services for the Orthodox Christians
living in Sweden.[7] In the same spirit the Russian missionaries, once
arrived in Peking, were expected to stave off the final submersion
of the Albazinians into the idolatrous Chinese world.

In practice, the Russian mission may have done as little for the Albazinians as for anyone else, especially after 1728, when it was relocated far away from the émigré quarter. Only twenty adherents were counted in 1756 and Shishkovskii, in 1784, saw only twelve men and two women regularly at the Nikolskii church.[8] By the time Timkovskii had reached Peking in 1820, the only faithful Albazinians were "an old man named Aleksei and two relatives."[9] But it was indeed a curious twist of missionary history that underlay the attempt—such as it was—to keep the Albazinians within the fold of the Orthodox church. Instead of Christianizing the Chinese, Russian missionaries were supposed to de-sinify their countrymen. If a Chinese Baptist in the mid-nineteenth century was often a suspicious character, how much more questionable were the Cossack offspring in eighteenth-century Peking who, whether they attended church or not, were obviously connected in the popular mind with those outlandish monks from the southern part of the city. This is one of the ironic tragedies of the mission, to which Russian historians have been oblivious. For Adoratskii it was a display of heroics that the Russian ecclesiastical mission could try to keep a pitiful ghetto of Albazinians from sinking into the "huge ethnographic laboratory" or the "heavy heathen gloom" of China, as it appeared to them in the late nineteenth century.[10]

Missionary Diplomacy

As much as the ecclesiastical activities of the Russian mission in Peking were reduced to appearances in the course of the eighteenth century, still more nominal was its function as a diplomatic outpost. In St. Petersburg the College of Foreign Affairs, which collaborated with the Synod in sending each new mission on its way, shared with the Synod the view that it was not so much what was accomplished in Peking that mattered, but simply the fact that the mission was there. The residence of both Izmailov and Vladislavich in the Hui-t'ung kuan, and Lange's use of it for his "consulate," had begun the process whereby Russia could persuade itself that it had a diplomatic establishment in the Ch'ing capital. The rationalization was not especially subtle, for after the treaty of Kiakhta no properly constituted or empowered ambassador set foot inside the Russian hostel until 1859.[11] But in the second quarter of the eighteenth century priests and church equipment had been dispatched to Russian embassies in Paris, Amsterdam, and Stockholm,[12] as well as to Peking; and afterwards the Synod was periodically instructed to ask the College of Foreign Affairs in what countries Russia was represented abroad, whether there were priests on hand to provide religious assistance, and if so, how they were being paid.[13] In China the Russian ecclesiastical mission gave St. Petersburg a means to syllogize this orderly pursuit of Russian foreign affairs: because Russian embassies always had priests, and because Russia had priests in Peking, it followed that an embassy also existed there. Throughout the eighteenth century the more one made reference to an embassy in Peking, the more it appeared that the mission was exactly that. Whatever the facts of the situation, the figure of speech had a historical momentum of its own.

Toward the end of the century Russia began to modify this pretense, not by insinuating diplomats into the mission in Peking, but by asking its archimandrites—Tsvet and Shishkovskii—to behave more like spies. Such a proposition undoubtedly gave these ecclesiastics an exciting sense of mission, now quite lacking in the prosecution of their other duties, but there is no evidence that it ever came to anything, at least not until the time of Bichurin in the early nineteenth century. Of course it was foolish to expect reliable espionage from people who could not learn enough Chinese to conduct baptisms; there is more significance in the simple-mindedness of the attempt to get around the problem of a diplomatic mission without diplomats.

Russian Sinology in the Eighteenth Century

During the eighteenth century officials in the Russian government became so inured to the expectation that their outpost in Peking would never amount to more than a verbalized importance that they were hardly in a frame of mind, when the mission did accomplish something of substance, to appreciate the fact. Such, at least, is one conclusion that may be drawn from the eighteenth-century history of this institution as a language school, to which we should now return. The O-lo-ssu hsueh was particularly noteworthy because, unlike most of Russia's foreign language schools, it was located abroad, in the very center of the country whose languages were supposed to be learned.[14] This simple difference was of great significance, for throughout the eighteenth century Russia had little success with language instruction in its own academies. Especially was this true of the languages of East Asia, and recounting something of the experience of trying to learn them within Russia may help to establish the historical importance of the O-lo-ssu hsueh.

Long before the instruction of Chinese and Manchu was undertaken, Russia had opened a Japanese school through the offices of a man named Dembei, whom Volodimir Atlasov had found shipwrecked on Kamchatka in 1697. Dembei was sent to the capital, received in audience by Peter the Great in 1702, and three years later, after enough time had passed for him to learn Russian, began teaching.[15] After five years he asked to return to Japan, as Peter purportedly had promised he could. Instead Dembei was forcibly baptized, given the Christian name of Gavriil, and his continued residence in Russia was thereby assured. Meanwhile, arrangements were already being made to locate more of these useful survivors of Japanese shipwrecks. A man named Sanima was found, christened with the name Ivan, and sent to St. Petersburg in 1714. In 1729 two more Japanese, Sozo and Gonzo,[16] were taken and presented (in 1734) to Tsarina Anna, who ordered that they be baptized. In the process Sozo became Kuzma Shulz and Gonzo, Demian Pomortsev. In June, 1736, Shulz and Pomortsev began teaching Japanese to two students at the Academy of Sciences; Shulz, however, died the same year and Pomortsev lasted only until 1739. With the exception of three small primers that they had left behind, Russia was once again without any means of Japanese instruction. During the 1740s several more Japanese were brought to the St. Petersburg school, but none, it turned out, had any aptitude for teaching. Before he left for Peking in 1744 Archimandrite Gervasii

Lintsevskii was therefore given the hopeless assignment by the College of Foreign Affairs of finding a man in China who knew Japanese to teach the Russian students there; or failing that, to send two or more of the students to a Chinese coastal town "near Japan" or to Japan itself.[17] Instead, in 1753, the Japanese school was moved nearer Japan—to Irkutsk—where it remained until 1816. Its moment of supreme opportunity had come in 1792, almost a century after the teaching of Japanese began in Russia, when one of its students was chosen to accompany the Laxman embassy to Japan. The Japanese were unable to understand him. Barthold concludes of this school that "during all this time it produced no one competent in Japanese and left no trace in the history of Russian Orientalism."[18]

Not until 1725 was the study of Mongolian begun seriously; it was undertaken in the Voznesenskii monastery outside Irkutsk by Archimandrite Antonii Platkovskii. Platkovskii, it will be remembered, had accompanied Izmailov's embassy to Peking in 1720, before leading his own mission there at the end of the decade. Evidently it was on the road to China that Izmailov suggested to Platkovskii that he initiate the instruction of Mongolian; like most envoys before him, Izmailov was dependent on the Jesuits, and although he had acquired three Mongol interpreters in Selenginsk[19] there is no evidence that they functioned effectively. Before crossing the frontier Izmailov had received an official paper from China written in Mongolian. His interpreters from Selenginsk notwithstanding, there was no one in the vicinity who could translate it for him. Finally a converted Mongol family was discovered; they were not exactly literate, and two days were required for a translation of the note to be presented. Even then no one knew for certain whether it was accurate. At this juncture Izmailov made his suggestion to Platkovskii, saying that if the Jesuits could learn Oriental languages coming all the way from Europe, then Russian priests could at least make no excuses for not trying.[20]

Afterwards, as Platkovskii conceived his plan, the Mongolian school would be established in the Preobrazhenskii monastery, and children of the clerical estate, as well as orphans, would be chosen as students, with the aim of training them as translators. At a later date the study of Chinese would begin. When permission for this enterprise was sought from Antonii Stakhovskii, the metropolitan of Tobolsk, it was refused. Never one to be outdone, Platkovskii thereupon presented his plan directly to the Synod, which agreed to it. In a series of ukases dating from late 1724, the Synod entrusted Platkovskii with the establishment of the school in the Voznesenskii monastery which was to open in the autumn of 1725. Among other measures, a christened lama named Ivan was to be hired as the teacher, and six soldiers would be provided to help construct the school and then collect the students for it.[21] Although Platkovskii took three of his students with him when he returned to Peking in 1729, the school itself soon failed and closed down completely in 1739. In 1744 the idea of a Mongolian school in the monastery was revived for a short while, but rejected on the unimaginative precedent of the earlier failure. At the end of the century, in 1790, classes in Mongolian, Chinese, and Manchu were successively opened in the provincial academy in Irkutsk, but after four years these too were abandoned "because of their difficulty and awkwardness."[22]

The initial Russian efforts to learn Chinese and Manchu were quite as haphazard. In 1725, the year in which it was being decided to send Russian students to Peking, and when Platkovskii's Mongolian school had opened its doors far away in Irkutsk, a German philologist, Theofile Siegfried Bayer, was invited to Russia to join the newly established Academy of Sciences in St. Petersburg. Bayer soon set to work on a Chinese-Latin dictionary which, when completed in 1734, included ten thousand characters. The academicians, who had so far approved this project, now realized that in order to publish the dictionary, and thereby make it available to students who would be departing for or returning from China, it would be necessary to engrave ten thousand wood blocks in Chinese calligraphy. No one, apart from Bayer, could see any redeeming value in going to this effort. The project was dropped and the dictionary remained in single copy in the Academy library.[23] In the same year, however, St. Petersburg suddenly had its first returned student from China. This was Ivan Pukhort, who had left the capital with Vladislavich and whom Lange had redeemed from Peking in the fall of 1732. Upon his arrival two years later, Pukhort was immediately put to work in the Academy. But since the German import, Bayer, seemed to have sinological matters well in hand, Pukhort was assigned in turn to the German section as a copyist. There he promptly forgot everything he had learned in Peking.[24]

The problem with Bayer, who was a reactionary by present-day Soviet standards and very likely deserves this label, was that his strait-laced philological investigations permitted no interest in Chinese as a living language which, like French or German, it might conceivably be useful to Russians to speak and read. For these dubious practical pursuits the Academy was entirely unsuited and therefore had nothing to do with the first Russian instruction in the languages of China, which came about the same time that Bayer's dictionary was shelved and Pukhort's German was displacing his Manchu and Chinese. In the early 1730s a Manchu named Chou Ko had been sent on an espionage assignment to the camp of Chereng Dondub, the son of Ayuki Khan, in order to ascertain where his loyalties lay and thereby improve the Ch'ing estimate of the power of the Zunghar *kontaisha*. He was confined in Chereng's camp until 1733, when a Russian emissary, Major Ugrimov, happened to be passing through the Turghud *ulus* on the return from a visit to the Zunghars. For some reason, the sister of Chereng Dondub caused Chou Ko to be sent to Tobolsk with Ugrimov, hoping that the Russians would be able to arrange his passage back to China. In Tobolsk, however, these plans were changed. Chou Ko, possessing information inimical to the interests of Russia in Central Asia, was sent in the opposite direction, to Moscow, where he arrived under guard in 1734. Here, however, the situation was sensitive for the reason that there remained a group of Kalmuks who had accompanied a Ch'ing embassy to Russia in 1731. If word of Chou Ko's whereabouts reached them it would certainly also reach Peking, a contingency to be strenuously avoided. Therefore Chou Ko was led over a long and circuitous detour to St. Petersburg, arriving two years later in 1736. On September 11, 1737, he was baptized,

renamed Fedor Petrov, and given the daughter of an Orthodox
Kalmuk in marriage. A year later he applied for permission to
return to China, which was obviously refused. Instead Chou Ko was
put to worthwhile service: he was returned to Moscow, given two
students, and began a short career as an instructor in Manchu and
Chinese at the College of Foreign Affairs. His class consisted of
Andrei Kanaev and Aleksei Leont'ev, students who learned very
quickly and in the space of two years—according to the claim made
by Chou Ko—had completely exhausted his competence to teach
them any more, since he, a soldier by profession, was not very
literate. Obtaining instructional materials had also been a problem,
but most acute was the fact that this arrangement was not making
anyone any money, both teacher and students being very poorly
paid. In 1741, therefore, Kanaev and Leont'ev were sent off to
Peking. As for Chou Ko he was made an ensign and assigned to
the garrison of Arkhangel, as far from the Chinese frontier as one
could be. For his efforts over the previous two years he received a
total of fifty rubles. He died on March 9, 1751.[25]

The inconsequential career of Chou Ko, or Fedor Petrov, like
that of Theofile Bayer, left Russia by 1741 with nothing but the
O-lo-ssu hsueh in Peking to provide the state with people who knew
the Chinese and Manchu languages. Of course not every student
who went to Peking to study managed to graduate; that much has
already been established. Over a third of them died there in the
course of the eighteenth century; of the remainder only a handful
came back knowing enough to make themselves useful, and of
these few, finally, the tsarist government often showed a curious
want of intelligence in placing them in practical positions. Such
conditions, however, were expectable. The exceptional feature of
the O-lo-ssu hsueh was that, inasmuch as it was attached to a durable
institution in Peking, it did not suffer the fate of extinction that
befell most Oriental language schools in eighteenth-century Russia.
Therefore it could be argued that even under the adverse circumstances of the time chance alone favored the emergence of several
good students who, by their heroic labors, succeeded in putting
Russian sinology in a competitive position with that of the rest of

Europe by the end of the eighteenth century. The tragedy was that
no one realized it.

The greatest of these was Ilarion Kalinovich Rossokhin, the
son of a priest, who was born, probably in 1707, in either Irkutsk,
Nerchinsk, Selenginsk, or the village of Khilok.[26] In 1725 he began
the study of Mongolian in the Voznesenskii monastery; four years
later he accompanied his archimandrite, Antonii Platkovskii, to
China. By 1735 his studies had proceeded well enough to qualify
him for service as a translator for the Li-fan yuan and as a teacher
on the faculty of the O-lo-ssu wen kuan, a position respectably
salaried at forty taels a year. At the same time Lorents Lange suggested to the College of Foreign Affairs that Rossokhin be awarded
the rank of ensign with a yearly income of one hundred and fifty
rubles for his success in obtaining a map of China and translating
its place names into Russian. Of Rossokhin's spare time in Peking
it is said that while his colleagues caroused together he was busily
learning the technique of Chinese rocketry.[27] Once he had also
taken the trouble to steal Platkovskii's diary.

In 1740 Rossokhin left Peking with the courier Mikhail
Shokurov. He arrived in St. Petersburg on March 5, 1741, and was
assigned immediately to the Academy of Sciences to translate from
Chinese and Manchu. Rossokhin also received permission to open
a language school at the Academy. Four students were drafted for
this purpose, but they were obtained from garrison schools and
were quite probably sons of common soldiers. The school lasted
ten years, until 1751, and then it simply closed its doors, having
achieved no results.[28] The students might well have been sent to
Peking, as Leont'ev and Kanaev had been after studying under
Chou Ko, but they were not and instead disappear entirely from
view. Rossokhin's most significant work was in making translations
from Chinese and Manchu. When he returned from Peking he
brought more than a hundred books with him. These, added to the
few materials that Vladislavich and Lange[29] had brought back and
those that had been acquired from Jesuits, gave Russia a not
inconsiderable collection of Chinese and Manchu texts. But by
this time T. S. Bayer had been dead for three years, and there was

no one in the Academy of Sciences, to say nothing of the empire at large, capable of recognizing the value of these holdings. Moreover there was no one to give support and patronage to the task of translation. Thus Rossokhin labored largely on his own, without guidance and without help. The academician closest to his work was G. F. Müller, but when the question arose of whether to proceed with a translation of a Chinese text, Müller could only compare the abstract Rossokhin had prepared with the books on China in other European languages in the academy library. A judgment would then be made, presumably, if no likeness were discovered.[30] It was not a very scientific method for determining the value of a translation enterprise.

It should also be pointed out that until the return of Aleksei Leont'ev from China Rossokhin had no assistance in his work, apart from what his students could provide. In 1741, as he was beginning his employment, Rossokhin asked that Chou Ko (Fedor Petrov) be attached to the Academy with him. To this the Academy replied that it had no need of Chou Ko, and was not even certain of being able to maintain Rossokhin in his present position.[31] At last he succeeded in having Ivan Pukhort, his fellow-student from the second mission in China, transferred to his department. But Pukhort's services to Rossokhin were painfully limited, and he soon petitioned to be relieved of his position, to which the Academy acceded, agreeing that he was "not capable of anything." Pukhort was back at work as a copyist when he became involved in an imbroglio which attempted the removal of Johann Schumacher, a German, from his powerful position as permanent secretary of the Academy. Pukhort was arrested and confined, and when Schumacher was restored in 1744, was severed from the Academy. The last one hears of him, this returned student from Peking was employed as a "stable clerk" in a detachment of Polish cadets. A somewhat similar fate befell another returned student, Ivan Bykov, whose literary Manchu was quite acceptable for a career of teaching and translating. But in 1748, when he presented himself to the College of Foreign Affairs for assignment, there happened to be no particular correspondence with China, at least none that required translating, and Bykov was dismissed. What became of him is a mystery.[32]

Rossokhin, meanwhile, employing his unprecedented abilities in Manchu, Chinese, and Mongolian, compiled altogether more than thirty annotated translations during his lifetime.[33] Often he would ask the Academy to publish his works, no doubt considering them of some importance. But either such a request was denied outright, or returned with the notation that an "examination" of the material was necessary first—a long and slow process which often meant, in fact, that the manuscripts remained forever buried in the archives of the Academy. For sixteen years Rossokhin remained at his starting salary, unhealthy, in debt, unappreciated by the European professors around him, receiving from the Academy pens, paper, a pound of candles a week, and little else. In 1757 he was at last given a raise to three hundred rubles with the rank of second lieutenant. During the lifetime of this remarkable man of little formal education, unquestionably Russia's first and still one of its greatest sinologues, not one of his translations was published. He died on February 10, 1761. A small annuity was given to his wife and daughter.[34]

Notwithstanding the oblivion to which Rossokhin's career seemed consigned, there had been some promising developments. Most important, the Academy of Sciences and the College of Foreign Affairs were beginning to entertain the possibility that their respective interests in China might well overlap. This was good news for any China expert in search of employment, for it meant not only that the college would perhaps find something useful for a returned student from Peking to do, but also that translation enterprises could have a value hitherto uncontemplated. These horizons had sufficiently broadened by 1747 to open a position of translator of Chinese and Manchu in the College of Foreign Affairs, promptly filled by Aleksei Vladykin when he returned, in that year, from China. Soon Vladykin was appointed to lead the caravan of 1753 to Peking, an occasion that the Academy of Sciences thereupon took in order to send along one of its own members (a European, Frants Elachich) with a list of books to acquire which had been carefully prepared by Rossokhin.[35] Among

them was the *Pa-ch'i t'ung-chih,* or the *Annals of the Eight Banners.*
This was a major work on early Manchu history, recondite enough
to be of interest to the Academy, and yet obviously dealing with
the forbears of those contemporary rulers of China with whom the
College of Foreign Affairs was trying to get along. (Indeed, if it
were read closely enough, Russians would discover how adroitly
K'ang-hsi had used their expatriate countrymen in winning the
battles of Albazin.) Rossokhin, who was already undertaking the
translation of Tulishen's account of the Manchu embassy to Ayuki
Khan, the *I-yü-lu,* had made another good choice, and soon the
translation of the *Annals* was to occupy most of the remaining
years of his life. Vladykin's caravan was admitted at the frontier
without any trouble, but once it arrived in Peking the Li-fan yuan
was unhappy to see Vladykin a second time. When he had left
China earlier he had carried away a map of the empire and a plan
of the capital (for which he had paid 1500 rubles); now he was
employing his expertise to help Russian merchants demand fair
prices for their furs. This was an inconvenient situation; the
Manchu means of dealing with it was to state that Vladykin was
obviously "an inexperienced and stupid man in matters of trade,"
and to express the wish that people like him, "and especially those
who had been students in Peking," not be sent as caravan leaders.[36]
Elachich did, however, get his books, which included the *Annals
of the Eight Banners.*[37]

Vladykin also brought back to Russia Aleksei Leont'ev, who
became the successor to Rossokhin and the second noteworthy
Russian sinologist of the day. Leont'ev was born in 1716 into the
family of a church servant. He attended the Moscow Academy and
then, when he was twenty-three, began the study of Chinese under
Chou Ko. In 1742 he was sent to Peking along with his fellow-
student Andrei Kanaev. Back in St. Petersburg Leont'ev was designated a translator for the College of Foreign Affairs, but soon was
sent to the Academy of Sciences to collaborate with Rossokhin on
the *Annals.* After the latter's death in 1761, Leont'ev continued on
his own. He was now a very busy man, having taken a great deal of
other work upon himself—some of it rather unnecessarily, it would

appear, for he set out to translate Tulishen's narrative in spite of
the fact that G. F. Müller had finally published Rossokhin's rendi-
tion of it in his *Monthly Notices* for 1764.[38] Leont'ev also proposed
to the College of Foreign Affairs the opening of a new school of
Chinese and Manchu—a more important undertaking, for there were
then no students in Peking with Archimandrite Amvrosii Yumatov,
and not yet any assurances that students would again be admitted
to China. The college agreed and gave him one thousand rubles for
the enterprise. Leont'ev conscripted as his assistant a baptized
Chinese named "Vasiliev" who had been found in Stavropol, and
four students.[39] Classes began in Leont'ev's school in May, 1763.
Although information on its further history is scarce, it does appear
as if the school suffered a now familiar fate. Two of the four students were sent away in 1765 because they themselves insisted on
being incapable of further study. A third disappears from the record
completely. The last student, Iakov Korkin, went to Kiakhta in
1767 and was included in the sixth ecclesiastical mission to Peking.[40]
There he made a bad impression on the people, and his name came
to be invoked by Manchu mothers who wished to scold or frighten
their children.[41] Korkin died in China on September 8, 1779, at the
age of thirty-four.

Leont'ev himself left for the Chinese frontier again in 1767 as
secretary and interpreter to the Russian envoy, Ivan Kropotov;[42]
out of this mission came the Sino-Russian protocol of 1768, which
Leont'ev had the satisfaction of translating into and out of Manchu,
far outdistancing the now meager abilities of his counterparts on the
other side of the border. Afterwards, in St. Petersburg, he continued
his work at the Academy of Sciences and the College of Foreign
Affairs, and occasionally even advised Catherine II.[43] Less than a
generation separated him from Rossokhin but he was employed
more practically and remunerated more handsomely for his
services. He died in 1786, two years after the publication of the
joint translation of the *Pa-ch'i t'ung-chih*.[44]

Leont'ev's death fortuitously followed the return of several
other students of promise from Peking. He was replaced at the
College of Foreign Affairs by Fedor Baksheev, a member of the

sixth ecclesiastical mission of Nikolai Tsvet. While Tsvet's mission had amounted to little, the students—of whom Baksheev was one—had taken to heart the new interest of the College of Foreign Affairs in learning all that it could about the state of things in China. They came back with a manuscript, importantly titled "A Journal of the Secret Activities, Intentions, Events, and Changes in the Ch'ing Empire from 1772–1782," at the beginning of which they write that "On various occasions we had cordial relations with both Manchus and Chinese, and in those friendly, frequent relationships we saw a lot of each other, and whether through kindnesses or gifts we acquired many friends of whom some were always open with us while many revealed to us secrets which pertained particularly to the empire."[45] This was the language Russia wanted to hear—not the sinological digressions of a Rossokhin! Although Baksheev died in 1787, after a year of employment at the college, his place was taken by another student from the sixth mission, Aleksei Semeno-vich Agafonov. A third student, Aleksei Paryshev, remained in the service of Governor Iakobi in Irkutsk.[46] Before he died, Baksheev had compiled a Manchu-Russian dictionary, and Paryshev was the author of some twenty manuscripts, but none of the works of either man were ever published. Agafonov, however, had more success, managing to find a publisher for six of his translations of Chinese pieces that dealt, rather repetitiously, with the moral philosophy of the Confucian school.

From the seventh mission (1781–1794) under Ioakim Shishkovskii emerged another student who was able to take over the position of translator at the College of Foreign Affairs, which probably had lain vacant since the death of Agafonov in 1792. This was Anton Grigor'evich Vladykin, by birth a Kalmuk, and the only survivor among the students of this mission's thirteen years in Peking. In China Vladykin had distinguished himself by trans-lating for the Li-fan yuan and by drafting a plan of the city of Peking which he presented to the college on his return. In 1798, partly perhaps as a result of suggestions that Vladykin had made since first attempting to learn Chinese and Manchu in Peking, the college again established a language school, with a theoretical capability of instruction in Persian, Turkish, and Tatar, besides Manchu and Chinese. The school was generously funded with three thousand rubles and Vladykin was invited to teach in it. Three students attended his classes in the Ch'ing languages, beginning in 1799. Progress was made: after a year the students were able to write a thousand characters. Vladykin, for his part, was a devoted teacher, compiling three textbooks of Manchu and five dictionaries for the use of his students. Unaccountably, the school closed in 1801. Four years later Anton Vladykin was attached to Count Golovkin's abortive embassy to China. In 1808 he presented Tsar Alexander I with a portion of his translated works, which included a history of the Yuan dynasty, and a Chinese novel.[47] Nothing, however, came of this gesture. Having failed, like most of his predecessors, to get anything published, Vladykin perished in 1811.

What we are left with, as the eighteenth century at last gave way to the nineteenth, is the conclusion that there was little the Russian mission could do to break out of the intellectual fetters in which its existence was bound. It may have done no less than was expected of it, but rarely was it allowed to do more. This was particularly true of its academic function, for despite the ability and industry of some of the graduates of the O-lo-ssu hsueh, the narrow purposes of the College of Foreign Affairs and the Academy of Sciences continued to describe the limits of Russian expertise on China. To be sure, a narrow purpose was better than no purpose at all, but the full extent of what had been accomplished would have revealed itself only to anyone taking the trouble to poke through the basement of the Academy. The existence of a Russian appetite for a more encyclopedic knowledge about China cannot be in doubt, because there were, in the latter eighteenth century, at least half a dozen instances of major publications on the subject that had been translated from French.[48] This was the problem—that the interest remained Europocentric and the field of sinology therefore remained a European preserve. Whenever Montesquieu or Voltaire, or Jesuit letters, had something to say on China it would be infinitely more interesting to the salons of St. Petersburg than anything

Ilarion Rossokhin could ever expect to write. Indeed, their national energies were so wholly absorbed in the process of "Westernization" that Russians were unable to focus attention on their *own* experience in China. Systematic exploration of even less Westernized societies outside of the Russian empire seemed irrelevant, or at least of little intrinsic importance.

The institutional weakness of the Russian mission in Peking was certainly a consequence, not a cause, of such a prejudice. At any point, had St. Petersburg so desired, more competent people could have been sent to China. Their expenses could have been better managed, and their needs better attended to. Their purposes could have been better defined and their work given more encouragement. They could have been better employed upon their return. Even internal bureaucratic difficulties could have been overcome, if someone high enough in the state councils had decided to press the issue. But no one in St. Petersburg was looking eastward. The intellectual frontiers within Russia acted more rigidly than the Sino-Russian border itself in limiting the opportunities of a missionary presence in Peking, for they made unimaginable the idea that members of the Russian mission might enter an open competition with either the Jesuits in China or their Enlightened equals in Paris. The growth of a Russian "national consciousness,"[49] which may have begun in this century, did not reach the ecclesiastical mission until well into the next.

Chapter VIII

SINO-RUSSIAN RELATIONS
IN THE EIGHTEENTH CENTURY

The Russian ecclesiastical mission in Peking has been understood, in this essay, as an institution that owed its origins to peculiar
historical circumstances, but which thereafter became one of those
essential means whereby the Sino-Russian treaty system, in Mancall's words, "permitted each side . . . to interpret the relationship in
terms of its own traditions."[1] Since this book is preponderantly
about the eighteenth century, it would perhaps be useful to return
to a consideration of the larger historical events of the time in Sino-
Russian relations and, as a conclusion, to reiterate the simple proposition that this mission was the thread—often the only thread—on
which those relations were suspended.

The "Kiakhta System"

As we have been at pains to observe, the geography of Inner
Asia had been responsible for the enormity of the problems in
Sino-Russian relations and had made all the more imperative the
need to find solutions to them. What came out of this need was the
"Kiakhta System," or a treaty relationship that held out the possibility of giving to both Russia and China more or less what they
were looking for. The provisions for trade at the frontier and in
Peking, the drawing of the boundary, the practice of returning
fugitives, the correspondence between the Senate and the Li-fan
yuan, and the Russian mission in Peking were all parts of the same
system, operating in various ways to satisfy the demands of stability
in Sino-Russian relations. Another example was the custom, appearing in the eighteenth century, of paying respects to a new emperor.
This practice, although soon observed more in the breach, had
served as a partial pretext for the Vladislavich mission to China
after the death of K'ang-hsi, and the Manchus reciprocated in 1729
and 1731, when missions were sent to Moscow and St. Petersburg

to congratulate Tsar Peter II and Tsarina Anna Ioannovna on their respective accessions to the throne.[2] Obviously in none of these cases were the aims of the embassies confined only to the ceremonial celebration of an accession; they also served as a convenient cover for the testing of important decisions. Not only did the Manchu missions alert Russia to the Ch'ing intention of resuming the campaign against the Zunghars, but the pattern of the earlier embassy in 1713–1715 was repeated: the Turghud Mongols living on the Volga were again visited in 1729, to be coaxed into an anti-Zunghar frame of mind. In Moscow and St. Petersburg both embassies agreeably observed Russian court ritual. They may stand out in Ch'ing history as noteworthy exceptions to usual tributary practice, long before Anson Burlingame was sent abroad by the T'ung-chih emperor, but it would hardly suffice to attribute this apparent aberration to the inexperience of the Yung-cheng emperor in his role as the son of heaven.[3] It has already been established that the early Manchu approach to Russia was a strand of Inner Asian history that ought not be braided into larger generalizations about Sino-Western relations during the Ch'ing period.

To be sure, neither Russia nor China was willing to entertain an embassy that did not adhere to established forms inside their frontiers. In 1731 the Manchus also dispatched a mission to Russia that was directed only to the Turghud. It waited at Kiakhta for more than three years and never received permission to proceed. In 1740 the Russians asked the Li-fan yuan to admit an embassy of Kalmuks who were on their way to pay tribute to the Dalai Lama, but since the Kalmuks were listed as "Russian subjects" they were refused.[4] Nevertheless, between one court and the other the idea persisted that embassies could be exchanged, and that new emperors should be visited. When Shokurov was in Peking in 1745, after announcing the accession of Elizabeth Petrovna, he asked the Li-fan yuan if China intended to send an embassy to celebrate the occasion. To this the Manchus replied that it was impossible since no Russian embassy had come to congratulate the Ch'ien-lung emperor ten years earlier. Shokurov then stated that one had to be informed of such things in order to observe them, and that Russia had not been properly informed.[5] Later on, the enormous embassy of Count Golovkin to China in 1805 was explained by a wish to congratulate the Chia-ch'ing emperor on his accession although he, like Ch'ien-lung in 1745, had already been ruling for ten years.

What the Treaty of Kiakhta did not supply an immediate answer to was the question of whether this system, once begun, would continue to work to the advantage of either side. This was the more true because Russia and China were interested in different results, some of which were mutually quite incompatible. One of these was the caravan trade in Peking: Russia wanted it, China did not. Lange had already complained about the difficulties of the caravan of 1727–1728; the caravan of 1732 survived largely because of a gift of ten thousand taels from the Board of Revenue.[6] In 1736 Lange complained again about the restrictions being applied to his caravan of that year.[7] And it was because the Lebratovskii caravan of 1745 sold so badly that the Sibirskii Prikaz decided to employ Aleksei Vladykin, a former student at the Russian mission who had contacts and expertise, as the director of the caravan of 1755. Otherwise nothing was done, for the border trade was going on throughout this time, with little interruption, and Russia was, in any case, anxious to give its new relationship with China a chance before the storm warnings of a disconsolate Vladislavich would be taken seriously. Indeed, the 1730s were experienced as a time of new commercial opportunity, when Russia could feel free to dispatch to the Chinese frontier a variety of expeditions, from one that sought to discover how to make gold and silver from lead, to another that purported to investigate the cultivation of rhubarb.[8] To smooth the way for commercial adventures like these, the College of Foreign Affairs had, in 1730, informed its frontier commandant that he must observe the provisions of the treaty and send back to China anyone wandering, whether intentionally or not, onto the Russian side. Russian compliance was further attested by an obliging note sent to the Li-fan yuan in 1733, and, later in the decade, by repeated instructions to the new governor of Eastern Siberia, Bibikov, to repatriate all border-crossers.[9] During these years many fugitive Mongols were indeed run down and returned to China. Russia was obviously prepared to be a peaceful, not to say docile, neighbor.

To the Manchus the single-minded Russian attention to the question of trade was good news, for it meant that the "Kiakhta System" was, at the very least, functioning successfully in the tradition of border horse markets, using the promises of the China market to discredit the aggressive ideas of barbarians like Vladis-lavich.[10] But it did more than that. Kiakhta soon gave the Yung-cheng emperor his long awaited opportunity for being aggressive himself by resuming the dynastic war of attrition against the Zunghars. Many of his ministers still demurred, being mistrustful not so much of the strength of the Kiakhta Treaty (for here Manchu intelligence was very good) as of the odds of gaining a rapid verdict on a battlefield that was bound to be much further from the center of Manchu power than, for example, Jao Modo had been. But Yung-cheng persisted with his preparations, appointed fifty generals, and sent off his Northern Route army in 1730. The eagerly awaited results of this campaign were not long in reaching Peking: in 1731, at Hoton Nor, the Manchu army was stalled by the Zunghar *kontaisha* Galdan Tsereng, son and successor of Tsewang Arabtan. A peace was finally signed in 1739, three years after the death of Yung-cheng, making the Altai mountains the boundary between Zungharia and China. Ch'ing troops did not cross them again until 1755. If anything could be retrieved from this disaster, it was Russia that turned out to be the most consoling, for it had dutifully expelled all the Mongols who, caught in the path of the plundering Manchu troops, attempted to find protection across the frontier.[11]

Russia's cooperative policy drowned out all dissenting voices, to which Lorents Lange had now added his own: "At this moment—he wrote in 1733—the Chinese are in a critical position. They are afraid of Russia and at the same time look to us to supply their armies with provisions and horses for the war with the Zunghars. The moment is most opportune to intervene in Peking and demand that all restrictions placed upon our caravans be removed, that the Russian house be freed of the insufferable surveillance of the Mandarins, which hinders all trade, and that the dispute concerning frontiers be settled favorably ... We even believe that this is an excellent time to seek the extension of our frontier to the Amur River."[12] But Old China Hands are notoriously unable to get their points across, and Lange had nothing to do but suffer the conviction that he was right and almost everyone else was wrong.

Amursana

Galdan Tsereng himself died in 1745, and soon the Khanate was torn apart by civil war between two of his sons. How quickly the tables had turned—from that period of prosperity and development in Ili that had begun under Tsewang Arabtan and withstood an invasion from China, to a situation that practically invited the Manchus to reappear. In the middle of 1755 the Northern Route army, now led by two Mongols, Bandi and Amursana, finally made good its entrance into Ili. There was little resistance, but the Manchus, with many memories of scores that needed evening, proceeded to massacre the population anyway. From these ashes no nomadic empire was ever again to rise in Inner Asia. Back in Peking, now in the twentieth year of his reign, the Ch'ien-lung emperor was ready to enjoy this final victory, left to him by his father and grandfather, when the news suddenly came that Amursana was being troublesome. The latter, a maternal grandson of Tsewang Arabtan, had derived in himself a proprietary claim to Ili, and none of the rewards that the emperor had given him for his important part in the Manchu campaign (least of all the portrait of him that had been commissioned of Giuseppe Catiglione[13]) could stay the independent ambitions of this Mongol.

After the bulk of the Manchu army had withdrawn from Zungharia, Amursana and his followers rebelled. For half a year he was master of Ili; then, when the Manchus re-entered, he fled westward to Kazakhstan. Notwithstanding the emperor's displeasure at not capturing him, the troops were again withdrawn. This opened up an opportunity for another insurrection, which Amursana returned to lead. In 1757 the rebels were routed for the last time, but Amursana still made good his escape, not to the

Kazakhs, who were now less hospitable toward him, but into Siberia.

In sudden possession of Amursana Russia did not act at all expectably, for its fugitive was not straightway returned to China. Had the alarming conquest of Ili had the effect of opening Russian eyes at last to the insidious Manchu designs on Inner Asia? To be sure, Amursana was not being treated very importantly inside Russia, where he was confined to a prison in Tobolsk. But with the first Manchu notification that he had fled to Russia, and then upon the repeated demands that he be extradited, the value of the prisoner began to rise. Russia did nothing. Soon Amursana contracted smallpox and died—a small matter, for it was principle that counted, and the Manchus continued to demand the extradition of his remains. At last Russia, which had taken the position that Amursana, having fled across an as yet undefined border, did not have to be given back, consented to pack the variolous corpse in ice and send it to the frontier for viewing. There the body of Amursana remained, the Russians unwilling to give it up, the Ch'ing officials unwilling to be without it. In the late Spring of 1758, as the weather warmed up, it was necessary to put Amursana underground. By now Ch'ien-lung had expressed his satisfaction that Russia had been so compliant as to send the remains to the frontier, and on April 6 he ostensibly issued a final edict disposing of the whole affair: "It matters little whether Russia delivers his corpse to us or not, and we should not pursue this matter further."[14] But this ridiculous affair was still far from having spent itself. According to documents printed by Bantysh-Kamenskii,[15] the Li-fan yuan continued to pester Russia with the demand to surrender Amursana. To its letter of July 30, 1758, the Senate replied that since the corpse had already "turned into earth," there was no point in talking any further about it. The Manchus answered that even if the body had putrefied, the Russians had said nothing about the bones, which would not decompose for a long time. In its reply the Senate stated, almost eloquently, that "Amursana's bones, contemptible things in themselves, are not worth the dissolution of the friendship between two empires. And when, by an unusual circumstance, it would appear that these bones, interred within the borders of the Russian empire, are to be exhumed and examined by another state, then would it not be better to bury the whole affair in oblivion?"

The Li-fan yuan did not agree. "We are intolerably embarrassed that the Senate—the government of an entire country—does not understand such a matter and does not preserve its own honor. Obviously his body has become putrid but his bones cannot have decomposed and, according to the custom of the Chinese empire, the bones of such knaves and traitors are broken in several places and shown to all the people." Throughout 1759 the Li-fan yuan continued to write in this vein about Amursana to Russia, until the Senate answered a last time (on June 13, 1760) that "the whole world realizes that to satisfy such a superfluous whim of the Chinese court as to demand the return of a dead man's bones would neither compliment mankind nor suit the honor of the Russian empire." With that the argument appears to end, the Li-fan yuan probably having come to the opinion, after this length of time, that the bones would have decayed beyond their demonstration value anyway. Amursana was not disturbed again.

The Late Eighteenth Century

With the two empires now completely face to face, the Sino-Russian alliance against the peoples of the steppe began to decompose as relentlessly as Amursana's remains. As early as 1755, when the Manchu armies had first taken Ili, there had been a noticeable stiffening in the attitude of officials from the Li-fan yuan who were receiving the Russian caravan of that year in Peking. Aleksei Vladykin, leader of the caravan, wrote that "the Manchus had now received the submission of the Zunghars and begun to act very arrogantly toward Russia, displaying their displeasure and enmity."[16] In the flush of his conquest, the Ch'ien-lung emperor wrote several long edicts which contributed the opinion that barbarians—including Russian barbarians—should be handled, if at all, with a mixture of power and condescension.[17] This was the spirit, taken to heart by the Li-fan yuan, that had moved the Manchu attitude toward

Vladykin (who, as we have seen, was "stupid") and its correspondence over Amursana. As it turned out, Vladykin's caravan
was the last to go to Peking. After 1755 only the Russian mission
remained to fill the otherwise soundless spaces of the Hui-t'ung
kuan.

As for Amursana, the exhibition of his remains within China
would have been a gratuitous signal of Ch'ing ascendency in Inner
Asia, but for Russia there was an equally important angle to be
considered: if what was being demonstrated was not only the fate
that was in store for knaves and traitors (as had befallen another
Mongol rebel of the time, Chinggunjab[18]), but also the fact that
the Russian empire was prepared to submit, as it were, to the
petulant demands of a Manchu emperor, then the time had indeed
come for Russia to resist. It was in order to avoid leaving this
unpleasant impression that Amursana was sent only to the frontier.
For Ch'ien-lung, however, even this act was submission enough to
inspire a piece of doggerel which was not, fortunately, translated
and sent to the Russian Senate: "Who would expect the *lo-ch'a* to
observe the peace treaty so faithfully/That they would travel the
distance of ten thousand li to present to us/The frozen corpse of
our traitor?"[19] The emperor's pejorative reference to *lo-cha*, a
term unused for years in China, suggests that he had read his history
well. No more need Ghantimur rankle Manchu minds, for the eighteenth century *lo-ch'a* had sent back an even bigger fish! Hardly a
decade passed before this self-confidence was repaid by the decision
of the Volga Turghud, in 1771, to transhume to China.[20] Russian
troops chased them all the way, but some tens of thousands of
Turghud families managed their exodus into Ili where they were
welcomed and settled onto grazing grounds so recently depopu-
lated of their Zunghar tenants. The Turghud chieftains—grandsons
and great-grandsons of Ayuki Khan—were received by Ch'ien-lung
at Jehol, invited on the great hunt, and expensively entertained, for
they had brought with them more substantial proof than could be
found in the emperor's poetry that history was on the Manchu side.
Not only that; several of the Russian cavalry who had made the
mistake of pursuing the Turghud fugitives into areas occupied by

Manchu troops were taken prisoner, brought to Peking (where members of the ecclesiastical mission graciously allowed themselves to be used as interpreters), and then exiled to banner garrisons in Fukien and Kwangtung. Here they remained for the rest of their lives, eighteenth-century counterparts of those Russians who had first strayed across the uncertain frontier beyond Albazin almost a hundred years before.[21] And with the passage of another decade (we are now in the year 1783), the Manchu reputation for being a source of protection for the persecuted peoples of Inner Asia had reached even to a colony of harried Old Believers in Siberia, who suddenly appeared in Kobdo with the intention of submitting to Ch'ien-lung.[22] But they were politely refused. As much as Peking wished to patronize the Yellow sect, it was not yet ready to offer itself to a group of Russian dissenters, least of all with the Russian mission already there. In any event, it was not until the twentieth century, when the Manchu empire was collapsing, that this tide of history was reversed and Russia could at last assume that protective position toward Mongolian national interests which, had it seen things differently, it might well have occupied much earlier. Of course it followed that the Chinese government, after the October Revolution, was then quite willing to let Peking act as a refugee center for Russian old believers of another sort.

Not to be blinded by the Manchu successes in Mongol Inner Asia, one must remember that Russia in the eighteenth century remained an expansionist power. This was particularly true in Eastern Siberia and beyond, where a number of expeditions, beginning with that of Vitus Bering in 1725, had been dispatched to explore routes to the sea. Under these circumstances it became more and more difficult to accept the fact that the Amur River, with its deep currents flowing eastward somewhere into the Pacific, was unnavigable only because it lay entirely within Chinese territory by the terms of the treaty of Nerchinsk. Here Lange was quite right. If Mongol fugitives were important to China, the Amur had become important to Russia, and it was while Amursana was dying of smallpox in a Tobolsk jail that the tsarina Elizabeth Petrovna sent an envoy, Vasilii Bratishchev, to Peking to seek permission for limited navigation rights. He was given his instructions on December 31, 1756, in fifteen points, the most important of which bore on the question of the Amur. If necessary, a full, formal embassy would be sent to China to negotiate the issue. Bratishchev arrived in Peking in 1757, and had an audience with the emperor at Jehol, but his demand for navigation rights made no impression on Ch'ien-lung. The idea of an embassy from Russia was also turned down on the grounds that "only a courier and not a proper ambassador was [earlier] sent from Russia to announce the change of rule—a courier who was, at that, unwilling to accept from Our kindness the gifts that were to be sent with him."[23]

This technicality, however, upon which Bratishchev had been sent away, soon provided Russia with the means for returning to Peking. When Catherine II gained the throne in 1762, a new envoy, Ivan Kropotov, was quickly sent to China to make the proper announcement of her accession, inquire about the ecclesiastical mission (which, as we know, had been under siege in the fall of 1759), and, incidentally, raise again the question of the Amur. But he had no apologies to make over Amursana and therefore left Peking with less than ever, for upon his departure Ch'ien-lung promptly suspended the border trade at Kiakhta. Although her reign had scarcely begun, Catherine was already sufficiently impatient with this Manchu monarch to issue a secret ukase putting her armies on the ready. Then, in the summer of 1764, she undertook a long discussion among her ministers of the question of war or peace. A majority continued to prefer the latter, not wanting to gamble the certain loss of the Kiakhta trade for whatever profits might come from being able, finally, to disembogue out of Siberia into the Pacific. Catherine submitted, and instead sent Kropotov off to China again to see what could be done through diplomacy. This time negotiations were held on the frontier with Hu-t'u-ling-a, a Mongol who held the honorary title of vice-president of the Li-fan yuan. The result of these meetings was a new agreement, signed on October 18, 1768, which brought Sino-Russian relations back to their essentials: trade would be re-opened on the frontier, and a new ecclesiastical mission would replace the old.[24] Neither side suggested the possibility of exchanging Amursana for the Amur, for it was now much too late to contemplate digging him up. But it would not have worked in any case, because the issues were not equivalent. With or without Amursana, the Manchus had gotten what they wanted in Inner Asia. The eighteenth-century Russian interest in the Amur was something different, the start of a new historic contest which would take another century to play out and would, of course, have another ending.

The latter eighteenth century, however, belonged to Ch'ien-lung and he made as much as he could of it, skittishly interrupting the border trade with Russia for a total of fifteen of the last forty years of his reign.[25] In 1792, after a seven-year suspension, the trade was restored with the signing of another protocol, phrased in language that made painfully clear the bases on which Sino-Russian relations now rested: "The trade at Kiakhta is of absolutely no benefit to China, but because the great emperor loves all human beings and sympathizes with your poor and miserable people, and because your Senate has appealed to His Imperial Majesty, He has deigned to approve its petition. If you do not respect this friendly relationship you must never dream of being allowed to trade again." Russia was also reminded to keep its lawless tribes and unruly merchants in check, and told to appoint only proper officers who would deal "politely and deferentially" with the Ch'ing border officials.[26]

Looking at what was accomplished during his reign, Ch'ien-lung can of course be excused a high opinion of himself. The opinion was shared by Sinophiles in the West, not least by Voltaire, who sent him several letters and concluded that here indeed was an enlightened despot, as capable of writing poetry as he was of building an empire. And never having seen Ch'ien-lung's poem on the lo-ch'a, Voltaire had no way of knowing, when he wrote to Catherine the Great about the versifier-emperor he had discovered in China, that he was making his announcement to the wrong person. She replied that "if destiny requires that I have a rival over you, in the name of the Virgin Mary let it not be the King of China, against whom I have an old grudge." With this chilling answer, in which it was readily apparent that Catherine had not only discovered Ch'ien-lung for herself but seemed to have a rather different opinion of him, Voltaire did not pursue the matter. "There, there madame, [he wrote back] you are the foremost person of the universe and I make no exceptions—not even for your neighbor Ch'ien-lung, even though he is a poet."[27]

From what is known of the vicissitudes of Sino-Russian relations in the eighteenth century one would certainly not wish to make the argument that the Russian ecclesiastical mission had, like the boundary that was ultimately drawn from Manchuria into Central Asia, an inexorable destiny to interpose itself among the affairs of these two empires. Too many accidents had contributed to its beginnings, and too few helped sustain it through the long haul of the century, to permit the contention that some insurgent historical force was driving it onwards into modern times. But neither can the fact that it managed to endure these vicissitudes be attributed merely to its defiance of the odds against it. Once the mission was formally established under the Kiakhta provisions it was at least assured a place in the bureaucratic business of both the Russian and Manchu governments; and since its existence depended upon compromise not in territory but in attitude, it remained thereafter a standard of the unique relationship that China and Russia had worked out together—something that seemed to justify the motions of keeping it going and coming every decade or so. Amid the stormier events of the time, the unprovocative life of the Russian mission, set in unrepaired buildings amid an unregenerate Orthodox flock—all of which gave rise to the smaller problems on which bureaucracies thrive—supplied Russia and China with the pleasant alternative of relating with each other over matters that neither would have considered crucial. It was this kind of need that the mission came to fill—that however badly things were going, the bottom should never be allowed to drop out from Sino-Russian relations.

Occasionally it would of course be necessary to recall why the mission was there in the first place. When the Earl of Macartney asked for an English copy of the Russian original,[28] the Manchu government had to explain carefully that the Russian mission owed its presence in Peking to a peculiar history in which England, as yet, had no part. But as far as both Russia and China were concerned, the less said about the peculiarities of this institution the better. Indeed, if that charade in which each side was guessing, to its own satisfaction, what the mission represented was to continue, neither would want to peek at the other's answer. After Kiakhta both countries were therefore agreed that this lamasery-embassy should be considered a thoroughly unexceptional affair. By the end of the century it had become yawningly "routine," as Ch'ien-lung himself once remarked in a message to the Tüshiyetü Khan.[29] The only protest would have come from those ingenuous Russian missionaries who endured a fate that was by no means routine and for whom there was, at the time, no available historian to impress them with the meaning of their existence.

Appendix A

RUSSIAN MISSIONARIES AND STUDENTS IN PEKING
IN THE EIGHTEENTH CENTURY

1. First mission (1716-et seq.)
   Archimandrite Ilarion Lezhaiskii
   Hieromonk Lavrentii (last name?)
   Deacon Filimon (last name?)
   Osip D'iakonov, Nikanor Kliusov, Petr Maksimov Iakutov,
   Grigorii Smagin, Fedor Kolesnikov, Andrei Popov, Iosif
   Afanasev.

2. Second mission (1729-1736)
   Archimandrite Antonii Platkovskii
   Priest Ioann Filimonov
   Hierodeacon Ioasaf Ivanovskii
   Students: Luka Voeikov, Ivan Pukhort, Stepan Tret'iakov,
   Ilarion Rossokhin, Gerasim Shulgin, Mikhail Ponomarev;
   (with Lange in 1732) Aleksei Vladykin, Ivan Bykov;
   (with Lange in 1736) Ivan Shikhirev.

3. Third mission (1736-1745)
   Archimandrite Ilarion Trusov
   Hieromonk Lavrentii Uvarov
   Hieromonk Antonii L'khovskii
   Hieromonk Lavrentii Bobrovnikov (after 1741)
   Students: (with Shokurov in 1742) Aleksei Leont'ev, Andrei
   Kanaev, Nikita Chekanov.

4. Fourth mission (1745-1755)
   Archimandrite Gervasii Lintsevskii
   Hieromonk Ioil' Vrublevskii
   Hieromonk Feodosii Smorzhenskii
   Students: Efim Sakhnovksii.

5. Fifth mission (1755–1771)
   Archimandrite Amvrosii Yumatov
   Hieromonk Silvestr Spitsyn
   Hieromonk Sofronii Argievskii
   Hierodeacon Sergei (last name?).

6. Sixth mission (1771–1781)
   Archimandrite Nikolai Tsvet
   Hieromonk Iust (last name?)
   Hieromonk Ioannikii (last name Protopopov?)
   Hierodeacon Nikifor (last name?)
   Students: Aleksei Agafonov, Feodor Baksheev, Aleksei
   Paryshev, Iakov Korkin.

7. Seventh mission (1781–1794)
   Archimandrite Ioakim Shishkovskii
   Hieromonk Antonii Sedel'nikov
   Hieromonk Aleksei Bogolepov
   Hierodeacon Israil (last name?)
   Students: Egor Salertovskii, Ivan Filonov, Anton Vladykin.

Appendix B

RULERS OF RUSSIA AND CHINA IN THE
17TH AND 18TH CENTURIES

Tsars of the Romanov Dynasty (1613–1917)	Emperors of the Ch'ing Dynasty (1644–1911)
Michael 1613–1645 (between 1619 and 1633 his father, Patriarch Filaret, was co-ruler)	Shun-chih 1644–1661
Alexis 1645–1676	K'ang-hsi 1662–1722
Fedor III 1676–1682	
Regency of Sophia 1682–1689 (for tsars Peter and Ivan)	
Peter I 1689–1725 (Ivan nominally co-ruler until 1696)	
Catherine I 1725–1727	Yung-cheng 1723–1735
Peter II 1727–1730	
Anna 1730–1740	Ch'ien-lung 1736–1795
Elizabeth 1741–1761	
Peter III 1761–1762	
Catherine II 1762–1796	Chia-ch'ing 1796–1820
Paul 1796–1801	

NOTES

Abbreviations Used in the Notes

AI   *Akty istoricheskie*

DAI   *Dopolneniia k aktam istoricheskim*

KSLK   Yü Cheng-hsieh, *Kuei-ssu lei-kao*

KSTK   Yü Cheng-hsieh, *Kuei-ssu ts'un-kao*

PSI   *Pamiatniki sibirskoi istorii xviii v.*

PSP   *Polnoe sobranie postanovlenii i rasporiazhenii po vedomstvu pravoslavnago ispovedaniia rossiiskoi imperii*

PSZ   *Polnoe sobranie zakonov rossiiskoi imperii s 1649 goda*

RKO   *Russko-kitaiskie otnosheniia v xvii veke*

TKDA   "Istoricheskii ocherk khristianskoi propovedi v Kitae," *Trudy Kievskoi Dukhovnoi Akademii*

Introduction

1. *RKO*, I, 9–12. I would also like to record here, and throughout this book, my debt to the pioneering work of Mark Mancall on early Sino-Russian relations. His treatment of Poiarkov and Khabarov may be found on pp. 21–27 of his *Russia and China: Their Diplomatic Relations to 1728* (Cambridge, Mass., 1971).

2. *RKO*, I, 268–269.

3. The record of Spafarii's embassy is now given in full in ibid., pp. 346–458.

4. For materials relating to the capture of Grigorii Mylnikov, the two

185

volumes of *RKO* are of no help. I have gotten them from *DAI*, X, 234-239; XI, 80, 218-219.

5.   Ibid., X, 239.

6.   *K'ang-hsi shih-lu*, 3:7b.

7.   Ibid., 112:4b.

8.   See, for example, the Ch'ien-lung edict allowing in Peking only those Westerners who plan to take up permanent residence there, in *CLSL*, 962:15a-16a. It is translated by Lo-shu Fu, *A Documentary Chronicle of Sino-Western Relations, 1644-1820* (Tucson, 1966), I, 273.

9.   R. Montgomery Martin, *China: Political, Commercial and Social in an Official Report to Her Majesty's Government* (London, 1847), I, 395-396.

10. Kenneth Scott Latourette, *A History of Christian Missions in China* (London, 1929).

11. Adoratskii's history, "Pravoslavnaia missiia v kitae za 200 let eia sushchestvovaniia," ran monthly in the *Pravoslavnyi Sobesednik* (Orthodox interlocutor) from February to November, 1887, and remains the standard work on the subject for the eighteenth century. Citations from Adoratskii's work are given by the monthly number and page of the *Pravoslavnyi Sobesednik*.

12. Adoratskii (July), p. 311.

13. V. G. Shcheben'kov, *Russko-kitaiskie otnosheniia v xvii v.* (Moscow, 1960), pp. 215-216.

14. P. T. Iakovleva, *Pervyi russko-kitaiskii dogovor 1689 goda* (Moscow, 1958), p. 197.

15. Fang Hsiu, "Tsarist Russia's Tool of Aggression against China: The Mission of the Russian Orthodox Church," *Li-shih yen-chiu*, no. 3 (June 20, 1975); translated in *Selections from PRC Magazines*, no. 847:31, 35, 41 (Nov. 24, 1975; American Consulate General, Hong Kong).

16. R. K. I. Quested, *The Expansion of Russia in East Asia, 1857-1860* (Singapore, 1968), p. 2.

17. Clifford M. Foust, *Muscovite and Mandarin: Russia's Trade with China and Its Setting, 1727-1805* (Chapel Hill, 1969), p. 51. In making this point, Foust is himself citing the work of Albert Parry "Russian (Greek Orthodox) Missionaries in China: Their Cultural, Political, and Economic Role" (Ph.D. dissertation, University of Chicago, 1938). Parry's study was very helpful to me, and I should not let this opportunity pass without making known my frequent reference to it on matters of bibliography, translation, and interpretation.

18. Norris and Ross McWhirter, eds., *Guinness Book of World Records, 1976 Edition* (New York, 1975), p. 248.

I. The Beginnings of the Ecclesiastical Mission in China

1. For information on the Sibirskii Prikaz readers may be referred to George V. Lantzeff, *Siberia in the Seventeenth Century: A Study of the Colonial Administration* (Berkeley and Los Angeles, 1943). On the Li-fan yuan, see John K. Fairbank and Ssu-yü Teng, *Ch'ing Administration: Three Studies* (Cambridge, Mass., 1960), p. 130; and David Farquhar, "The Ch'ing Administration of Mongolia up to the Nineteenth Century" (Ph.D. dissertation, Harvard University, 1960).

2. Yü Cheng-hsieh discusses this term in *KSTK*, pp. 160-166.

3. *KSTK*, p. 169.

4. For the Manchus, this was the most important consequence of Ignatii Milovanov's Mission to Peking in this year. *RKO*, I, 270-271, 273-274, 277-280, 283-287.

5. *RKO*, I, 276.

6. See my article " 'Kitai' and the Ch'ing Empire in Seventeenth Century Russian Documents on China," *Ch'ing-shih wen-t'i*, 2.4:21-39 (November 1970).

7. Ibid., pp. 24-25. See also, for example, the journal of Baikov's embassy in *RKO*, I, esp. pp. 179, 189.

8. Again, this is my own interpretation, based on documents collected in *RKO*, vol. 1.

9. For Russia this was the most important consequence of the Milovanov mission. See note 4, above.

10. *RKO*, I, 476, 497, 515; Mancall, *Russia and China*, pp. 79-80.

11. See the note to this effect in *RKO*, II, 762.

12. The texts of the treaty are printed in *RKO*, II, 645-659. The editors of *RKO* summarize their opinions of Nerchinsk on pp. 53-54.

13. *KSLK*, p. 332. In Manchu, Uruslanov, or "Wu-lang-ko-li," became "Ulangger," from which subsequent Russian translations of Manchu documents reproduced him as "Ulanger'," making his identification almost impossible. See A. Liubimov, "Nekotorye man'chzhurskie dokumenty iz istorii russko-kitaiskikh snoshenii v xvii veke," *Zapiski vostochnago otdeleniia imperatorskago russkago arkheologicheskago obshchestva*, 21. 2-3:65-94 (St. Petersburg, 1911-1912). According to the *Ming-Ch'ing tang-an ts'un-chen hsuan-chi* compiled by Li Kuang-t'ao (Taipei, 1959, p. 118), on February 6, 1654, the Board of Rites reported that the newly surrendered Russian (Uruslanov) refused to marry any of the widows of the Solons, from whom the Board had given him permission to select a bride. He insisted on marrying a virgin of good family.

14. *RKO*, I, 287.

15. Cited in *KSLK*, p. 332. Michel Pavlovsky, in his *Chinese-Russian Relations* (New York, 1949), p. 179, suggests that this I-fan was Ivan Pereleshin, a Cossack who had fled to Eastern Siberia with Nikifor Chernigovskii. This is impossible. "Ivashko" Pereleshin is mentioned in *DAI* (VIII, 348) carrying the tsar's salaries to the Albazinians in 1679. In Albazin he apparently functioned as the "village petitioner." The background of the I-fan in question remains a mystery, but it may be supposed that his name was in fact Ivan Artem'ev. As the second principal deserter to China he was given rank second only to Uruslanov in 1684. In 1683 a Manchu document mentions Ivan as an "elder" associate of another deserter, Agafon. (Liubimov, p. 84.) In two places *DAI* cites an "Ivashko Artem'ev" as a prominent interrogator of Russian captives, along with Agafon and others (X, 238; XI, 80). No other Ivans or Ivashkos are mentioned in such a connection.

16. *RKO,* I, 416-417.

17. Ho Ch'iu-t'ao, *Shuo-Fang pei-sheng* (compiled around 1860, published in 1881), 4:8b. K'ang-hsi's military historians reflected that "since the nature [of the Russians] was rather like that of animals, they could be handled only by employing a mixture of favor and awe." See also Mancall, *Russia and China,* p. 162.

18. Ho Ch'iu-t'ao, 2:1b-2a. This desertion was prompted by another turn-coat, also named "I-fan," but not Artem'ev. Yü Cheng-hsieh, in *KSLK,* p. 133, remarks parenthetically that "there are many I-fans among the *lo-ch'a.*"

19. *DAI,* X, 260-261.

20. See, for example, N. I. Veselovskii, ed., *Materialy dlia istorii rossiiskoi dukhovnoi missii v Pekine* (St. Petersburg, 1905), p. 5. The editors of *RKO* insist (II, 769) that all those Russians who entered China after the destruction of Albazin had been "seized" (*zakhvacheny*) by the Manchus.

21. Certainly, however, there were more than the "several" that Iu. V. Barten'ev acknowledges in his chauvinistic article, "Geroi Albazina i daurskoi zemli," *Russkii Arkhiv,* 1889, I, 321.

22. *RKO,* I, 490.

23. *RKO,* I, 417.

24. *DAI,* XI, 80.

25. Ho Ch'iu-t'ao, 1:17a-b; see also *K'ang-hsi shih-lu,* 113:9b-10a.

26. See for example, *RKO,* II, 108-109.

27. *DAI,* XII, 120-121.

28. *RKO,* II, 769.

29. Ho Ch'iu-t'ao, 2:20b. In the Russian translation of this letter, "Chi-erh-meng-a" is transcribed as "Kirmunta" (*DAI,* X, 261-262).

30. *RKO*, I, 485; II, 405.

31. *AI*, V, 306, 307.

32. Nikolai Bantysh-Kamenskii, *Diplomaticheskoe sobranie del' mezhdu rossiiskim i kitaiskim gosudarstvami 1619 po 1792 god* (Kazan, 1882), p. 48. Verbiest had already received one promotion for the excellent cannon he was making. Fu, I, 58.

33. *RKO*, II, 646, 650.

34. Bantysh-Kamenskii, p. 84. The treatment of Albazin and the Albazinians in Chinese works, besides that of Yü Cheng-hsieh, may be found in Ho Ch'iu-t'ao, chüan 14 ("Ya-k'o-sa ch'eng k'ao"), and in the collection *Hsiao-fang-hu-chai-yü-ti ts'ung-ch'ao* (first published in 1877; reprinted in Taiwan, 1962), 2:417a–423b. This article, somewhat longer than the first, is also by Ho Ch'iu-t'ao. In English, Michel Pavlovsky's research (pp. 145–164) has easily withstood whatever tests have been put upon it in the twenty-five years since his book was published. In Russian, *RKO* does not pay much attention to the problem of Albazin, and includes none of the many documents in *AI* and *DAI* that, to my mind at least, bear very crucially on those seventeenth-century relations that the editors of *RKO* purport to be covering so comprehensively.

35. *K'ang-hsi shih-lu*, 112:17b–18a.

36. This information comes from a variety of sources: *Ch'ien-lung hui-tien*, 95:2b, *KSLK*, p. 333; Ho Ch'iu-t'ao, 1:17a–b; *K'ang-hsi shih-lu*, p. 113: 9b–10a; Adoratskii (March), p. 339; *TKDA*, p. 300; and *Ching-shih wu-ch'eng fang-hsiang hu-t'ung chi; ching-shih fang-hsiang chih-kao* (Peking, 1962), p. 157.

37. Lo-to-hun had very likely accompanied Father Gerbillon to Nerchinsk for the negotiations with Russia. See Pavlovsky, p. 178.

38. *KSLK*, p. 333.

39. This speculation comes from "Lt. Colonel" Chernozubov, "Zavoevanie Amura russkimi i Albazinskaia sideniia," *Voennyi Sbornik*, 11:9 (1907); and I. I. Serebrennikov, *Albazintsy* (Peking, 1922), p. 9.

40. For this piece of news I am indebted to Dr. Marianne Bastid, of the University of Paris.

41. Gaston Cahen, *Histoire des relations de la Russie avec la Chine sous Pierre le Grand, 1689-1730* (Paris, 1911), p. xxxv. For V. V. Barthold's interpretation, see his *La decouverte de l'Asie* (Paris, 1947), p. 226. On the Ides mission see also E. Isbrants Ides, *Three Years Travels from Moscow Over-land to China: thro' Great Ustiga, Siriana, Permia, Siberia, Daour, Great Tartary, etc., to Peking* (London, 1706); and M. I. Kazanina, ed., *Izbrant Ides i Adam Brand: zapiski o russkom posol'stve v Kitai* (Moscow, 1967).

42. Cahen, *Histoire,* p. xxxiii. Letter of the Li-fan yuan, dated March 1, 1694.

43. Bantysh-Kamenskii, p. 73.

44. *RKO,* I, 432.

45. John F. Baddeley, *Russia, Mongolia, China,* II, 430. On the Greek chapel in Peking, see *DAI,* VI, 43.

46. Cahen, *Histoire,* pp. 248-249; Adoratskii (March), p. 346. The priests' names were Lavrentii Ivanov and Grigorii Navitskii. They did not remain in China, contrary to what Cahen and Parry say. For information on the Lobanov caravan, see "Iz istorii russko-kitaiskikh otnoshenii 1695-1720 gg." *Istoricheskii Arkhiv,* 3:174 (1957).

47. Cahen, *Histoire,* pp. 247-248; Adoratskii (March), pp. 346-347.

48. William Palmer, *The Patriarch and the Tsar: Services of the Patriarch Nicon to the Church and State of his Country, and their Requital by the Creation of a Merely National or State Church in Russia* (London, 1876), V, 981. For the importance of Vinius's position, see S. K. Bogoiavlenskii, *Prikaznye sud'i xvii veka* (Moscow-Leningrad, 1946), p. 162.

49. *Pis'ma i bumagi Imperatora Petra Velikago* (St. Petersburg and Moscow, 1887-1910, 1964), I, 694-695.

50. Quoted in Wolfgang Franke, *China and the West* (New York, 1967), p. 62.

51. Noted by Donald Lach, *The Preface to Leibniz' Novissima Sinica* (Honolulu, 1957), IV, 53-54. Brand's book appeared the following year: Adam Brand, *A journal of the embassies from their Majesties John*

and Peter Alexievitz, Emperors of Muscovy, etc., over land into China through Ustiugha, Siberia, Dauri, and the Great Tartary to Peking, the capital city of the Chinese empire. By Everard Isbrand, their ambassador in the years 1693, 1694, and 1695 (London, 1698).

52. Quoted in Franke, p. 62.

53. On Witsen and his relationship with Leibniz and Peter, see Kurt Müller, "Gottfried Wilhelm Leibniz und Nicolaas Witsen," *Sitzungsberichte der Deutschen Akademie der Wissenschaften zu Berlin,* 1955, 1:1-46; and W. Guerrier, *Leibniz in seinen Beziehungen zu Russland und Peter dem Grossen* (St. Petersburg und Leipzig, 1873).

54. *Pis'ma i bumagi,* I, 738-739. Witsen's letter to Leibniz is printed in Guerrier, p. 41.

55. *Pis'ma i bumagi,* I, 253-254. The letter was received by Vinius on July 10 (ibid., p. 729). Peter's reference is to the Jesuit demise in Japan earlier in the century.

56. Lach, p. 19; Guerrier, p. 45.

57. Guerrier, p. 60.

58. E. F. Shmurlo, ed., *Pis'ma i doneseniia Iezuitov o Rossii kontsa xvii i nachala xviii veka* (St. Petersburg, 1904), pp. 26-27. The "schism" of course refers not to that within the Russian church, but to the division between the Roman Catholic and Eastern Orthodox churches.

59. Quoted in Franke, p. 63.

60. As implied by Reinhard Wittram, in his *Peter I, Czar und Kaiser: Zur Geschichte Peters des Grossen in seiner Zeit* (Göttingen, 1964), II, 180, 479-480.

61. *PSZ,* vol. 4, no. 1800.

62. Here my reference is to the Schism, or *raskol,* within the Russian church that had begun in the 1660s. A very helpful account of Peter's church reforms at the end of the century has been James Cracraft, *The Church Reform of Peter the Great* (Stanford, 1971).

63. Patriarch Adrian died in the fall of 1700, and Peter appointed no one
     to replace him, thereby taking upon himself authority over the Russian
     church.

64. (Grumelevskii) Filaret, *Istoriia russkoi tserkvi* (St. Petersburg, 1894),
     p. 517.

65. Ibid., p. 518.

66. Ibid., pp. 518-519.

67. *PSZ*, vol. 4, no. 1800. Cracraft (p. 66) also translates this part of the
     edict of 1700.

68. Petr Andreevich Slovtsov, *Istoricheskoe obozrenie Sibiri* (St. Petersburg,
     1886), p. 201.

69. *AI*, V, 537-538.

70. Baddeley, II, 430-431. The original Russian is in *DAI*, X, 292-293.

71. G. F. Miller [Müller], *Istoriia Sibiri* (Moscow, 1937), II, 80; Adoratskii
     (April), p. 464.

72. Adoratskii (March), p. 350.

     II. Ilarion Lezhaiskii: The First Ecclesiastical Mission to China

1.   Cahen, *Histoire*, pp. 249-250.

2.   *Sibirskii Vestnik*, pp. 115-116.

3.   Veselovskii, p. 10.

4.   Ibid., p. 11.

5.   Ibid., p. 12. See also (Arkhimandrit) Amvrosii, *Istoriia rossiiskoi
     ierarkhii* (Moscow, 1810), II, 447-448; *Sibirskii Vestnik*, pp. 116-117;
     Adoratskii (April), pp. 466-467; *TKDA*, p. 301. These accounts do not
     agree in all points relating to this sequence of events. I have tried to

put together as probable a reconstruction as the documents can support.

6. The *I-yü-lu* (first published in Peking, 1723). The text is contained in chüan 43 and 44 of Ho Ch'iu-t'ao, although the Manchu and Chinese are now given together by Shunju Imanishi in *Tulishen's I-yü-lu Revised and Annotated* (in Japanese; Nara, 1964). An English translation of the *I-yü-lu* was made by G. T. Staunton (*Narrative of the Chinese Embassy to the Khan of the Tourgouth Tartars in the years 1712, 13, 14, and 15* [London, 1821]), but it has a number of errors, as for example, in the case of Grigorii Oskolkov, mentioned above. His patronymic was Afanasevich. Tulishen refers to him as "Ha-mi-sa-erh O-fa-na-ssu-yeh-wei-ch'ih," i.e., Commissar Afansevich. Staunton, however (p. 39), presents "Ha-mi-sa-erh" and "Go-fo-nas-se-ye-fi-che" as two different people.

7. Cahen, *Histoire*, pp. 128–133.

8. *Sibirskii Vestnik*, p. 118.

9. Filofei Leshchinskii was away being tonsured, and had temporarily left his see to Maksimovich.

10. Imanishi, p. 254.

11. Here I translated from the Chinese and Manchu texts of ibid., pp. 253–254, 364. I am indebted to my Manchu teacher, Hugjintai, of Taipei, Taiwan, for assistance. Of the many Western translations of the *I-yü-lu* the best would seem to be that done by Ilarion Rossokhin in G. F. Müller, ed., *Ezhemesiachnyia sochineniia i izvestiia o uchenykh delakh* (July–December 1764). The passage quoted here occurs in the September issue, pp. 201–203. The "Dmitri" that Tulishen refers to in the quoted passage ("Mi-ti'li" in Chinese and "Mi-ti-ri" in Manchu) is the old Cossack from Albazin, Dmitri Nestorovich Grigor'ev. He is often confused with Maksim Leont'ev, for whom he acted as church warden. Aleksei Pozdneev, for example, in *Mongoliia i Mongoly* (St. Petersburg, 1896–1898), II, xxiii–xxiv, states that "the first Russians in Peking arrived there in 1686, and their priest was Dmitri, who died about 1700." Although Amvrosii is also wrong in stating (II, 447) that Dmitri was the Albazinians' first priest, he mentions that it was Dmitri who brought the icon of St. Nicholas to Peking in 1685. This is quite possible, since, as we have seen, Leont'ev's entry into China predates the fall of Albazin. As for Grigor'ev's presence in Albazin between 1683 and 1685, there is a reference to a "Mishka Grigor'ev" in *DAI*, X, 237, who carried K'ang-

hsi's first letter to the Albazinians from Albazin to the voevoda of
Nerchinsk, Fedor Voeikov, on December 15, 1683. Cahen reports
(p. 248) that he lived at least until 1731.

12. Friedrich Christian Weber, *The Present State of Russia* (London, 1723),
I, 101; II, 25. Garvine and Lange had entered China in 1716 with the
caravan of Gusiatnikov, which had awaited their arrival at Selenginsk
(*PSI*, II, 34-35). Other estimates of this man's name are: "Korfin"
(Adoratskii [November], p. 325); "Garwin" (Weber, I, 101); "Harwing"
(Cahen, *Histoire,* p. 107); "Carwin" (Imanishi, p. 104); "Garfin" (P. E.
Skachkov, "Russkie vrachi pri rossiiskoi dukhovnoi missii v Pekine,"
Sovetskoe Kitaevendenie, no. 4:137 (1958); "Garwin" again (Julius
Heinrich von Klaproth, *Memoires relatifs a l'Asie* [Paris, 1824], I, 4).
I get "Garvine" from Rev. Robert Paul, ed., "Letters and Documents
relating to Robert Erskine, Physician to Peter the Great, Czar of Russia,
1677-1720," *Miscellany of the Scottish History Society,* 2:403 (1940):
"The Earl of Loudoun to Sir John Erskine or his brother Charles
(October 31, 1713): "Sir—I give you the trouble of this to desire a
letter of recommendation from you to Doctor Areskine in favors of
Tomas Garvine who is now a surgeon in the hospital at Petersbourg.
I have had obligations to some of his near relations in this Country,
and would be glad to do him a favour, let the bearer have your letters
which will verry much oblige, Dear Pap, your most humble servant,
Loudoun."
    What became of Garvine after his interview with K'ang-hsi is unclear.
Some suppose that he returned to Russia with Lange in 1717 (P. E.
Skachkov, "Russkie vrachi," p. 137). Lange (whose journal of this trip
is included in Weber) himself makes no mention of whether Garvine
was with him or not on his return. Adoratskii (November), p. 325,
maintains that Garvine "very successfully treated K'ang-hsi, from which
he was held in great esteem, on account of which he became very proud.
The cunning Jesuits by their flattery got all the best medicines out of
Korfin [*sic*] and he was obliged to leave Peking although even K'ang-hsi
wanted to have him by his side." But Adoratskii is also silent on when
Garvine left. Chinese records are of no help. They merely report that a
doctor from Russia came "to study medicine" in Peking in 1715 (Ho
Ch'iu-t'ao, 40:3b).

13. Adoratskii (April), pp. 467-468.

14. Ibid., pp. 468-469. Information on the personnel of this first mission is
contradictory. I have chosen to cite Adoratskii because he worked in

the archives of the Holy Synod, as well as in those of the Irkutsk
eparchy. He, Veselovskii, and Bantysh-Kamenskii all agree on Lezhaiskii
and his two chief subordinates, Lavrentii and Filimon. John Dudgeon, in
his *Historical Sketch of the Ecclesiastical, Political, and Commercial
Relations of Russia with China* (Peking, 1872), agrees with Adoratskii
that there were seven additional members of the mission, but their lists
wholly disagree. Dudgeon's members are "Gregory, a student, Voyekoff,
Pulart and Traitzukoff, students at the Academy of Moscow; Pulart understood medicine; two inferior church officers and Peter Kamensky, bedellus" (pt. 2, p. 29). Parry (p. 17) and Lo-shu Fu (II, 490) seem to be following Dudgeon, at least as far as the presence of a "Pulart" in Peking at
that time is concerned. But it is known that students became part of the
mission only after the treaty of Kiakhta. Here Dudgeon seems to be
confused with the students who were sent to Peking upon the conclusion
of the treaty, who were Luka Voeikov, Feodor Tret'iakov, and Ivan
Pukhort (Veselovskii, p. 36). The identity of Dudgeon's "Gregory"
remains unknown, unless it was Grigorii Smagin, one of those whom
Adoratskii mentions. As for the "bedellus," Peter Kamensky (presumably,
the "procession leader"), he apparently did not arrive until the third
mission, under Ilarion Trusov, in 1736 (Ibid., p. 34). Veselovskii's list
contains only five lesser members. He agrees with Adoratskii on Afans'ev,
Kliusov, and Iakutov, but two other names—"Feodor Belka and Petr
Kalmak"—remain a mystery.

15. Ibid., p. 470. While generally following Adoratskii's account of the
     arrangements for Lezhaiskii's mission, I will continue to note dif-
     ferences of fact and opinion where they occur. The *Sibirskii Vestnik*,
     for example, states that Lavrentii was a hieromonk (i.e., not a parochial
     priest) and that he was to receive thirty rubles from Irkutsk (p. 119).
     Filimon is termed a hierodeacon, not simply a deacon; his salary was
     twenty rubles, and the remaining members got fifteen rubles each (ibid.).
     Veselovskii agrees (p. 12) that Lavrentii and Filimon were a hieromonk
     and hierodeacon respectively; he also claims (p. 15) that they both
     received thirty rubles, and that the rest received twenty apiece.
     Adoratskii notes (April), p. 469, that Lavrentii, at least, may have
     become a member of the black clergy while he was in Peking.

16. Veselovskii, p. 13. I have chosen this date over that given by the
     Sibirskii Vestnik (p. 120) of April 20, 1716. The returning Manchu
     embassy had left Tobolsk early in the previous spring, and it does not
     seem likely that it would have taken it over a year to reach Peking.
     Adoratskii (April), p. 473, states that it arrived at the end of 1715 or

beginning of 1716. He also mentions that two members of the Manchu embassy, Tulishen and Naian, had left Tobolsk earlier and arrived in Peking on April 20, 1715. It may be this date that the *Sibirskii Vestnik* has confused with that of Lezhaiskii's arrival. The *I-yü-lu* does not mention the independent return of Tulishen and Naian.

17. The frequency of these visits is uncertain. The *Sibirskii Vestnik* (p. 122) says they occurred every day. Adoratskii maintains that it was a monthly event (April), p. 475. Veselovskii (p. 14) states that it was not just a court official who made these visits, but K'ang-hsi's favorite "grandee," who happened also to be a general. As for their frequency, his account simply says that they occurred "often."

18. Adoratskii (April), p. 478, *TKDA*, p. 302.

19. Veselovskii, p. 15.

20. Adoratskii (April), pp. 476–477.

21. Veselovskii, p. 15.

22. Ibid., pp. 15–16.

23. Adoratskii (April), p. 477; *Sibirskii Vestnik*, p. 122. Veselovskii states (p. 16) that Lezhaiskii died on October 14, 1717, thus having him in Peking less than a year. For this figure Veselovskii seems to be depending on a Chinese source, since the date is also given as being in the fifty-seventh year of the K'ang-hsi reign. That, of course, is 1718, not 1716. Both Bantysh-Kamenskii (p. 84) and Amvrosii (II, 449) give the year of Lezhaiskii's death as 1719. This is probably too late. Lezhaiskii was buried in the Russian cemetery slightly to the north of the Tartar City wall, probably close to the grave of Maksim Leont'ev. By the nineteenth century no traces of Leont'ev's grave remained, but Dudgeon, writing soon after the Tientsin massacres, reports that he found Lezhaiskii's gravestone desecrated by Chinese graffiti (II, 29–30).

24. Matteo Ripa, *Memoirs of Father Ripa, during Thirteen Years' Residence at the Court of Peking in the Service of the Emperor of China,* tr. Fortunato Prandi (New York, 1846), pp. 102–103.

25. Ho Ch'iu-t'ao, 2:17a; 4:7b.

26. See V. A. Aleksandrov's *Rossiia na dal'nevostochnykh rubezhakh,
     vtoraia polovina xvii v.* (Moscow, 1969); and Joseph Fletcher's review of
     it in *Kritika,* 7.3:138-170.

27. See chap. 8.

28. Liu Ta-nien, "Lun K'ang-hsi," *Li-shih yen-chiu,* no. 3:7-8 (1961).

29. See, for example, the article by E. D. Kostikov, "Velikoderzhavnye
     ambitsii i pogranichnaia politika pekinskogo rukovodstva," *Problemy
     dal'nego vostoka,* no. 1:53-63 (1973); or S. L. Tikhvinskii, ed.,
     Man'chzhurskoe vladychestvo v Kitae (Moscow, 1966), pp. 5-76. Both
     writers are critical of the views of Liu Ta-nien (Kostikov, p. 55;
     Tikhvinskii, pp. 67-68).

III. Izmailov, Lange, and Kul'chitskii: Back to the Beginning

1. Bantysh-Kamenskii, pp. 84-85; *Sibirskii Vestnik,* p. 124.

2. Mancall, *Russia and China,* p. 221.

3. Klaproth, I, 4.

4. On March 30, 1720, Izmailov picked up Platkovskii at the Voznesenskii
    monastery. Bantysh-Kamenskii, pp. 90 and 99; Cahen, *Histoire,* p. 160,
    n. 5.

5. *TKDA,* 308. Platkovskii also made the dubious statement that over fifty
    Chinese and Manchus had been baptized, not counting the wives of the
    Albazinians. Ibid., pp. 310-311.

6. John Bell of Antermony, *Travels from St. Petersburgh in Russia to Various
    Ports of Asia,* II, 23, 53-54.

7. Veselovskii, p. 11, note.

8. Bell, II, 262. (Lange's journal of his residence in Peking is included in the
    second volume of Bell's work.) The debt came to 82 *liang* 26 *fen* silver
    (ibid., p. 279).

9. Ibid., p. 255. "The 16th, after having received the news of the perpetual

peace, concluded between his Czarish Majesty and the Ottoman Porte, I caused Te Deum to be sung in the church of St. Nicholas, and celebrated the rest of the day in festivity."

10. It does not appear true, however, that Izmailov won his point on a second Russian church in Peking, contrary to the common assumption that he did (Parry, p. 18; Edward H. Parker, *China and Religion* [London, 1905], p. 235; I. V. Shcheglov, *Khronologicheskii perechen' vazhneishikh dannykh iz istorii Sibiri* [Irkutsk, 1883], p. 174; A. Thomas, *Histoire de la mission de Pékin* [Paris, 1923], p. 287; Cahen, *Histoire,* p. 169). Whatever in fact took place during this brief and badly documented mission, it is quite clear that no concessions for another church were made for the simple reason that the subsequent embassy of Sava Vladislavich in 1726-1728 made precisely the same demand.

11. Bantysh-Kamenskii, p. 509.

12. Baddeley, II, 236.

13. Lange had noted in his journal (Bell, II, 253) that "the Coanne [Kuan] is in ruins and might not survive another rainy season." His doubts were soon confirmed on May 1, 1722: "all the wall of one side of my chamber fell, about midnight, into the courtyard, which made me very apprehensive for what remained" (ibid., pp. 280-281).

14. For more on the Hui-t'ung kuan, see chap. 5.

15. *Ch'ien-lung hui-tien tse-li,* 95:1b.

16. Bell, II, 413-415; see also pp. 391-393.

17. Ibid., p. 378.

18. Adoratskii (April), p. 480.

19. *TKDA,* p. 303. See also L. I. Denisov, *Pravoslavnyie monastyri rossiiskoi imperii* (Moscow, 1908), pp. 739-741. According to the *Opisanie arkhiva Aleksandro-Nevskoi lavry za vremia tsarstvovaniia Imeperatora Petra Velikago* (Petrograd, 1916), vols. 2 and 3, the name of the bishop-designate was Kul'chinskii. This work also lists an "Inokentii Kul'chitskii" on the register of the monastery, called there in the spring of 1719 from his job ministering to a corps of oarsmen. Kul'chinskii's previous post

was with the "Finnish Corps." I believe that the two–Kul'chinskii and Kul'chitskii–are probably one and the same. In any case, we will continue to refer to the bishop as "Kul'chitskii" (see ibid., II, 950, 988, 999; III, 85, 90, 269-270).

20. Established in January, 1721. See Cracraft, pp. 165 ff.

21. Established in 1711, and with the Synod, was one of "the two highest bodies of the realm" in late Petrine times (Michael T. Florinsky, *Russia: A History and an Interpretation* [New York, 1959], p. 334).

22. Adoratskii (April), p. 489.

23. *PSZ*, vol. 6, no. 3734. Cited also in Adoratskii (April), p. 489.

24. Adoratskii (April), pp. 489-490.

25. *PSP*, first series, I, 45-47; 53-54. Kul'chitskii also received 500 rubles for travel.

26. Bantysh-Kamenskii, p. 99.

27. *PSP*, first series, I, 45-47. The reply was dated March 8, 1721.

28. *Sibirskii Vestnik*, p. 128; Adoratskii (April), p. 491.

29. *PSP*, first series, I, 122-123.

30. Ibid., p. 121. See also Adoratskii (April), pp. 491-492, and *Sibirskii Vestnik*, p. 129.

31. *Sibirskii Vestnik*, p. 135.

32. Cahen, *Histoire*, p. 252, n. 5.

33. *Sibirskii Vestnik*, pp. 129-134.

34. *PSP*, first series, I, 121-122.

35. Adoratskii (April), pp. 494-495. The Filimon to whom Kul'chitskii refers is no doubt the same person who acted as courier of the news of Lezhaiskii's death.

36. Bantysh-Kamenskii, pp. 99-100. This reply was sent on to the College of Foreign Affairs on March 30, 1723.

37. Adoratskii (April), pp. 496-497.

38. Bantysh-Kamenskii, pp. 109-110, 112. The conductor of the survey was Stepan Fefilov, a *dvorianin* from Tobolsk.

39. *PSP,* first series, IV, 118.

40. On August 21, 1723. Cahen, *Histoire,* p. 253.

41. *PSP,* first series, IV, 119-120.

42. Ibid., p. 120.

43. Ibid., p. 236.

44. Ibid. The Synod ruled that none of Kul'chitskii's money should be withheld, in keeping with a ruling of the tsar on September 15, 1723, that those serving in certain remote places would be exempted from the deduction. *PSZ,* vol. 7, no. 4299.

45. O-lun-tai (or Olundai) was a second cousin of Yung-cheng. His father, T'ung Kuo-kang, was a maternal uncle of K'ang-hsi and one of the principal negotiators at Nerchinsk in 1689. See Arthur W. Hummel, *Eminent Chinese of the Ch'ing Period,* II, 794. T'e-ku-t'e (or Tegute) was the president of the Li-fan yuan. See the *Ch'ing-shih* (Taipei, 1961), 4:2612-2613. Bantysh-Kamenskii presents them (p. 110) as "Olondai" and "Tkut."

46. Adoratskii (April), p. 501. The letter was dated August 14, 1724.

47. *Sibirskii Vestnik,* p. 139.

IV. Vladislavich Platkovskii and the Kiakhta Treaty

1. This was the mission of Captain Ivan Unkovskii, which Mancall treats in *Russia and China,* pp. 214-215, and which Cahen, in *Histoire,* virtually ignores. Information may also be found in I. Ia. Zlatkin, *Istoriia dzhungarskogo khanstva, 1635-1758* (Moscow, 1964), esp. pp. 354-355.

2. Bantysh-Kamenskii has these instructions on pp. 434–455.

3. Ibid., p. 117.

4. *PSP*, first series, V, 157–158, 176. The priest's salary was one hundred rubles a year for two years, and one hundred and fifty rubles for travel. The field church, books, and vessels were to be obtained through the office of the College of Foreign Affairs in Moscow.

5. Ibid., p. 158.

6. Bantysh-Kamenskii, pp. 453–455.

7. *PSP*, first series, V, 157; Bantysh-Kamenskii, p. 120.

8. Ibid.

9. Lungkodo was a cousin of K'ang-hsi and an uncle of Yung-cheng on his mother's side. See his biography in Hummel, I, 552–554.

10. Ssu-ko, a Mongolian, was a member of the Manchu Plain Yellow Banner and a commander of the Imperial Guard. See ibid., p. 553; see also Fu, II, 511. Gaston Cahen, whose life ended before he was able to get to China and use Chinese sources for a revision of his history, presents Ssu-ko as four different people: "Seke" (p. 208, n. 5), "Sek" (p. 218, n. 3), "Besyga" (from Po Ssu-ko or "Earl" Ssu-ko—a rank he had inherited from his great-grandfather—p. 219, n. 3), and "Seki" (*Histoire,* p. cxxiv).

11. For the text of this letter see *PSP*, first series, V, 468–470, and *Sibirskii Vestnik,* pp. 140–141.

12. Bantysh-Kamenskii, p. 125.

13. Veselovskii, pp. 17–18; 68–69.

14. Bantysh-Kamenskii, pp. 125–126. See also *Sibirskii Vestnik,* pp. 141–142.

15. Veselovskii, p. 69.

16. *PSP*, first series, V, 468–470. A second ukase of similar content

was given on January 18 (Bantysh-Kamenskii, p. 127).

17. *PSP*, first series, V, 478.

18. Adoratskii (May), pp. 106-107.

19. *PSP*, first series, VI, 116, 276. Kul'chitskii had received the order to leave Selenginsk on March 24, 1727. He left on July 22.

20. For more biographical details on Innokentii Kul'chitskii see the *Slovar' istoricheskii o sviatykh proslavlennykh v rossiiskoi tserkvi* (St. Petersburg, 1836), pp. 120-122. The *Sibirskii Vestnik* (p. 146) and Adoratskii (April), p. 507 unaccountably give the year of his death as 1736. On the order for his immortalization on the calendar, see *PSZ*, vol. 28, no. 21540.

21. Chabina was Minister of the Imperial Household. See *Ch'ing-shih*, 5: 4105-4106. On Tulishen see Hummel, II, 784-787 and *Ch'ing-shih*, 4:2613. See also chap. 2. Tulishen was now vice-president of the Board of War. It might also be noted that Manchu "hard-soft" diplomacy alternated during the time of Vladislavich's visit in Peking. *Yung-cheng hui-tien*, 109:24b, states that in 1726 "an envoy named Sa-wa is a Russian high minister. It is specially ordered that every day his provisions should be doubled." By 1727 however, Vladislavich and the members of his embassy had been put on a salt-water diet. Bantysh-Kamenskii, p. 134.

22. Cahen, *Histoire*, pp. 213-214.

23. Ibid., pp. 214-215; Bantysh-Kamenskii, p. 138.

24. The clause providing for the Russian students is also omitted from the Chinese text of the treaty of Kiakhta that is reproduced in *Treaties, Conventions, etc. between China and Foreign States* (Shanghai, 1917), I, 33. But the full Chinese text, allowing for the students, is available in such places as Ho Ch'iu-t'ao 9:7a-7b and *Ch'ien-lung hui-tien tse-li*, 142:40a. While the negotiating for the students may have taken place on the frontier after Vladislavich left Peking (see Tsereng's memorial from the frontier to the emperor summing up the Kiakhta negotiations, in which Russian students are mentioned, but not the Russian mission, in *Yung-cheng shih-lu*, 60:23b), it is now clear that the subject had been at least tentatively raised by Vladislavich in Peking. See Antoine

Gaubil, S.J., *Correspondance de Pékin, 1722-1759* (Geneva, 1970), p. 175.

25. Bantysh-Kamenskii, p. 151.

26. See Adoratskii (May), pp. 116-117, and Bantysh-Kamenskii, p. 502. Vladislavich wrote to St. Petersburg to say that the church was being constructed. Bantysh-Kamenskii, p. 152.

27. In making this translation I have used the documents in L. I. Duman, ed., *Russko-kitaiskie otnosheniia, 1689-1916: ofitsialnye dokumenty* (Moscow, 1958), pp. 19-20.

28. Cahen, *Histoire,* pp. 199-200; 219; 231, n. 3. On p. 256 Cahen mistakenly presents Shestopalov-Iablontsev as two different people. He also maintains (p. 258) that Pukhort replaced Shestopalov-Iablontsev, but he does not account for how Voeikov, whom Vladislavich had renounced, suddenly appears again in his former role as a student.

29. Cahen, *Histoire,* p. 231. On Aleksei Tret'iakov, see [E. P.] Sychevskii, *Istoricheskaia zapiska o kitaiskoi granitse* (Moscow, 1875), pp. 60, 75.

30. Bantysh-Kamenskii, p. 142; Cahen, *Histoire,* p. 232; Adoratskii (May), p. 110. One contingent of the caravan had already left Selenginsk on September 5.

31. Cahen, *Histoire,* pp. 256-257. Although on January 9, 1727 the Synod had determined only that Platkovskii should receive between 500-600 rubles, and the other members of the mission only enough to subsist on, on January 18 it prescribed the salaries that Vladislavich eventually paid (Bantysh-Kemanskii, p. 127, n. 1). Each member of the mission was also to be given fifty rubles for "church expenses." But of the three students who went to Peking with the caravan of 1727, Cahen reports (*Histoire,* p. 231) that the two Latinists, Voeikov and Pukhort, received 200 rubles and Tret'iakov, 130 rubles, on specific instructions from Vladislavich to Lange. The *Sibirskii Vestnik* reports in one place (p. 147) that everyone under Platkovskii got 130 rubles, and in another (p. 150), that the students earned 200 rubles, with an extra hundred going to the one who best succeeded in his studies. Adoratskii (May), p. 109, states that the students at first received 130 rubles a year, but that the amount "later grew to 200." When Lange ultimately gave Platkovskii the two-year salary of the entire mission, except for the three students who were

already in Peking, it was on the order of 2660 rubles. This would have been exactly enough for Platkovskii and six others; but we know that there were only five others—two clerics and three students. If the extra amount was thus intended for everyone's "church expenses," it is ten rubles too much; if it was intended for the two servants, it is not enough. Perhaps Lange's own accounts, generally well-kept, had suffered a lapse.

32. Cahen, *Histoire*, p. 257, n. 2; 258; Bantysh-Kamenskii, pp. 144-145.

33. Bantysh-Kamenskii, pp. 144-145.

34. Cahen, *Histoire*, p. 258.

35. See the appendix in Dudgeon: "Journal of Lange's residence at Peking in 1727-28," p. 11. For the full text of Lange's journal of this third trip to Peking see P. S. Pallas, ed., *Neue nordische Beyträge zur physikalischen und geographischen Erd- und Völkerbeschreibung, Naturgeschichte und Oekonomie* (St. Petersburg und Leipzig, 1781-1783), 2.83:159 (1781).

36. Cahen, *Histoire*, pp. 235-236; Bantysh-Kamenskii, p. 502.

37. Dudgeon, app., p. 6. In monthly terms this worked out to three taels silver and four *liang* white millet (Bantysh-Kamenskii, p. 142, n. 3).

38. Cahen, *Histoire*, p. 236. Some information on the Albazinians with whom Lange dealt may be gotten from another work by Gaston Cahen, *Le Livre de comptes de la caravane Russe à Pekin en 1727-1728* (Paris, 1911).

39. On June 30, 1728, for example, Vladislavich wrote to Ivan Bukholts, who was to be left in charge of frontier affairs under the authority of the voevoda of Irkutsk, that "when Archimandrite Antonii Platkovskii and two priests, three students, and two servants arrive in Selenginsk wanting to make their journey to Peking, write about their entry, with a suitable translator, to the Urga authorities." Vladislavich then went on to say that Platkovskii was quite available to carry any letters from Bukholts to Lange or Molokov in Peking, in cipher if need be. Sychevskii, pp. 62-64.

40. Bantysh-Kamenskii, p. 156.

41.   Sychevskii, p. 73.

42.   Adoratskii (May), p. 108, Veselovskii, pp. 33, 36.

43.   The *Kuo-tzu-chien chih* (Peking, 1834), 18:3a-3b, mistakenly lists all
      the Russian students as having arrived in 1728. In fact, the first
      contingent arrived in 1727 and the last three did not reach Peking until
      1729.

44.   Cahen, *Histoire*, p. 258, n. 3; Bantysh-Kamenskii, p. 164. The latter gives
      August 12 as the date of arrival in Selenginsk (p. 159, n. 1).

45.   Adoratskii (May), p. 113; Bantysh-Kamenskii, p. 164.

46.   Bantysh-Kamenskii, pp. 373-375. See also Mancall, *Russia and China*,
      pp. 257-258.

V. The Institutions of the Russian Mission

1.   Apart from the very helpful article of Meng Ssu-ming, "The E-lo-ssu
      kuan (Russian hostel) in Peking," *Harvard Journal of Asiatic Studies*,
      23:19-46 (1960-1961), I would like to record my reliance on the fol-
      lowing works in outlining this chapter: Paul Pelliot, "Le Hoja et le
      Sayyid Husain de l'histoire des Ming," *T'oung pao*, 38. livr. 2-5:81-
      292 (Leiden, 1948), esp. pp. 207-292; Jinichi Yano, "Pekin no Rokoku
      koshikan ni tsuite," *Geibun*, 6.10:884-894 (August 1915); 6.1:1065-
      1091 (October 1915); and Ho Ch'iu-t'ao, esp. chüan 9, 12, 13.

2.   *Shun-t'ien-fu chih* (Peking, 1884), 13:13a-b; *Jih-hsia chiu-wen k'ao*
      (Peking, 1764), 63:5a; 15a-b. The southern Hui-t'ung kuan was thus
      called the "nan kuan" long before it had become the Russian hostel.

3.   *Jih-hsia chiu-wen k'ao* (Peking, 1781), 62:20a. To the northwest of the
      hostel buildings was a large open space, included in the property of the
      Hui-t'ung kuan by mid-Ch'ing. See *Shun-t'ien fu-chih*, 13:13b. See also
      le Rev. P. Hyacinthe (Iakinf Bichurin), *Description de Pékin* (St. Peters-
      burg, 1829), p. 80.

4.   *Jih-hsia chiu-wen k'ao*, 63:15a.

5.   In making this statement I am offering only a theoretical argument,

mindful of the view of scholars like Hae-jong Chun that a tributary relationship could certainly fail to pay its way. See his article, "Sino-Korean Tributary Relations in the Ch'ing Period," in John K. Fairbank, ed., *The Chinese World Order* (Cambridge, Mass., 1968), pp. 90-111.

6. *Chia-ch'ing hui-tien shih-li,* 401:4a.

7. For this summary of the regulations pertaining to the administration of the Hui-t'ung kuan see the *K'ang-hsi hui tien,* chüan 73; *Yung-cheng hui-tien,* chüan 104, 105, 108; *Ch'ien-lung hui-tien tse-li,* chüan 56, 95, 142.

8. Baddeley, II, 326; *RKO,* I, 180, 551.

9. On the embassy of Plotnikov shortly after the treaty of Nerchinsk, and his residence in Peking, see *DAI,* X, 276-283.

10. *Ch'ien-lung hui-tien tse-li,* 142:38a.

11. Bell, II, 291-292.

12. Ibid.

13. *Ch'ien-lung hui-tien tse-li,* 95:1-b.

14. Ibid., 2a.

15. See, for example, the instructions to Gervasii Lintsevskii (Adoratskii [July], p. 321). However, the reference to the "posol'skii dvor" is deleted from the official letter of the Senate to the Li-fan yuan (ibid., p. 318).

16. Baddeley, II, 326; *RKO,* I, 371.

17. Bell, I, 440.

18. Bell, II, 253.

19. Ibid., pp. 280-281.

20. See Dudgeon, app., p. 3.

21. Adoratskii (August), p. 433.

22. Veselovskii, pp. 44-45.

23. The so-called *t'a-tzu kuan.*

24. See the instructions to Ilarion Trusov, *PSP,* first series, VIII, 308-313.

25. George Timkowski, *Travels of the Russian Mission through Mongolia to China and Residence in Peking in the Years 1820-1821* (London, 1827), II, 163-164. In the Russian version of Timkowski (Egor Fedorovich Timkovskii, *Puteshestvie v Kitai cherez Mongoliiu v 1820 i 1821 godakh* [St. Petersburg, 1824], II, 334), this passage reads as follows: "I may boldly say that for the noble person who is not afraid of seclusion, who enjoys intellectual endeavor, and who is willing to devote himself to the fulfillment of the fatherland's expectations, for such a person life in Peking will never give rise to a period of boredom or suffering."

26. See Apollon Mozharovskii, "Arkhimandrit Petr Kamenskii," *Russkaia Starina,* 85:323 (February 1896). See also Timkovski, II, 104.

27. Adoratskii (August), pp. 419-420. The descendants of Nestorov contested his will, but the Li-fan yuan awarded his house to the pei kuan in 1766.

28. Bantysh-Kamenskii, pp. 173, 195.

29. *Sibirskii Vestnik,* p. 161.

30. Adoratskii (June), p. 181.

31. Ibid. (August), p. 418.

32. Ibid., p. 417.

33. Ibid., pp. 417-418.

34. Ibid. (September), pp. 41-42.

35. Ibid. (October), p. 198.

36. Ibid., p. 202.

37. Timkowski, II, 45.

38. Ibid., p. 104.

39. *Nagel's Encyclopedia Guide: China* (Geneva, 1968), p. 506.

40. Bantysh-Kamenskii, p. 502.

41. Veselovskii, p. 19.

42. Ibid., p. 22. On February 2 of the old calendar occurs the holiday of "sretenie gospodina" in the Russian Orthodox church.

43. *Sibirskii Vestnik,* p. 151.

44. Adoratskii (July), pp. 326-327.

45. Ibid. (August), p. 414.

46. Ibid., pp. 415-416.

47. Ibid., p. 414.

48. Ibid. (September), p. 41.

49. Ibid. (October), p. 198.

50. Ibid. (May), pp. 128-129.

51. Ibid. (July), p. 328.

52. Ibid.

53. Ibid. (September), p. 43.

54. Timkowski, II, 56.

55. Adoratskii (August), p. 419.

56. Ibid., p. 420.

57. Ibid. (October), pp. 198-199.

58. Ho Ch'iu-t'ao, 12:2a; 9; 19a-b. Escorts (*ling-ts'ui*) were also provided during the changing of the mission or for walks outside the compound. For other references to the *chien-tu* see Bell, II, 332, and Timkowski, II, 46.

59. Ho Ch'iu-t'ao, 12:2b; 9:21a.

60. Dudgeon, p. 20.

61. Ho Ch'iu-t'ao, 37:7b-8a. See also the *Ch'ing-ch'ao wen-hsien t'ung-k'ao* (compiled in 1787; reprinted Taipei, 1963), p. 7485. When Russian cara-vans were in town a special censor was appointed (*Ch'ien-lung hui-tien*, 81:10a) as well as a special escort and supervisor of the trade (*Ch'ien-lung hui-tien tse-li*, 142:40b; 147:21a).

62. Ho Ch'iu-t'ao, 37:7b.

63. *Ch'ien-lung hui tien tse-li*, 142:38b, 40a; Bell, 1:372-373.

64. Timkowski, II, 4. Dudgeon says: "For aught known to the contrary, the same sums are still disbursed yearly from the treasury for the same purposes; in fact it is said that the officials themselves now appropriate the sum formerly given to the ecclesiastical mission." (p. 36).

65. Dudgeon, p. 36.

66. *Sibirskii Vestnik*, p. 183.

67. Adoratskii (June), p. 183.

68. Timkowski, II, 38. There was also a well in the Russian hostel proper, but according to the notation on the plan of the mission provided by Timkowski in the Russian edition of his book (see page 201) neither well had potable water.

69. Sychevskii, p. 111.

70. Ho Ch'iu-t'ao, 37:7b-8a.

71. See Yao Yuan-chih, *Chu-yeh-t'ing tsa-chi* (1893; reprinted Taipei, 1969), 3:22b.

72. Adoratskii (July), p. 329.

73. Bantysh-Kamenskii, pp. 305-306.

74. Adoratskii (October), p. 210.

75. Timkowski, II, 123.

76. Baddeley, II, 245. Two of the letters were translated by a Chinese, or someone who knew Chinese, that Milescu found in Tobolsk (Bantysh-Kamenskii, pp. 6-7).

77. Bantysh-Kamenskii, p. 25.

78. Baddeley, II, 299, 310.

79. Iakovleva, p. 168.

80. Ides, for example, was asked in Peking in 1694 what languages he knew; his answer was "German, low-Dutch, a little Italian, and Muscovite" (Ides, p. 70). One person in the embassy knew a little Latin, but was unable to use it successfully in talking with the Jesuits, so Italian was employed as the language for negotiation (Brand, p. 137). In 1720 Izmailov's Latin translator died in Irkutsk, on the way to China (Bell, I, 313).

81. Hoo Chi-tsai, *Les Bases conventionnelles des relations modernes entre la Chine et la Russie* (Paris, 1918), p. 59.

82. Bantysh-Kamenskii, p. 123.

83. For more on the initial Russian effort at learning Japanese, see chap. 7.

84. C. K. Bulich, "Ocherk istorii iazykoznaniia v Rossii," *Zapiski istoriko-filologicheskago fakul'teta imperatorskago S. Peterburgskago universiteta*, 75:194 (St. Petersburg, 1904).

85. In Russia the first native teacher of Manchu, and perhaps Chinese as well, was a Manchu soldier named Chou Ko, who arrived in St. Petersburg in the late 1730s. For more on him, see chap. 7. The *PSI*, II, 365-367, carries this ukase dating from 1722: "In recent years a man came to us

from China, entered the Selenginsk monastery, near Irkutsk, took baptism, and now resides there. [Since] he knows how to read and write Manchu and Chinese, ... take that man and send him to St. Petersburg;" but nothing seems to have come of it.

86. A most helpful work on the Ming—Ch'ing experience with foreign language is that of Pelliot, pp. 207-292. For the training of translators the Ssu-i kuan was established in 1407, shortly after the return of Cheng Ho's fleet (see J. J. L. Duyvendak, "The True Dates of the Chinese Maritime Expeditions in the Early Fifteenth Century," *T'oung pao* 34.5:360 [1939]). For the preparation of interpreters, as well as for the accommodation of tribute missions, the institution of the Hui-t'ung kuan was, as we have seen, established in 1441 in Peking, but it actually dates from 1408, where it was first organized in Nanking (Pelliot, p. 253). The two institutions were combined into the Hui-t'ung ssu-i kuan under Ch'ien-lung in 1748. Unlike the O-lo-ssu wen kuan, they were under the administration of the Board of Rites, and daily operations were conducted by the Hanlin Academy. See also R. Hirth, "The Chinese Oriental College," *Journal of the China Branch of the Royal Asiatic Society* (Shanghai, 1887), new series, 22. 3-4:203-223; G. Deveria, "Histoire du college des interprètes de Peking," *Mélanges Charles de Harlez* (1896), pp. 34-102; and Knight Biggerstaff, *The Earliest Modern Government Schools in China* (Ithaca, N.Y., 1961).

87. My reference here is to the deserters, Ivan Artem'ev and Stenka Verkhotur'. See Liubimov.

88. Bantysh-Kamenskii, p. 47.

89. *K'ang-hsi shih-lu,* 160:26a-b.

90. Bell, II, 24.

91. J. L. Stevenson, ed., *John Bell of Antermony: A Journey from St. Petersburg to Pekin, 1719-1722* (Edinburgh, 1965), p. 97.

92. *Jih-hsia chiu-wen k'ao*, 62:20a. Timkowski confirms this location (II, 121).

93. *KSTK*, p. 160.

94. *Ch'ien-lung shih-lu,* 539:23a-b, contains the first set of regulations for

the school. The regulations were modified several times (Meng, pp. 42-43), making it more difficult by the nineteenth century for a graduate to become an official. For other sources, see *Chia-ch'ing hui-tien shih-li,* 12:22, and Ho Ch'iu-t'ao, 12:2a, where he lists only one proctor for the school. The precedent for the O-lo-ssu wen kuan would seem to go back to the Manchu "Eight Banner Schools" (pa-ch'i hsueh-kuan) which had, from the time of Shun-chih, trained Manchu students in the study of Chinese. Although the numbers of students and professors obviously varied, the organization of both institutions lay within the banner system; and professors in both cases were appointed from the faculty of the Imperial Academy (Kuo-tzu-chien). See the paper of Nancy Evans, "The Canton T'ung-wen Kuan: A Study of the Role of the Bannermen in One Area of Self-strengthening," in *Papers on China* (East Asian Research Center, Harvard University, 1969), 22a:89-103 (1969).

95. Timkowski, I, 338.

96. I am indebted to Mr. Li Hsueh-chih of the Institute of History and Philology, Academia Sinica, in Nankang, Taiwan, for showing me actual copies of examinations taken by the Ch'ing students in the O-lo-ssu wen kuan during Ch'ien-lung times.

97. Timkowski, I, 369.

98. Meng, pp. 40-41, states that because the Manchus were unable to translate Milovanov's official letter in 1670, but were able to translate that of Ides in 1693, it is likely that the O-lo-ssu wen kuan was established between 1670 and 1693. But the availability of native Russian translators has already been demonstrated.

99. Aleksandr Kazimirovich Korsak, *Istoriko-statisticheskoe obozrenie torgovykh snoshenii Rossii c Kitaem* (Kazan, 1857), p. 16.

100. P. E. Skachkov, "Istoriia izucheniia Kitaia v Rossii v xvii i viii vv," *Mezhdunarodnye sviazi Rossii v xvii-xviii vv.* (Moscow, 1966), p. 164.

101. Adoratskii (June), p. 127; (August), p. 423.

102. Ho Ch'iu-t'ao, 12:5b.

103. *Ch'ien-lung shih-lu,* 539:23a.

214 Notes to pages 107-110

104. Fu, I, 205; II, 540.

105. Meng, p. 42.

106. Veselovskii, p. 66.

107. Ibid., p. 40. The children were all apostates.

108. Stenka Kozmin was a fur trader from Yeniseisk.

109. Cahen, *Livre*, p. 10.

110. That Savin was literate is attested to by the fact that Antonii Platkovskii tried unsuccessfully to have him appointed to translate a Chinese book into Russian. Adoratskii (May), p. 128.

111. Cahen, *Livre*, passim.

112. *Sibirskii Vestnik*, p. 125.

113. Skachkov, "Istoriia izucheniia Kitaiia," p. 164.

114. Bantysh-Kamenskii, p. 81.

115. Bell, II, 374-375.

116. For information on the Latin school see Joseph Brucker S.J., "La Mission de Chine de 1722 à 1735," *Revue des questions historiques*, 58: 491-532 (Paris, Apr. 1, 1881); and M. L. Aimé-Martin, ed., *Lettres édifiantes et curieuses écrites des missions étrangères*, 23:324 (Paris, 1811).

117. Brucker, p. 518.

118. Bantysh-Kamenskii, p. 214.

119. See Adoratskii (August), p. 440. See also M. L. Aimé-Martin, ed., *Lettres édifiantes et curieuses concernant l'Asie, l'Afrique et l'Amérique avec quelque relations nouvelles des missions* (Paris, 1838-1843), IV, 67. When Vladislavich arrived in Peking in 1726 he carried a letter from the new tsarina, Catherine, to Yung-cheng, which Parrenin

was asked to translate for the emperor. The Latin copy of the letter ended *"tua bona amica Catharina."* According to Father Jacques, a confrère of Parrenin, "Les Chinois en sont fort surpris. Ils ne veulent point se mettre dans la tête que qui que ce soit au monde puisse se faire égal à leur souverain." See *Revue de l'extrême-Orient,* 3:69-70 (Paris, 1887).

120. Normally the Ch'ing prepared interpreters and translators (i.e., those who make written translations) in separate institutions. The O-lo-ssu wen kuan seems to have incorporated both purposes, but emphasized the latter. According to the memorial of Grand Secretary Fu-heng, seen by the emperor on July 12, 1757, "the students who learn the Russian language were originally meant to be used as translators of the official letters which we receive from and send to Russia." *Ch'ien-lung shih-lu,* 539:23a.

121. *Ch'ien-lung shih-lu,* 1375:16b-17a. See Fu, I, 312, from whom I have borrowed this translation.

122. Timkowski, I, 370.

123. Ibid., I, 52-53, 159; II, 431.

124. Ibid., I, 338, 368; II, 122.

125. Dudgeon, p. 26.

126. See the *Chia-ch'ing ch'ung-hsiu i-t'ung-chih* (published in 1812; reprinted Taipei, 1967), 4:13b.

127. See the *Kuo-tzu-chien chih,* 18:3a, Bantysh-Kamenskii, p. 164. Textbooks were also supplied (*Kuo-tzu-chien tse-li* [Peking, 1823], chüan 44). See Meng, p. 38, for the regulations governing the appointment of professors. According to Anton Vladykin, a student in Peking at the end of the eighteenth century, the teachers "recived no salary and were thus lazy and devious," Adoratskii (September), p. 57.

128. Timkowski, I, 351.

129. Ho Ch'iu-t'ao, 13:3b. Here the Russian students are said to be coming to study a "craft" or "trade."

130. *Ch'ien-lung hui-tien tse-li,* chüan 157. On the Liu-ch'iu students see also Ta-tuan Ch'en, "Investiture of Liu-ch'iu Kings in the Ch'ing Period," in Fairbank, ed., *The Chinese World Order,* pp. 136, 157, 160.

131. *Chia-ch'ing ch'ung-hsiu i-t'ung-chih,* 4:13a.

132. *Kuo-tzu-chien chih,* 18:3a. Here the students from Liu-ch'iu and Russia are listed under the section *"wai-fan ju hsueh"* (external vassals who come to study).

133. A. I. Kononov, "Stoletie vostochnogo fakul'teta Leningradskogo Universiteta (1855-1955)," *Sovetskoe Vostokovedenie,* 2:83 (1956).

134. See my paper, "Archimandrite Palladius and Chinese Control of Barbarians in 1858," *Papers on China,* 19:55-86 (East Asian Research Center, Harvard University, 1965).

VI. The Missionary Life in Eighteenth-Century Peking

1.   *Sibirskii Vestnik,* p. 147.

2.   *TKDA,* pp. 310-311.

3.   Adoratskii (May), pp. 123-124.

4.   Bantysh-Kamenskii, p. 194.

5.   Platkovskii had wanted the Albazinian Iakov Savin to translate the book (the *tzu lüeh,* an elementary school vocabulary) but he had no authority over Savin who was of course a Ch'ing subject. See Adoratskii (May), pp. 127-128. According to Cahen (pp. 259-260) Savin was also engaged as a private tutor by the students of the second mission, but never arrived.

6.   Veselovskii, p. 19.

7.   Adoratskii (May), p. 130.

8.   Ibid., p. 131; Bantysh-Kamenskii, p. 210; Veselovskii, pp. 70-71.

9.   *PSP,* first series, VIII, 299 (1898).

10. Veselovskii, pp. 65-66; Adoratskii (May), pp. 124-125, 131 n.

11. *PSP*, first series, VIII, 305; Cahen, *Histoire*, p. 262.

12. Bantysh-Kamenskii, p. 189; Adoratskii (May), p. 130. According to the students, Platkovskii's first request to return to Russia was made on the day he arrived in Peking.

13. Cahen, *Histoire*, p. 259.

14. Bantysh-Kamenskii, p. 189. The letter was received in St. Petersburg on February 19, 1732.

15. Ibid. See also Cahen, *Histoire*, p. 361; Adoratskii (May), p. 132.

16. Adoratskii (May), p. 133.

17. Cahen, *Histoire*, p. 263.

18. Hieromonk Lavrentii, it will be remembered, as a member of the first ecclesiastical mission to Peking, carried the rank of an eight-grade official.

19. Veselovskii, pp. 65-71. It should be noted that here Veselovskii is reproducing the reminiscences of Hieromonk Feodosii Smorzhenskii of the fourth mission.

20. For this information see Parry, p. 42; he cites several early volumes of the *Opis' dokumentov i del' khraniashchikhsia v arkhive sviateishago pravitel' stvuiushchago Synoda* (St. Petersburg, 1868-1914) that I have been unable to acquire.

21. Adoratskii (June), p. 167.

22. Bantysh-Kamenskii, p. 164.

23. Adoratskii (May), p. 128.

24. *PSP*, first series, VIII, 300.

25. Cahen, *Histoire*, p. 261.

26. Bantysh-Kamenskii, p. 212.

27. Letter to the College of Foreign Affairs, relayed to the Synod on
     February 19, 1734, *PSP*, first series, VIII, 301.

28. Veselovskii, p. 29.

29. Bantysh-Kamenskii, pp. 173, 194–195, 210, 218, 234.

30. For these details of Trusov's life see Veselovskii, p. 32; and Cahen,
     Histoire, pp. 262–263.

31. Veselovskii, p. 32.

32. Successor of Innokentii Kul'chitskii in 1731.

33. *PSP*, first series, VIII, 268–269.

34. Ibid., pp. 307–308.

35. Ibid., pp. 308–313.

36. On February 2 of the old calendar falls the holiday of Srentenie Gospodina.
     From this the Russians usually referred to their church in Peking as the
     "Sretenskii church."

37. By this system, the Russian caravan which, as stipulated, was admitted to
     Peking once every three years, would pay the missionaries and students
     their salaries in silver after the conclusion of the trade in the Russian
     hostel. The vouchers of the mission were kept on account in the Sibir-
     skii Prikaz. After 1755 this system broke down because no more cara-
     vans were sent to Peking. Instead the mission members would attempt
     to haul enough furs or silver to Peking to last them the length of their
     stay there.

38. The passport, of course, was for passage from one place to another
     inside of Russia.

39. Bantysh-Kamenskii, p. 217.

40. Here Platkovskii's point is that Lange is a non-Orthodox Protestant.

41. Veselovskii, pp. 21, 30-31.

42. Bantysh-Kamenskii, p. 217, 234.

43. *Sibirskii Vestnik,* p. 185; Veselovskii, pp. 20-21, 31; Adoratskii (May), pp. 134-135; (June), pp. 182-183.

44. Adoratskii (June), p. 187.

45. Bantysh-Kamenskii, pp. 244, 248-249.

46. Adoratskii (June), p. 185. According to Bantysh-Kamenskii (p. 244), however, Ivanov survived and returned to Russia in 1742. He was, in any case, replaced by someone named Koz'ma Bobrovkin.

47. Ibid. (June), p. 185; (July), p. 320. Ioasaf Ivanovskii died during the fourth mission (1745-1755).

48. Ibid. (June), pp. 187-188.

49. Bantysh-Kamenskii, pp. 242-243; Veselovskii, p. 22.

50. Bantysh-Kamenskii, p. 243.

51. On April 20, 1742. Ibid., p. 244.

52. Ibid., pp. 245-246.

53. Veselovskii, p. 22.

54. Ibid.

55. Adoratskii (July), p. 312.

56. At first a hieromonk named Symeon Shmigel'skii and a hierodeacon, Ioil' Vrublevskii, were chosen to accompany Lintsevskii to Peking (another deacon, Ioasaf, already being there since the second mission). But upon arriving in St. Petersburg to be inscribed in the fourth mission, these two implored the Synod to be released from going to China. On October 29, 1742 the Synod replaced them with two hierodeacons, Ilarion Zavalevich and Feodosii Smorzhenskii. Smorzhenskii (who later

contributed the first written history of the mission, which is contained in the work of Veselovskii) was very unhappy about going to Peking but had no compelling excuses. Zavalevich, however, was excused because he had not long before been a Uniat, and was, furthermore, experiencing nightly headaches. In his place Ioil' Vrublevskii was conscripted again and promoted to Hieromonk. There were, in addition, several assistants: Sozont Karpov, Kirilo Semenov, and Kirilo Ivanov; Aleksei Smol'nitskii was the private attendant of Archimandrite Gervasii; and two other servants, Timofei Andreev and Matfei Storozhenko. Only one student was selected: Efim Sakhnovskii. See Adoratskii (July), pp. 313-316; Bantysh-Kamenskii, p. 253.

57.   Later, one of the servants escaped from the mission (in Tomsk) and two others were left behind at the frontier because of illness. Adoratskii (July), p. 319 n. 1, 322.

58.   For this information on Lebratovskii, see Veselovskii, pp. 24-26; and Kh. Trusevich, *Posol'skiia i torgovliia snosheniia Rossii s Kitaem (do XIX veka)*, Moscow, 1882, pp. 125-126.

59.   Polycarpo de Souza (d. 1757), the last Roman Catholic bishop of Peking in the eighteenth century. See Joseph Krahl, S.J., *China Missions in Crisis: Bishop Laimbeckhoven and His Times 1738-1787* (Rome, 1964), p. 190.

60.   Bantysh-Kamenskii, pp. 253-254.

61.   Adoratskii (July), pp. 330-331. In Aimé-Martin, III, 64, it is noted by A. M. de L'isle (28 August 1752): "Je ne sais où sont les affaires des prêtres et disciples russes laissés ici; on dit qu'ils ne s'accordent guère ensemble."

62.   Yumatov's staff also consisted of Hieromonk Silvestr Spitsyn, a hierodeacon named Sergei; three assistants, Stepan Zimin, Il'iia Ivanov, and Aleksei Danilov; two servants, Vasilii Aleksandrov and Ivan Kozolavskii; Spitsyn's son Grigorii, and four students: Vavila Ermolaev, Stefan Sokolov, Stefan Iakimov, and Ivan Ozerov. See Bantysh-Kamenskii, pp. 260-261; Adoratskii (August), pp. 402-405.

63.   Bantysh-Kamenskii, pp. 262-263. One of the assistants, Il'iia Ivanov, and the servants had to return immediately to Russia, presumably because they exceeded the numbers prescribed by the Kiakhta treaty.

64. In explanation the Li-fan yuan wrote that there was nothing in the treaty stating that new students had to be accepted in exchange for the old ones. Ibid., p. 262.

65. See chap. 8.

66. For the text of this report, see Adoratskii (August), pp. 422 ff.

67. Bantysh-Kamenskii, pp. 277-278.

68. Veselovskii, pp. 26-28.

69. Apart from the missions of Vasilii Bratishchev and Ivan Kropotov, a number of messengers—Arbuzov, Streakalov, and Zamoshchikov—visited Peking with diplomatic business. See Bantysh-Kamenskii, pp. 271-288, passim.

70. Ibid., p. 277.

71. *Sibirskii Vestnik*, p. 172.

72. Adoratskii (August), p. 426.

73. The Ch'ing stated: "And inasmuch as the Russians have begun to behave respectably and submissively, the mission may be changed." Sychevskii, p. 287. See chap. 8.

74. Adoratskii (September), pp. 30-32. Tsvet's subordinates were two hiero-monks named Iust and Ioannikii; a hierodeacon named Nikifor; and two psalm readers, Semen Tsvet (a relative?) and Semen Kilevskii. They were all selected by Tsvet himself. No students were enlisted, because it was not yet known whether they would be accepted in China. Tsvet's monastery was evidently the same as that to which Antonii Platkovskii had been removed.

75. For a long time no copy of these instructions, which dated from 1734, could be found. A search was conducted in the offices of the Synod in St. Petersburg, and then of the typographer. They seemed to be in neither place, nor in the Synod chambers in Moscow. Finally it was decided to look for them in Irkutsk, and even in Peking, but before the search was continued they must have been located. At least it appears that Tsvet had them before he left St. Petersburg. Ibid., pp. 32-35.

76. They were Aleksei Agafonov, Feodor Baksheev, and Aleksei Paryshev (from Tobolsk), and Iakov Korkin. Ibid., pp. 37-38.

77. Ibid., p. 54. For some reason Tsvet sent this letter to Macao, from where it was sent to England, and finally to Russia. They were sent on January 7, 1778 and arrived on August 22.

78. Ibid., pp. 47-48.

79. These included the priest Ioann [ikii] Protopopov, the church assistant Petr Rodionov, and three of the four students: Agafonov, Baksheev, and Paryshev. Adoratskii (September), p. 55.

80. The mission, apart from Shishkovskii, consisted of Hieromonks Antonii Sedel'nikov and Aleksei Bogolepov, a hierodeacon named Israil, two assistants, Ivan Orlov and Semen Sokolovskii, students Egor Salertovskii, Ivan Filonov, and Anton Vladyikin, and one chorister, Aleksei Petrov Popov. Ibid. (October), pp. 190-191.

81. Ibid., pp. 192-195.

82. For the information on the passage of the mission to the frontier see ibid., pp. 196-197; for Shishkovskii's report (of May 13, 1783), ibid., p. 199.

83. Ibid., p. 210. Adoratskii comments that the students were also able to inform themselves on matters pertaining to the trade between China and Russia through the confidences of an official translator of Russian named "Iun' -chin." This may well have been Yuan Ch'eng-ning, who in 1791 was ordered by the emperor to remain in Peking, where his expertise was much in demand. See Fu, I, 312; Ch'ien-lung shih-lu, 1375; 16b-17a; and my note 121 to chap. 5.

84. Adoratskii (October), p. 209.

85. Timkowski, II, 56; Adoratskii (November), p. 305. Two days later, on May 25, Shishkovskii's young chorister, Aleksei Popov, also died.

VII. The Ecclesiastical Mission and the Problem of "China"
in Eighteenth-Century Russia

1. Primary documents relating to these, and other, missionary efforts of

the Russian church may be found in *PSP*, first series, IV, 145-150; V, 3-4, 20-21, 48, 416; VI, 127-131; VIII, 229-235, 335-339; second series, II, 15-16, 76-77, 97 ff., 143-145, 301-303, 383-385, 432-434; third series, I, 723-784. A useful book on the subject is Josef Glazik's *Die Russisch-Orthodoxe Heiden-mission seit Peter dem Grossen* (Münster, 1954).

2.   Adoratskii (July), p. 329.

3.   Ibid. (August), pp. 420-422; (September), pp. 48-49; (October), p. 199.

4.   Timkowski, II, 47.

5.   V. Mirotvortsev, "Materialy dlia istorii Pekinskoi dukhovnoi missii," *Pravoslavnyi Sobesednik* (October 1888), p. 262.

6.   Pavlovsky, p. 163.

7.   *PSP*, first series, II, 498; second series, II, 181-182; third series, I, 479-480. On April 21, 1733, having received a notice from the King of Prussia, the tsarina ordered that Russia give attention to the religious needs of the Orthodox soldiers serving in the Prussian army. On June 11 the Synod dispatched a priest named Vasilii Shcherbatskii, along with four choristers, a cook, prayer books, antimins, myrrh, wine, incense, candles, charcoal, and money, to Prussia. See ibid., first series, VIII, 65; 76-82; 91-92; 363-364.

8.   Adoratskii (August), p. 445; (October), p. 199.

9.   Timkowski, II, 103.

10.   Adoratskii (February), p. 254; (March), p. 350.

11.   Here I am not counting the arrivals in Peking of Bratishchev in 1757 or Kropotov in 1762. Neither were, properly speaking, ambassadors. When Kropotov returned to China in 1767, now with plenipotentiary powers, he did his negotiating on the border, not in Peking. A good example, incidentally, of the Russian view of its "diplomatic" outpost in Peking is V. A. Ulianitskii, *Russkiia konsul'stva za granitseiu v xviii veke* (Moscow, 1899).

12.   On March 5, 1744, Andrei Genevskii, a priest in Paris, asked the Synod to send him church equipment, assistants, and money. *PSP*, second

series, II, 31-32. On October 28, 1724, the College of Foreign Affairs relayed to the Synod the message from the Russian envoy to Holland, Prince Boris Kurakin, that a church and holy antimins were needed there. *PSP,* first series, IV, 256. See also ibid., second series, II, 300. The College of Foreign Affairs received a letter from Stockholm on May 22, 1722; it was written on April 30 by Kameriunker Mikhail Bezstuzhev, who related that "the Russian church that was in Sweden before the war is still in good condition and all the church vessels are still there, only there is not any priest. All the other foreign ministries have their chapels here, so please send a priest to direct the divine service, the more so since many Russian merchants are beginning to arrive and it is impossible for them to remain here without a priest." The college passed this letter on to the Synod on August 17, 1722; a priest, Davyd Skalub, was assigned to Stockholm. Ibid., first series, II, 297.

13. Ibid., second series, II, 297.

14. In the eighteenth century Russian students were also sent to France, England (where, among other things, they were to study Oriental languages at Oxford), and Constantinople (where they were housed in the Russian diplomatic mission).

15. For information on the Japanese school see Bulich, pp. 383-396; G. E. Lensen, *The Russian Push toward Japan: Russo-Japanese Relations, 1697-1875* (Princeton, 1959), pp. 29-43; O. P. Petrova, "Iaponskii iazyk v Rossii v pervoi polovine xviii veka," *Narody Azii i Afriki,* 1:163-177 (1965); N. N. Ogloblin, "Pervyi Iaponets v Rossii, 1701-1705 gg.," *Russkaia Starina,* no. 72 (1891), esp. p. 19; A. Sgibnev, "Ob obuchenii v Rossii iaponskomu iazyky," *Morskoi Sbornik* (1868), no. 12.

16. In *PSP,* first series, VIII, 259, his name is given as "Gomzo."

17. Adoratskii (July), p. 321.

18. Barthold, p. 230.

19. Cahen, *Histoire,* p. 155.

20. *PSP,* first series, IV, 227-229.

21. For information on the school of Mongolian see Bulich, pp. 194-195; 396-403; A. Likhovitskii, "Prosveshchenie v Sibiri v pervoi polovine xviii stoletiia," *Zhurnal Ministerstva Narodnago Prosveshcheniia*, 360.3:1-29 (July, 1905).

22. Shcheglov, p. 322.

23. On Bayer see Bulich, pp. 219-220; 368-371; Skachkov, "Istoriia izucheniia," p. 163.

24. On Pukhort see *PSP*, III, 536-537; IV, 487, 643-644; V, 377, 450-451, 645-647, 958-959; VII, passim; see also M. I. Radovskii, "Russkii kitaeved I. K. Rossokhin," *Iz istorii nauki i tekniki v stranakh vostoka* (Moscow, 1961), II, 88-99.

25. On Chou Ko, see Bantysh-Kamenskii, p. 245; *Materialy dlia istorii imperatorskoi akademii nauk*, vol. 4 (1887), pp. 643-644; vol. 5 (1889), pp. 341, 345; P. E. Skachkov, "Pervyi prepodavatel' kitaiskogo iazyka v Rossii," *Problemy Vostokovedeniia*, 3:198-201 (1960).

26. The precise details of Rossokhin's birth are still to be established. V. P. Taranovich, "Illarion Rossokhin i ego trudy po kitaevendeniiu," *Sovetskoe Vostokovedenie*, 3:225-226 (1945).

27. V. S. Starikov, "Larion Rossokhin i nachalo izucheniia kitaiskoi pirotekhniki v Rossii," *Iz istorii nauki i tekhniki v stranakh vostoka*, 2:100-125 (Moscow, 1961).

28. Taranovich, p. 227. It is reported, however, that in 1748 a visit was paid to Rossokhin's library and school by Marquis Sacramozo of Malta and another "Maltese cavalier." Rossokhin related to them the contents of several of the Chinese books and "his students carried on a conversation in Chinese and Manchu with exceptional competence." See Petr Pekarskii, *Istoriia imperatorskoi akademii nauk v. Peterburge* (St. Petersburg, 1870-1873), II, xxxvii.

29. T. K. Shafranovskii and K. I. Shafranovskii, "Priobretenie v nachale xviii v. kitaiskikh knig rossiiskim rezidentom v Kitae Lorentsom Langom," *Strany i narody vostoka*, 1:295 (Moscow, 1959).

30. R. V. Obchinikov, " 'Rapport' M. V. Lomonosova i drugikh akademikov

v senat o perevode 'istorii kitaiskogo gosudarstva'," *Istoricheskii Arkhiv,*
6:234 (1961).

31. *Materialy dlia istorii akademii nauk,* V, 345.

32. On Bykov see Bulich, p. 378; *Materialy dlia istorii akademii nauk,* IX,
     163-164, 221-222, 304.

33. Taranovich, pp. 229-239, gives a full compilation of Rossokhin's
     translations.

34. *Materialy dlia istorii akademii nauk,* VII, 294. See also Taranovich, pp.
     227-228.

35. See P. E. Skachkov, "O neizvestnykh rukopisiakh Lariona Rossokhina,"
     Narody Azii i Afriki, 1:158-159 (1965); T. K. Shafranovskaia, "Peozdka
     lekaria Frantsa Elachicha v 1753-1756 gg. v Pekin dlia popolneniia
     kitaishkikh kollektsii kunst (-) kamery," *Iz istorii nauki i tekhniki v
     stranakh vostoka* (Moscow, 1961), II, 126-131.

36. Bantysh-Kamenskii, p. 262. See also Sergei M. Solov'ev, *Istoriia Rossii
     s drevneishikh vremen* (Moscow, 1959-1966), XII, 390. The Senate
     reimbursed Vladykin.

37. R. V. Obchinikov, p. 234.

38. G. F. Müller, ed., *Ezhemesiachnyia sochineniia i izvestiia uchenykh
     delakh* (July-December, 1764).

39. No more is known about the Chinese "Vasiliev" except that his father
     was said to be an important general in Fukien (Skachkov, "Istoriia
     izucheniia," p. 169). On Leont'ev's school see *PSP* third series, 1:56.
     Information on Leont'ev is also obtainable from A. V. Strenina, "U
     istokov russkogo i mirovogo kitaevedeniia," *Sovetskaia Etnografiia,*
     1:170-177 (1950).

40. Skachkov, "Istoriia izucheniia," p. 170.

41. Veselovskii, p. 37.

42. Skachkov, "Istoriia izucheniia," p. 170.

43. V. P. Vasil'ev, "Vospominanie ob I. I. Zakharov," *Zhurnal Ministerstva Narodnago Prosveshcheniia* (November 1885), p. 94.

44. In Russian: "Obstoiatel'nogo opisaniia prosikhozhdeniia i sostoianiia manchzhurskogo naroda i voiska." The *Pa-ch'i t'ung-chih* was printed in China in 1739. The Russian translation runs to sixteen volumes (five by Rossokhin and eleven by Leont'ev), with a seventeenth volume of notes. See Z. I. Gorbacheva and D. I. Tikhonov, "Iz istorii izucheniia Kitaia v Rossii," *Sovetskoe Vostokovedenie,* 2:141 (1955); Skachkov, "Istoriia izucheniia," pp. 168-169. For a summary of Leont'ev's translations see Strenina, pp. 170-171; Skachkov, "Istoriia izucheniia," pp. 170-173.

45. Adoratskii (September), p. 49.

46. See Skachkov, "Istoriia izucheniia," p. 173, for treatment of these three students.

47. Ibid., pp. 174-175; Adoratskii (October), pp. 209-210.

48. For drawing my attention to these works, cited in P. E. Skachkov's *Bibliografiia Kitaia* (Moscow, 1960), I am indebted to Ms. Alison Dray-Novey.

49. See Hans Rogger, *National Consciousness in Eighteenth-Century Russia* (Cambridge, Mass., 1960).

VIII. Sino-Russian Relations in the Eighteenth Century

1.   Mark Mancall, "Russia and China: the Structure of Contact," in Wayne S. Vucinich, ed., *Russia and Asia: Essays on the Influence of Russia on the Asian Peoples* (Stanford, 1972), p. 321.

2.   For information on these missions see Bantysh-Kamenskii, pp. 174-187; Fu, pp. 160-161, 516-517; Liu Tse-jung and Wang Chih-hsiang, eds., *Ku-kung O-wen shih-liao* (Peiping, 1936), no. 23; Mark Mancall, "China's First Missions to Russia, 1729-1731," *Papers on China,* 9:75-110 (East Asian Research Center, Harvard University, 1955). When the second Manchu embassy was entertained in St. Petersburg its presence at the Russian court was recorded by Mrs. William Vigor, *Letters from Russia* (New York, 1970), pp. 81-85. Although conversation was very polite, one of the Manchu envoys did yield the opinion that the eyes of Princess Elizabeth were too large for her face.

3.   The paper of Joseph F. Fletcher, "China and Central Asia, 1368-1884," in Fairbank, ed., *Chinese World Order,* pp. 206-224, takes up this question on the basis of impressive research into Ming and Manchu history.

4.   Bantysh-Kamenskii, pp. 187, 190, 193, 240-241. For the memorial from the Li-fan yuan and the edict of the emperor on this matter, see *Ch'ien-lung shih-lu,* 100:14a-15a.

5.   Bantysh-Kamenskii, pp. 245-247.

6.   *Yung-cheng shih-lu,* 110:9b.

7.   Bantysh-Kamenskii, p. 229. Lange's journal of this, his last visit to Peking is reproduced in Pallas, II, chap. 8.

8.   M. P. Putsillo, *Ukazatel' delam i rukopisiam otnosiashchimsia do Sibiri i prinadlezhashchikh Moskovskomu Glavnomu Arkhivu Min. Ino. Del'* (Moscow, 1879), p. 71; Shcheglov, p. 222. Later in the century, China stopped the rhubarb trade with Russia, believing that "it was a necessity" there. The export of rhubarb was even prohibited along the China coast by the emperor, who believed it would be resold to the Russians. See *Ch'ien-lung shih-lu* for 1789, esp. 1320:7b-9b; 1323:32a-32b.

9.   Bantysh-Kamenskii, pp. 169, 206, 224-225.

10. For evidence that this was in fact the Ch'ing view and not just a simplification of modern Chinese history, see the later edict of Ch'ien-lung on October 10, 1763 (*Ch'ien-lung shih-lu,* 694:4b-5a).

11. Bantysh-Kamenskii, pp. 215-217; Pavlovsky, p. 32; P. I. Kabanov, *Amurskii vopros* (Blagoveshchensk, 1959), p. 29.

12. Bantysh-Kamenskii, p. 199.

13. Mikinosuke Ishida, "A Biographical Study of Giuseppe Castiglione (Lang Shih-ning), a Jesuit Painter in the Court of Peking under the Ch'ing Dynasty," *Memoirs of the Research Department of the Toyo Bunko,* 19:99 (1960). See also Henri Cordier, "Les Conquêtes de l'Empereur de la Chine," in *Memoires concernant l'Asie Orientale* (Paris, 1913).

14. *Ch'ien-lung shih-lu,* 555:33a.

15. See Bantysh-Kamenskii, pp. 285-297.

16. Ibid., p. 262.

17. Translations may be found in Fu, I, 211-212; 277-280.

18. On Chinggunzab see the article by Charles R. Bawden, "The Mongol Rebellion of 1756-1757," *Journal of Asian History,* 2.1:1-31 (1968).

19. For this poem see the *Hsi-yü t'u-chih* of Fu-heng et al. (published in 1762), chüan shou 2, 25b. I am borrowing this translation from Lo-shu Fu, II, 543.

20. On the return of the Turghud to China see *Ch'ien-lung shih-lu* for 1771, esp. chüan 887-894. See also Bantysh-Kamenskii, pp. 279 ff.; Shcheglov, p. 256; C. D. Barkman, "The Return of the Torghuts from Russia to China," *The Journal of Oriental Studies,* 2:89-115 (Hong Kong, 1955); and John Mish, "The Return of the Turgut, a Manchu Inscription from Jehol," *Journal of Asian History,* 4.1:80-82 (1970).

21. The history of these eighteenth-century Russian fugitives and prisoners in China, paralleling so closely the experiences of the late seventeenth century, remains to be studied. Apparently, in 1764, Ch'ien-lung decided to begin harboring Russian deserters in China, in violation of the treaty of Kiakhta (see *Ch'ien-lung shih-lu,* 710:7b-9a). Not only were the Turghud welcomed in 1771 (and also a group of Urianghais in 1772), but some sixty Russians were kept in China between 1764 and 1771, and never returned. These included a drifter named Petr Kalman who provided information to the Manchus and was compensated with a wife, rank, and position (as a teacher in the O-lo-ssu wen kuan, the Russian language school in Peking). Four other drifters in 1764 were enrolled in the Russian Company; and three captured fur traders were turned over to the Russian mission as servants. As the numbers of Russians increased, however, most were exiled to the south. They included simple drifters, exiled Cossacks who were fleeing from forced labor in the Nerchinsk silver mines, persecuted *raskolniki* (religious dissenters), and so forth. Some became mounted soldiers in the provincial garrison in Fukien; others were sent to Kwangtung as servants of Manchu bannermen there. Occasionally some would escape,

as three did in Fukien in 1773 (these were "Fei-yueh-to-erh, So-erh-chi, and Mi-yeh-lun-k'u-su-erh-tsao; see *Ch'ien-lung shih-lu*, 944:2a–2b); and one "I-fan" from Kwangtung in 1776. (With respect to I-fan, the emperor asked, "since I-fan cannot speak Chinese and his countenance is so different, how could he have escaped?" See *Ch'ien-lung shih-lu*, 997:9b.) Finally, it should be noted that these sixty-odd Russians do not include the company of Captain Dudin, which was overtaken by the Turghud when they returned to China, evidently brought to China, and left there. The Ch'ing likewise refused to surrender this group, which may have consisted of as many as one hundred and fifty people. The fate of Dudin (in Chinese "Tu-tang"—cf. *Ch'ien-lung shih-lu*, 914: 5a) is unknown. The last group of Russians arrived in 1779; it was a group of nineteen, for whom the students of the sixth ecclesiastical mission—Agafonov, Baksheev, and Paryshev—acted as interpreters. Their fate is also a mystery. For most of this information I am indebted to the lengthy report of the church assistant Stepan Zimin, of the fifth mission. It is an unpublished document and is available to me only through the extensive citations of Adoratskii (August), pp. 423 ff. On the Chinese side, Lo-shu Fu has translated a number of imperial edicts on these Russians (I, 237–238, 271, 274). When A. J. von Krusenstern called at Canton in 1805 (see *Voyage Round the World in the years 1803, 1804, 1805, and 1806, by order of his Imperial Majesty Alexander the First, on board the ships Nadeshda and Neva, under the command of Captain A. J. von Krusenstern, of the Imperial Navy* [London, 1813]) he noted (p. 324) that a Moslem merchant had informed him that there were two Russians in Canton "whose residence is of a compulsory nature. They have been in Canton these five and twenty years—he wrote—and will in all probability terminate their existence there. The Mahomedan knew them both very well: and according to his description, one of them is a handsome, tall man, whose behavior evinces a good education. On his once asking him by what accident he came to Canton, his only reply was a flood of tears, an answer which sufficiently proves that he does not belong to any inferior class of people. They are neither of them kept in confinement, but allowed to walk freely about the Tartar town, taking care, however, not to proceed beyond its boundaries. One of them, about four years ago, was compelled by the viceroy to marry; they were both apprised of our being so near by the Mahomedan; but much as the idea was impressed upon my mind, I thought it too daring an attempt to endeavor to speak to them, or to release them from their confinement." R. M. Martin (I, 396) also wrote: "A Russian, or a Russian Pole, dressed as a Chinese, and speaking the language, was at Canton and Hong Kong in 1844."

22. *Ch'ien-lung shih-lu,* 1188:1b-3b; Fu, I, 293-296.

23. The reference is to Mikhail Shokurov's visit to Peking in 1745. With Bratishchev were Efim Sakhnovskii, who had been a student in Peking two years before, in the position of the embassy's interpreter of Manchu and Chinese. The interpreter of Mongol was a man named Shalin. The Russians distinguished between the two by calling Sakhnovskii a *perevodchik,* and Shalin a *tolmach* (from the Mongolian *tolmachi,* "interpreter"). For Bratishchev's mission see Bantysh-Kamenskii, pp. 276 ff.

24. As the Manchus put it, "because the Russians have begun to behave with respect and submissiveness, thus it would seem that they may change the mission." Sychevskii, p. 287. For more information on this agreement, and the events leading up to it, see Trusevich, pp. 55-56; Bantysh-Kamenskii, pp. 308 ff.; and *Ch'ien-lung shih-lu,* 814:35b-36b. The best treatment in English, beyond any doubt, is the work of Clifford Foust.

25. Foust, who has probably counted more carefully, writes (p. 277) that legal trade was curtailed or suspended for seventeen of the thirty-four years of Catherine's reign.

26. Ho Ch'iu-t'ao, 46:8b-9a. (This is the summary of Sung-yün, amban at Urga and a delegate to the conference of 1792.) See also Duman, pp. 24-26.

27. W. F. Reddaway, ed., *Documents of Catherine the Great* (Cambridge, England, 1931), pp. 94, 119.

28. Sychevskii, p. 10; Adoratskii (October), pp. 210-211; Hosea Ballou Morse, *The Chronicles of the East India Company Trading to China, 1635-1834* (Oxford, 1926), II, 249.

29. *Ch'ien-lung shih-lu,* 1123:10b. In the same edict, the Sino-Russian trade is taken by Ch'ien-lung as a "vexatious" matter.

BIBLIOGRAPHY

Adoratskii, Nikolai. "Pravoslavnaia missiia v Kitae za 200 let eia sushchestvovaniia," *Pravoslavnyi Sobesednik* (Kazan, February–November, 1887).

Aimé-Martin, M. L., ed. *Lettres édifiantes et curieuses concernant l'Asie, l'Afrique, et l'Amerique avec quelque relations nouvelles des missions.* 4 vols. Paris, 1838–1843.

Akty istoricheskie sobrannye i izdannye Arkheograficheskoiu Kommissieiu, vols. 1–6, St. Petersburg, 1841–1843.

Aleksandrov, V. A. *Rossiia na dal'nevostochnykh rubezhakh, vtoraia polovina xvii v.* Moscow, 1969.

Amvrosii, Arkhimandrit. *Istoriia rossiiskoi ierarkhii.* 6 vols. Moscow, 1807–1815.

Andrievich, Vladimir K. *Istoriia Sibiri.* St. Petersburg, 1889.

Arlington, L. C. and William Lewisohn. *In Search of Old Peking.* First published 1935; New York, 1967.

Baddeley, John F. *Russia, Mongolia, China.* 2 vols. London, 1919.

Bakhrushin, Sergei V. *Ocherki po istorii kolonizatsii Sibiri v xvi i xvii vv.* Moscow, 1927.

Bantysh-Kamenskii, Nikolai. *Diplomaticheskoe sobranie del' mezhdu rossiiskim i kitaiskim gosudarstvami s 1619 po 1792 god.* V. M. Florinskii, ed. Kazan, 1882.

Barkman, C. D. "The Return of the Torghuts from Russia to China," *Journal of Oriental Studies,* 2:89–115 (1955).

Barten'ev, Iu. V. "Geroi Albazina i daurskoi zemli," *Russkii Arkhiv,* no. 1: 304–336 (1899).

Barthold, V. V. *La découverte de l'Asie: histoire de l'orientalism en Europe et en Russie.* Paris, 1947

Basnin, V. N. "O posol'stve v Kitai Grafa Golovkina," *Chteniia v imperatorskom obshchestve istorii i drevnostei rossiskikh pri Moskovskom Universitete,* 95, Bk. 5: 1–103 (1875).

Bawden, Charles R. "The Jebtsundamba Khutukhtus of Urga," *Asiatische Forschungen,* no. 9 (1961).

——— "The Mongol Rebellion of 1756–1757," *Journal of Asian History,* 2.1: 1–31 (1968).

Bei-guan': russkaia dukhovnaia missiia v Kitae. Tientsin, 1939.

Bell, John, of Antermony. *Travels from St. Petersburgh in Russia to Various Parts of Asia.* 2 vols. Edinburgh, 1788.

Biggerstaff, Knight. *The Earliest Modern Government Schools in China.* Ithaca, New York, 1961.

Bogoiavlenskii, S. K. *Prikaznye sud'i xvii veka.* Moscow-Leningrad, 1946.

Bol'shaia sovetskaia entsiklopediia. 53 vols. Moscow, 1950–1959.

Brand, Adam. *A journal of the embassies from Their Majesties John and Peter Alexievitz, Emperors of Muscovy, etc., over land into China through Ustiugha, Siberia, Dauri, and the Great Tartary to Peking, the capital city of the Chinese Empire, by Everard Isbrand, their ambassador in the years 1693, 1694, and 1695.* London, 1698.

Brucker, Joseph, S.J. "La Mission de Chine de 1722 à 1735," *Revue des questions historiques,* 58: 491–532 (Paris, Apr. 1, 1881).

Bulich, C. K. "Ocherk istorii iazykoznaniia v Rossii," *Zapiski istoriko-filologicheskago fakul'teta imperatorskago S. Peterburgskago Universiteta,* 75: 149–1228 (1904).

Cahen, Gaston. *Histoire des relations de la Russie avec la Chine sous Pierre le Grand, 1689–1730.* Paris, 1911.

——— *Le Livre de comptes de la caravane russe à Pékin en 1727–1728.* Paris, 1911.

Ch'en Ta-tuan. "Investiture of Liu-ch'iu Kings in the Ch'ing Period," in John K. Fairbank, ed., *The Chinese World Order*. Cambridge, Mass., 1968.

Chernozubov, Lt. Colonel. "Zavoevanie Amura russkimi i Albazin-skaia sideniia," *Voennyi Sbornik* (1907), 10: 1–18; 11: 1–18; 12: 1–18.

Chia-ch'ing ch'ung-hsiu i-t'ung-chih 嘉慶重修一統志. Published in 1812; Taipei, Taiwan, 1967.

Chia-ch'ing hui-tien shih-li. See *Ta-Ch'ing hui-tien.*

Ch'ien-lung hui-tien and *Ch'ien-lung hui-tien tse-li.* See *Ta-Ch'ing hui-tien.*

Ch'ien-lung shih-lu. See *Ta-Ch'ing li-ch'ao shih-lu.*

Ch'ing-ch'ao wai-chiao shih-liao. 清朝外交史料. Peiping, 1932.

Ch'ing-ch'ao wen-hsien t'ung-k'ao 清朝文獻通考. Compiled in 1787. Taipei, Taiwan, 1963.

Ch'ing-shih 清史. 8 vols. Taipei, 1961.

Ch'ing-shih lieh-chuan 清史列傳. Shanghai, 1928.

Ching-shih wu-ch'eng fang-hsiang hu-t'ung chi: ching-shih fang-hsiang chih-kao 京師五城坊巷衚衕集京師坊巷志稿. Peking, 1962.

Chun, Hae-jong. "Sino-Korean Tributary Relations in the Ch'ing Period," in *The Chinese World Order,* John K. Fairbank, ed. Cambridge, Mass., 1968.

Cordier, Henri. "Les Conquêtes de l'Empereur de la Chine," *Memoires concernant l'Asie Orientale.* Paris, 1913.

Cracraft, James. *The Church Reform of Peter the Great.* Stanford, 1971.

Dantsig, B. M. *Izuchenie blizhnego vostoka v Rossii.* Moscow, 1968.

de Guignes, Joseph. *Voyages à Pékin et l'Ile de France faits dans l'intervelle des années 1784 à 1801.* 3 vols. Paris, 1808.

Dehergne, J., S.J. "Les biens de la maison française de Peking en 1776–1778," *Monumenta Serica,* 20: 246–265 (1961).

Demidova, N. F. "Biurokratizatsiia gosudarstvennago apparata absoliutizma v xvii–xviii vv., in B. B. Kafengauz, ed., *Absoliutizm v Rossii (xvii–xviii vv.),* pp. 206–242. Moscow, 1964.

Denisov, L. I. *Pravoslavnyie monastyri rossiiskoi imperii.* Moscow, 1908.

Deveria, G. "Histoire du college des interprètes de Peking," *Mélanges Charles de Harlez,* 1896, pp. 34–102.

Dopolneniia k aktam istoricheskim, vols. 1–12, St. Petersburg, 1846–1875.

Dudgeon, John. *Historical Sketch of the Ecclesiastical, Political, and Commercial Relations of Russia with China.* Peking, 1872; reprinted in anastatic edition, 1940.

Duman, L. I., ed. *Russko-kitaiskie otnosheniia, 1689–1916: ofitsialnye dokumenty.* Moscow, 1958.

Duyvendak, J. J. L. "The True Dates of the Chinese Maritime Expeditions in the Early Fifteenth Century," *T'oung pao,* 34.5: 341–412 (1939).

Ermachenko, I. S. *Politika man'chzhurskoi dinastii Tsin v iuzhnoi i severnoi Mongolii v 17 veke.* Moscow, 1974.

Evans, Nancy. "The Canton T'ung-wen Kuan: A Study of the Role of the Bannermen in One Area of Self-strengthening," *Papers on China,* 22a: 89–103, East Asian Research Center, Harvard University, 1969.

Fairbank, John K., ed. *The Chinese World Order.* Cambridge, Mass., 1968.

——— and Ssu-yü Teng. *Ch'ing Administration: Three Studies.* Cambridge, Mass., 1960.

Fang, Chao-ying. "A Technique for Estimating the Numerical Strength of the Early Manchu Military Forces," *Harvard Journal of Asiatic Studies*, 13.1–2: 192–215 (1950).

Fang Hsiu. "Tsarist Russia's Tool of Aggression against China: The Mission of the Russian Orthodox Church," *Li-shih yen-chiu*, no. 3 (June 20, 1975). Translated in *Selections from PRC Magazines*, 847:31–43 (American Consulate General, Hong Kong; November 24, 1975).

Farquhar, David. "The Ch'ing Administration of Mongolia up to the Nineteenth Century." Ph.D. dissertation, Harvard University, 1960.

Fletcher, Joseph F. "China and Central Asia, 1368–1884," in *The Chinese World Order*, John K. Fairbank, ed. Cambridge, Mass., 1968.

——— "V. A. Aleksandrov on Russo-Ch'ing Relations in the Seventeenth Century," *Kritika*, 7.3: 138–170 (1971).

Florinsky, Michael T. *Russia: A History and an Interpretation.* 2 vols. New York, 1959.

Foust, Clifford M. *Muscovite and Mandarin: Russia's Trade with China and Its Setting.* Chapel Hill, North Carolina, 1969.

Franke, Wolfgang. *China and the West.* New York, 1967.

Fu-heng 傅恒 . *Huang-yü his-yü t'u-chih* 皇輿西域圖志. N.p., n.d.

Fu, Lo-shu. *A Documentary Chronicle of Sino-Western Relations, 1644-1820.* 20 vols. Tucson, Arizona, 1966.

Gaubil, Antoine, S.J. *Correspondance de Pékin, 1722–1759.* Geneva, 1970.

Glazik, Josef. *Die Russisch-Orthodoxe Heidenmission seit Peter dem Grossen.* Münster, 1954.

Golder, F. A. *Russian Expansion on the Pacific, 1641–1850.* First published 1914; reprint Gloucester, 1960.

Gorbacheva, A. I. and D. I. Tikhonov. "Iz istoriia izucheniia Kitaia v Rossii," *Sovetskoe Vostokovedenie,* 2: 140–147 (1955).

(Grumelevskii), Filaret. *Istoriia russkoi tserkvi.* St. Petersburg, 1894.

Guerrier, W. *Leibniz in seinen Beziehungen zu Russland under Peter dem Grossen.* St. Petersburg and Leipzig, 1873.

Hertslet, Sir Edward. *Hertslet's China Treaties.* 2 vols. London, 1908.

Hirth, F. "The Chinese Oriental College," *Journal of the China Branch of the Royal Asiatic Society,* new series, 22. 3–4: 203–223 (1887).

Ho Ch'iu-t'ao 何秋濤 . *Shuo-fang pei-sheng* 朔方備乘 (including the *P'ing-ting lo-ch'a fang-lueh* 平定羅剎方略 in *chüan-shou* 5–8). Peking, 1881.

Hoo Chi-tsai. *Les Bases conventionnelles des relations modernes entre la Chine et la Russie.* Paris, 1918.

Howorth, Henry H. *History of the Mongols from the Ninth to the Nineteenth Century.* 4 vols. London and New York, 1876–1928.

Hsiao-fang-hu-chai-yü-ti ts'ung-ch'ao 小方壺齋輿地叢鈔 First published 1877; reprinted in Taiwan, 1962.

Hugon, J., S.J. "Les premiers missionaires français en Chine (1688–1720)," *Revue d'Histoire des Missions,* 3: 40–52 (1926).

Hummel, Arthur W. *Eminent Chinese of the Ch'ing Period.* 2 vols. Washington, 1943–1944.

Hyacinthe, le Rev. P. (Iakinf Bichurin). *Description de Pékin.* St. Petersburg, 1829.

Iakovleva, P. T. *Pervyi russko-kitaiskii dogovor 1689 goda.* Moscow, Academy of Sciences, 1958.

Ides, E. Isbrants. *Three Years Travels from Moscow Over-land to China: thro' Great Ustiga, Siriana, Permia, Siberia, Daour, Great Tartary, etc. to Peking.* London, 1706.

Imanishi Shunju. *Tulisen's I-yü-lu Revised and Annotated* (in Japanese). Nara, Japan, 1964.

Innocent, Archimandrite. "The Russian Orthodox Mission in China," *The Chinese Recorder*, 47.10: 678–685 (October 1916).

Ishida Mikinosuke, "A Biographical Study of Giuseppe Castiglione (Lang Shih-ning), a Jesuit Painter in the Court of Peking Under the Ch'ing Dynasty," *Memoirs of the Research Department of the Toyo Bunko*, 19: 79–121 (1960).

"Istoricheskii ocherk khristianskoi propovedi v Kitae," *Trudy Kievskoi Dukhovnoi Akademii*, kn. 3: 112–172; 241–366 (1860).

Ivanov, P. *Opisanie gosudarstvennago arkhiva starykh del'.* Moscow, 1850.

"Iz istorii russko-kitaiskikh otnoshenii 1695–1720 gg." *Istoricheskii Arkhiv* (1957).

Jih-hsia chiu-wen k'ao 日下舊聞考 . Peking, 1781.

Josson, H. and L. Willaert, eds. *Correspondance de Ferdinand Verbiest de la Compagnie de Jésus, 1623–1688.* Brussels, 1938.

Kabanov, P. I. *Amurskii vopros.* Blagoveshchensk, 1959.

K'ang-hsi hui-tien. See *Ta-Ch'ing hui-tien.*

K'ang-hsi shih-lu. See *Ta-Ch'ing li-ch'ao shih-lu.*

Kazanina, M. I., ed. *Izbrant Ides i Adam Brand: zapiski o russkom posol'stve v Kitai (1692–1695).* Moscow, 1967.

240

Klaproth, M. J. (Julius Heinrich von). *Memoires relatifs à l'Asie.* 3 vols. Paris, 1824–1828.

Kononov, A. I. "Stoletie vostochnogo fakul'teta Leningradskogo Universiteta (1855–1955)," *Sovetskoe Vostokovedenie,* 2: 83–90 (1956).

Korostovets, I. "Russkaia dukhovnaia missiia v Pekine," *Russkii Arkhiv,* 9: 57–86 (1893).

Korsak, Aleksandr Kazimirovich. *Istoriko-statisticheskoe obozrenie torgovykh snoshenii Rossii c Kitaem.* Kazan, 1857.

Kostikov, E. D. "Velikoderzhavnye ambitsii i pogranichnaia politika pekinskogo rukovodstva," *Problemy dal'nego vostoka,* no. 1: 53–63 (1973).

Kotoshikhin, Grogor'. *O Rossii v tsarstvovanie Alekseia Mikhailovicha.* St. Petersburg, 1906.

Krahl, Joseph, S.J. *China Missions in Crisis: Bishop Laimbeckhoven and His Times, 1738-1787.* Rome, 1964.

Krusenstern, A. J. von. *Voyage Round the World in the Years 1803, 1804, 1805, and 1806, by Order of his Imperial Majesty Alexander the First, on Board the Ships Nadeshda and Neva, under the Command of Captain A. J. von Krusenstern of the Imperial Navy.* London, 1813.

Kudriavtsev, F. A. *Istoriia buriat-mongol'skogo naroda.* Moscow and Leningrad, 1940.

Kuo-tzu-chien chih 國子監志 . Peking, 1834.

Kuo-tzu-chien tse-li 國子監則例 . Peking, 1823.

Kurts, B. G. *Russko-kitaiskie snoshenie v xvi, xvii, i xviii stoletiiakh.* 1929.

Lach, Donald F. *The Preface to Leibniz' Novissima Sinica.* Honolulu, 1957.

Lantzeff, George V. *Siberia in the Seventeenth Century: A Study of the Colonial Administration.* Berkeley and Los Angeles, 1943.

Latourette, Kenneth Scott. *A History of Christian Missions in China.* London, 1929.

Lensen, G. E. *The Russian Push toward Japan: Russo-Japanese Relations 1697–1875.* Princeton, 1959.

Lettres édifiantes et curieuses écrites des missions étrangères, vol. 23, Paris, 1811.

Li-fan Yuan tse-li 理藩院則例 . Peking, 1811.

Li Kuang-t'ao 李光濤 comp. *Ming-Ch'ing tang-an ts'un-chen hsuan-chi* 明清檔案存真選輯 . Taipei, 1959.

Li Yü-shu 李毓澍 . *Wai-meng cheng-chiao chih-tu k'ao* 外蒙政教制度考 . Taipei, 1962.

Likhovitskii, A. "Prosveshchenie v Sibiri v pervoi polovine xviii stoletiia," *Zhurnal Ministerstva Narodnago Prosveshcheniia,* 360.3: 1–29 (July 1905).

L'Isle, J. N. and A. G. Pingre. *Description de la ville de Peking.* Paris, 1765.

Liu Ta-nien 劉大年 . "Lun K'ang-hsi 論康熙 ," *Li-shih yen-chiu* 歷史研究 , no. 3: 5–21 (1961).

Liu Tse-jung 劉澤榮 and Wang Chih-hsiang 王之相 , eds. *Ku-kung O-wen shih-liao* 故宮俄文史料 . Peiping, 1936,

Liubimov, A. "Nekotorye man'chzhurskie dokumenty iz istorii russko-kitaiskikh snoshenii v xvii veke," *Zapiski vostochnago otdeleniia imperatorskago russkogo arkheologicheskago obshchestva,* 21.2–3: 65–94 (St. Petersburg, 1911–1912).

Maggs, Barbara Widenor. "China in the Literature of Eighteenth-Century Russia." Ph.D. dissertation, University of Illinois, 1973.

242

——— " 'The Jesuits in China.' Views of an Eighteenth-Century Russian Observer," *Eighteenth-Century Studies*, 8.2: 137–152 (Winter, 1974, 1975).

Mancall, Mark. "China's First Missions to Russia, 1729–1731," *Papers on China*, 9: 75–110 (East Asian Research Center, Harvard University, 1955).

——— "Russia and China: the Structure of Contact," in Wayne S. Vucinich, ed., *Russia and Asia: Essays on the Influence of Russia on the Asian Peoples*. Stanford, 1972.

——— *Russia and China: Their Diplomatic Relations to 1728*. Cambridge, Mass., 1971.

——— "Sino-Russian Relations to 1729: The Search for Stability." 2 vols. Ph.D. thesis, Harvard University, 1963.

Martin, R. Montgomery. *China: Political, Commercial, and Social, in an Official Report to Her Majesty's Government*. 2 vols. London, 1847.

Materialy dlia istorii imperatorskoi akademii nauk, vols. 3–7, St. Petersburg, 1886–1895.

McWhirter, Norris, and Ross McWhirter, eds. *Guinness Book of World Records*, 1976 Edition. New York, 1975.

Melikhov, G. V. *Man'chzhury na severo-vostoke (xviiv.)*. Moscow, 1974.

Meng Ssu-ming. "The E-lo-ssu kuan (Russian hostel) in Peking," *Harvard Journal of Asiatic Studies*, 23: 19–46 (1960–1961).

Miller [Müller], G. F. *Istoriia Sibiri*. 2 vols. Moscow, 1937–1941.

Mirotvortsev, V. "Materialy dlia istorii Pekinskoi dukhovnoi missii," *Pravoslavnyi Sobesednik* (September and October 1888).

Mish, John L. "The Return of the Turgut, a Manchu Inscription from Jehol," *Journal of Asian History*, 4.1: 80–82 (1970).

Morse, Hosea Ballou. *The Chronicles of the East India Company Trading to China, 1635–1834*. 4 vols. Oxford, 1926. Vol. 5 for 1742–1774; Oxford, 1929.

Mozharovskii, Apollon. "Izloshenie khoda missionerskago dela po prosveshcheniiu kazanskikh inorodtsev, s 1552 po 1867 god," *Chteniia v imperatorskom obshchestve istorii i drevnostei rossiskikh pri Moskovskom Universitete,* 1: 1–261 (1880).

——— "K istorii nashei dukhovnoi missii v Kitae," *Russkii Arkhiv,* 2: 405–437 (1886).

——— "Arkhimandrit Petr Kamenskii," *Russkaia Starina,* 85: 317–342 (February 1896).

Müller, G. F., ed. *Ezhemesiachnyia sochineniia i izvestiia o uchenykh delakh.* July–December, 1764.

Müller, Kurt. "Gottfried Wilhelm Leibniz und Nicolaas Witsen," *Sitzungsberichte der Deutschen Akademie der Wissenschaften zu Berlin,* no. 1: 1–46 (1955).

Nagel's Encyclopedia-Guide: China. Geneva, 1968.

"O nachale torgovykh i gosudarstvennykh snoshenii Rossii s Kitaem i o dukhovnoi missii v Pekine," *Sibirskii Vestnik,* 18: [99]– 164; 19: 165–196 (1822).

Obchinikov, R. V. " 'Rapport' M. V. Lomonosova i drugikh akademi- kov v senat o perevode 'Istorii kitaiskogo gosudarstva'," *Istoricheskii Arkhiv,* 6: 234–235 (1961).

Ocherki po istorii russkogo vostokovedeniia. 6 vols. Moscow, 1955– 1963.

Ogloblin, N. N. "Pervyi Iaponets v Rossii, 1701–1705 gg.," *Russkaia Starina,* no. 72 (1891).

Opis' dokumentov i del' khraniashchikhsia v arkhive sviateishago pravitel'stvyiushchago Synoda. 30 vols. St. Petersburg, 1868– 1914.

Opisanie arkhiva Aleksandro-Nevskoi lavry za vremia tsarstvovaniia Imperatora Petra Velikago, vols. 2 and 3. Petrograd, 1916.

244

Pallas, P. S., ed. *Neue nordische Beyträge zur physikalischen und geographischen Erd- und Völkerbeschreibung, Naturgeschichte, und Oekonomie.* St. Petersburg und Leipzig, 1781–1783.

Palmer, William. *The Patriarch and the Tsar: Services of the Patriarch Nicon to the Church and State of his Country, and their Requital by the Creation of a Merely National or State Church in Russia.* 6 vols. London, 1871–1876.

Pamiatniki sibirskoi istorii xviii v. 2 vols. St. Petersburg, 1882–1885.

Parker, Edward H. *China and Religion.* London, 1905.

Parry, Albert. "Russian (Greek Orthodox) Missionaries in China, 1689–1917: Their Cultural, Political, and Economic Role." Ph.D. dissertation, University of Chicago, 1938.

Paul, Rev. Robert, ed. "Letters and Documents relating to Robert Erskine, Physician to Peter the Great, Czar of Russia, 1677–1720," *Miscellany of the Scottish History Society,* 2: 373–430 (1904).

Pavlovsky, Michel N. *Chinese-Russian Relations.* New York, Philosophical Library, 1949.

Pekarskii, Petr. *Istoriia imperatorskoi akademii nauk v Peterburge.* 2 vols. St. Petersburg, 1870–1873.

Pelliot, Paul. "Le Hoja et le Sayyid Husain de l'histoire des Ming," *T'oung pao,* 38 (livr. 2–5): [81]–292 (Leiden, 1948).

Petech, Luciano. *China and Tibet in the Early Eighteenth Century.* Leiden, 1950.

Petrova, O. P. "Iaponskii iazyk v Rossii v pervoi polovine xviii veka," *Narody Azii i Afriki,* 1: 163–177 (1965).

Pfister, Aloys. *Notices biographiques et bibliographiques sur les jésuites de l'ancienne mission de la Chine, 1552–1773.* 2 vols. Shanghai, 1932–1934.

Pis'ma i bumagi Imperatora Petra Velikago. 11 vols. St. Petersburg and Moscow, 1887–1910, 1964.

Polnoe sobranie postanovlenii i rasporiazhenii po vedomstvu pravoslavnago ispovedaniia rossiiskoi imperii. First series, vols. 1–8; second series, vol. 2; third series, vol. 1. St. Petersburg, 1879–1910.

Polnoe sobranie zakonov rossiiskoi imperii s 1649 goda. First series, 1649, 1825. 45 vols. St. Petersburg, 1830.

Pozdneev, Aleksei. *Mongoliia i Mongoly.* 2 vols. St. Petersburg, 1896–1898.

Putsillo, M. P. *Ukazatel' delam i rukopisiam otnosiashchimsia do Sibiri i prinadlezhashchikh Moskovskomu Glavnomu Arkhivu Min. Ino. Del'.* Moscow, 1879.

Quested, R. K. I. *The Expansion of Russia in East Asia, 1857–1860.* Singapore, 1968.

Radovskii, M. I. "Russkii kitaeved I. K. Rossokhin," *Iz istorii nauki i tekhniki v stranakh vostoka.* 2 vols. Moscow, 1961.

Reddaway, W. F., ed. *Documents of Catherine the Great.* Cambridge, Eng., 1931.

Revue de l'extreme-Orient, vol. 3, Paris, 1887.

Ripa, Matteo. *Memoirs of Father Ripa, during Thirteen Years' Residence at the Court of Peking in the Service of the Emperor of China,* tr. Fortunato Prandi. New York, 1846.

Rochemonteix, Camille de. *Joseph Amiot et les derniers survivants de la Mission Francaise a Pekin.* Paris, 1915.

Rogger, Hans. *National Consciousness in Eighteenth-Century Russia.* Cambridge, Mass., 1960.

Russko-kitaiskie otnosheniia v xvii veke, N. F. Demidova, V. S. Miasnikov, S. L. Tikhvinskii, L. I. Duman, eds. 2 vols. Moscow, 1969–1972.

Sebes, Joseph, S.J. *The Jesuits and the Sino-Russian Treaty of Nerchinsk (1689): The Diary of Thomas Pereira, S.J.* Rome, 1961.

Serebrennikov, I. I. *Albazintsy.* Peking, 1922.

———*Moia vospominaniia.* 2 vols. Tientsin, 193?.

Sgibnev, A. "Ob obuchenii v Rossii iaponskomu iazyku," *Morskoi Sbornik,* no. 12 (1868).

Shafranovskaia, T. K. "Poezdka lekaria Frantsa Elachicha v 1753–1756 gg. v Pekin dlia popolneniia kitaiskikh kollektsii kunst (-) kamery," *Iz istorii nauki i tekhniki v stranakh vostoka.* 2 vols. Moscow, 1961.

Shafranovskii, T. K. and K. I. Shafranovskii. "Priobretenie v nachale xviii v. kitaishkikh knig rossiiskim rezidentom v Kitae Lorentsom Langom," *Strany i narody vostoka,* 1: 295–301 (Moscow, 1959).

Shcheben'kov, V. G. *Russko-kitaiskie otnosheniia v xvii v.* Moscow, 1960.

Shcheglov, I. V. *Khronologicheskii perechen' vazhneishikh dannykh iz istorii Sibiri.* Irkutsk, 1883.

Shmurlo, E. F., ed. *Pis'ma i doneseniia Iezuitov o Rossii kontsa xvii i nachala xviii veka.* St. Petersburg, 1904.

Shumakher, P. V. "Nashi snosheniia c Kitaem (1567–1805)," *Russkii Arkhiv,* 6: 145–183 (1879).

——— "Pervyia russkiia poseleniia na sibirskom vostoke," *Russkii Arkhiv,* 5: 5–36 (1879).

Shun-t'ien fu-chih 順天府志 . Peking, 1884.

Shunkov, V. I. *Ocherki po istorii kolonizatsii Sibiri v xvii–nachale xviii v.* Moscow, 1946.

Sibirskii Vestnik. See "O nachale torgovykh i gosudarstvennykh snoshenii Rossii s Kitaem i o dukhovnoi missii v Pekine."

Skachkov, P. E. *Bibliografiia Kitaia.* Moscow, 1960.

—— "Istoriia izucheniia Kitaia v Rossii v xvii i xviii vv."
Mezhdunarodnye sviazi Rossii v xvii–xviii vv. L. G. Beskrovnyi,
ed. Moscow, 1966.

—— "O neizvestnykh rukopisiakh Lariona Rossokhina," *Narody
Azii i Afriki,* 1: 158–159 (1965).

—— "Pervyi prepodavatel' kitaiskogo i man'chzhurskogo iazykov
v Rossii," *Problemy Vostokovedeniia,* 3: 198–201 (1960).

—— "Russkie vrachi pri rossiiskoi dukhovnoi missii v Pekine,"
Sovetskoe Kitaevedenie, 4: 136–148 (1958).

Sladkovskii, M. I. *Istoriia torgovo-ekonomicheskikh otnoshenii
narodov Rossii s Kitaem (do 1917 g.)* Moscow, 1974.

Slovar' istoricheskii o sviatykh proslavlennykh v rossiiskoi tserkvi.
St. Petersburg, 1836.

Slovtsov, Petr Andreevich. *Istoricheskoe obozrenie Sibiri.* St.
Petersburg, 1886.

Smorzhenskii, Feodosii. "Ob Iezuitakh v Kitae," *Sibirskii vestnik,*
19: 107–132, 181–210; 20: 227–254, 295–310, 329–356
(1822).

Solov'ev, Sergei M. *Istoriia Rossii s drevneishikh vremen.* 15 vols.
Moscow, 1959–1966.

Starikov, V. S. "Larion Rossokhin i nachalo izucheniia kitaiskoi
pirotekhniki v Rossii," *Iz istorii nauki i tekhniki v stranakh
vostoka.* 2 vols. Moscow, 1961.

Staunton, G. T., tr. *Narrative of the Chinese Embassy to the Khan
of the Tourgouth Tartars in the Years 1712, 13, 14 and 15.*
London, 1821.

Stevenson, J. L., ed. *John Bell of Antermony; A Journey from St.
Petersburg to Pekin, 1719–1722.* Edinburgh, 1965.

Strenina, A. V. "U istokov russkogo i mirovogo kitaevedeniia,"
Sovetskaiia Etnografiia, 1: 170–177 (1950).

Sychevskii, [E. P.]. *Istoricheskaia zapiska o kitaiskoi granitse.*
Moscow, 1875.

Ta-Ch'ing hui-tien 大清會典 . *K'ang-hsi* 康熙 *hui-tien* (Completed 1695–1696); *Yung-cheng* 雍正 *hui-tien* (completed 1734); *Ch'ien-lung* 乾隆 *hui-tien* and *Ch'ien-lung hui-tien tse-li* 則例 (completed 1768); *Chia-ch'ing* 嘉慶 *hui-tien* and *Chia-ch'ing hui-tien shih-li* 事例 (completed 1822).

Ta-Ch'ing li-ch'ao shih-lu 大清歷朝實錄 . Series for the reigns of Sheng-tsu 聖祖 (K'ang-hsi emperor), Shih-tsung 世宗 (Yung-cheng emperor), and Kao-tsung 高宗 (Ch'ien-lung emperor). Tokyo, 1937–1938.

Taranovich, V. P. "Illarion Rossokhin i ego trudy po kitaevendeniiu," *Sovetskoe Vostokovedenie*, 3: 225–241 (1945).

Thomas, A. *Histoire de la mission de Pékin*. Paris, 1923.

Tikhvinskii, S. L., "Man'chzhurskoe vladychestvo v Kitae," in *Man'-chzhurskoe vladychestvo v Kitae*, ed. S. L. Tikhvinskii. Moscow, 1966, pp. 5–76.

Timkovskii, Egor Fedorovich. *Puteshestvie v Kitai cherez Mongoliiu v 1820 i 1821 godakh*. 3 vols. St. Petersburg, 1824.

Timkowski, George [E. F. Timkovskii]. *Travels of the Russian Mission through Mongolia to China and Residence in Peking in the Years 1820–1821*. 2 vols. London, 1827.

Treaties, Conventions, etc. between China and Foreign States. 2 vols. 2nd ed.: Shanghai, 1917.

Trusevich, Kh. *Posol'skiia i torgovliia snosheniia Rossii s Kitaem*. Moscow, 1882.

Ulianitskii, V. A. *Russkiia konsul'stva za granitseiu v xviii veke*. Moscow, 1899.

Vasil'ev, V. P. "Vospominanie ob I. I. Zakharov," *Zhurnal Ministerstva Narodnago Prosveshcheniia* (November 1885), pp. 94–110.

Veselovskii, N. I. *Materialy dlia istorii rossiiskoi dukhovnoi missii v Pekine.* St. Petersburg, 1905.

Vigor, Mrs. William. *Letters from Russia* (originally published as *Letters from a Lady who Resided Some Years in Russia;* London, 1777). New York, 1970.

Vucinich, Wayne S., ed. *Russia and Asia: Essays on the Influence of Russia on the Asian Peoples.* Stanford, California, 1972.

Weber, Friedrich Christian. *The Present State of Russia.* 2 vols. London, 1723.

Widmer, Eric. "Archimandrite Palladius and Chinese Control of Barbarians in 1858," *Papers on China,* 19: 55–86 (East Asian Research Center, Harvard University, 1965).

——— " 'Kitai' and the Ch'ing Empire in Seventeenth Century Russian Documents on China." *Ch'ing-shih wen-t'i,* 2.4: 21–39 (November 1970).

Wills, John E., Jr. *Pepper, Guns, and Parleys: The Dutch East India Company and China, 1662-1681.* Cambridge, Mass., 1974.

Wittram, Reinhard. *Peter I, Czar, und Kaiser: Zur Geschichte Peters des Grossen in seiner Zeit.* 2 vols. Göttingen, 1964.

Yano Jinichi 矢野仁一. "Pekin no Rokoku koshikan ni tsuite," *Geibun* 藝文, 6.8: 884–894; 6.10: 1065–1091 (August and October, 1915).

Yao Yuan-chih 姚元之. *Chu-yeh-t'ing tsa-chi* 竹葉亭雜記 n.p., 1893; reprinted Taipei, 1969.

Yü Cheng-hsieh 俞正燮. *Kuei-ssu lei-kao* 癸巳類稿 Peking, 1833; reprint Shanghai, 1957.

——— *Kuei-ssu ts'un-kao* 癸巳存稿 Ling-shih, 1848; reprint Shanghai, 1957.

Yung-cheng hui-tien. See *Ta-Ch'ing hui-tien.*
Yung-cheng shih-lu. See *Ta-Ch'ing li-ch'ao shih-lu.*

Zlatkin, I. Ia. *Istoriia dzhungarskogo khanstva (1635–1758).* Moscow, 1964.

INDEX

Ablin, 10

Academy of Learning (Kuo-tzu-chien), Russian students in, 112-113

Academy of Sciences, St. Petersburg: Chinese-Latin dictionary compiled at, 157; Pukhort at, 158; Rossokhin at, 160-162; Chinese books requested by, 103, 162; Leont'ev at, 163-164; narrow aims of, 166

Adoratskii, Nikolai, 6; on decadence of Russian Company, 22; on founding of language school, 106; on Albazinians, 153

Afanasev, Iosif, 40

Agafonov, Aleksei Semenovich, 165

Albazin, Siberian garrison at, 1; fall of, 4, 13, 163; pacification of, 13-19; Russians from, 19; cloister in, 29; significance of for China, 46, 48

Albazinians: "prisoners" in China, 13-19; in early 18th century, 35; and Nikolskii church, 95; as interpreters, 104, 105, 106; in mid-18th century, 140; saving of, 151-153

Aleksandro-Nevskii Monastery, 59

Aleksandrov, Vasilii, 32, 35

Aleksei Mikhailovich, 11

Alexander I, 166

Altai mountains, border of Zunghuria and China, 171

Amsterdam, Russian embassy at, 154

Amur River, 1; Sino-Russian contacts in valley of, 10, 14, 16; confusions concerning, 12; importance of for Russia, 176; negotiations on, 176-178

Amursana, 47, 172-174, 176; significance of corpse of, 175

Anna Ioannovna, Tsarina, 155, 169, appointment of Trusov by, 125, 126

Annals of the Eight Banners. See Pa-ch'i t'ung-chih

Argievskii, Sofronii, 139

Argun, R., 1

Armiansk, bishop of, 62

Artem'ev, Ivashko (I-fan), 16, 21

Astrakhan, mission to, 148

Atlasov, Volodimir, 155

Ayuki Khan, Petr Petrovich Taishin, 148, 158; Manchu mission to, 36-39, 175; account of, 163

Baikov, Ivan, 10, 12, 48; housing of, 89

Baksheev, Feodor, 164-165

Bandi, leader of Northern Route army, 172

Bantysh-Kamenskii, Nikolai, 77, 108, 173

Barshchenkov, student, 123

Barthold, V. V., 23

Bayer, Theofile Siegfried: compiler of Chinese-Latin dictionary, 157, 158; death of, 160

Bell, John of Antermony, 55, 92, 105

252

HARVARD EAST ASIAN MONOGRAPHS